14 00 used

DERRIDA

DERRIDA

_____

Deconstruction from Phenomenology to Ethics

Christina Howells

Polity Press

First published in 1998 by Polity Press in association with Blackwell Publishers Ltd.

Editorial office:
Polity Press
65 Bridge Street
Cambridge CB2 1UR, UK

Marketing and production:
Blackwell Publishers Ltd
108 Cowley Road
Oxford OX4 1JF, UK

Published in the USA by
Blackwell Publishers Inc.
Commerce Place
350 Main Street
Malden, MA 02148, USA

ISBN 0-7456-1167-2
ISBN 0-7456-1168-0 (pbk)

A catalogue record for this book is available from the British Library and has been applied for from the Library of Congress.

Typeset in 10½ on 12 pt Palatino
by Best-set Typesetter Ltd., Hong Kong
Printed in Great Britain by MPG Books, Victoria Square, Bodmin, Cornwall

This book is printed on acid-free paper.

Key Contemporary Thinkers

Published

Forthcoming

Contents

Acknowledgements

My thanks are due to many friends and colleagues who contributed to this study, in particular by reading draft versions of the various chapters and helping me to clarify my ideas and understanding. I am especially grateful to Michael Ayers, Malcolm Bowie, Colin Davis and Alan Montefiore, and most of all to my husband, Bernard, who read the whole text with an extremely vigilant eye and suggested many vital improvements. The errors that remain are, of course, 'all my own work'. I would also like to thank Lydia Rainford for her meticulous work on the Bibliography and Index. I thank Wadham College, the University of Oxford and the British Academy for the extended period of leave which enabled me to finish the project. Finally, I thank my children, Marie-Elise and Dominic, for their tolerance and good-humour, as well as for their refreshingly deflating remarks about the 'deconstruction of the (l)ego'.

Abbreviations

References to most works are given in the text. Translations from French are my own, and references are therefore to the French editions.

Works by Derrida

Adieu	*Adieu: à Emmanuel Levinas*
CP	*La Carte postale*
Diss	*La Dissémination*
Droit	*Du droit à la philosophie*
ED	*L'Écriture et la différence*
Force	*Force de loi*
Gram	*De la Grammatologie*
Marges	*Marges: de la philosophie*
Politiques	*Politiques de l'amitié*
Pos	*Positions*
Spectres	*Spectres de Marx*
VP	*La Voix et le phénomène*

Works by Other Writers

EN	*L'Être et le Néant* (Sartre)
Essai	*Essai sur l'origine des connaissances humaines* (Condillac)
OG	*L'Origine de la géometrie* (Husserl)
SG	*Saint Genet* (Sartre)
TE	*La Transcendance de l'ego* (Sartre)
TI	*Totalité et infini* (Levinas)

Apologia

Derrida is one of the most significant and brilliant French philosophers of the twentieth century. He is also one of the most prolific and currently one of the most popular, though not of course in the sense that he is easily accessible. It is not possible today to be a well-educated intellectual without knowing at least something about Derrida and the way of reading most closely associated with him: deconstruction. Indeed the vogue for deconstruction has spread from France to England and the United States and far beyond, and Derrida may well be more appreciated outside France than inside it, though at the same time the sharpest attacks on his thinking have come from philosophers belonging to the Anglo-Saxon analytical tradition. In the Continental context, on the other hand, in which his work is embedded, it might appear less contestatory and therefore be less contested, with the result that if his prestige is undisputed his pre-eminence is not taken for granted. The sheer difficulty of Derrida's texts is legendary, and this too has been held against him by critics suspicious of mystification and unwilling to make the effort required to respond to writing that can sometimes be Mallarmean in its verbal density. It is my aim here to encourage and facilitate such an effort, in the conviction that the reward may be a mind-expanding delight rarely equalled elsewhere.

Derrida is an unusual philosopher, and hard to categorize, in that much of his best work constitutes an extensive critique of other texts, literary, philosophical, psychoanalytic and political. The very term 'deconstruction' was, as Derrida explains in his 'Lettre à un ami japonais' (*Psyché*, 1987), chosen by him from Littré to translate Heidegger's *Destruktion* and *Abbau*, both of which imply a dismantling but not a destruction of the traditional organizing concepts of Western ontology and metaphysics (p. 388).[1] When he chose the term, Derrida suggests, he had little or no idea of the importance it would assume for his later thinking. Derrida's early work was primarily concerned, as we shall see, with a critique of Husserl and phenomenology. Soon Heidegger, Hegel, Nietzsche, Plato, Foucault, Lévi-Strauss, Rousseau, Freud, Levinas, Mallarmé, Artaud and Bataille, amongst others, were to become objects of the deconstructive strategy. In all his books and essays Derrida is a scrupulous, meticulous, patient reader, determined to disentangle what has been conflated, to bring to light what has been concealed, and to pay scrupulous attention to marginalia and footnotes, in the expectation that what has been relegated to the margins may prove paradoxically central to a less parochial understanding of the text.

In part because of historical coincidence, and in part because of theoretical misunderstanding, Derrida has sometimes been described as a postmodernist or a post-structuralist. It is true that he shares much with both postmodernism and post-structuralism, in particular an implacable opposition to the hegemony of the human subject as it is manifest in philosophical humanism, and a concomitant will to question the nature of the relationship between reality, language, history and the subject. None the less, both labels are potentially misleading: post-structuralism asserts that truth claims are ultimately dependent on the discourse or conceptual scheme from which they emanate; postmodernism further concludes that all epistemological enterprises – including those of science and philosophy – are merely operative fictions. For postmodernism even the very questions of relativism and indeterminacy are not matters of truth or falsehood but rather 'performative utterances'. In other words, the 'baby' of truth has been thrown out with the 'bathwater' of positivist certainty. Derrida, as will become progressively clearer in the course of this book, is not part of the move to debunk truth. For this reason amongst others, critics[2] who imagine they are turning the tables on Derrida when they point out that in taking issue with a particular argument or textual interpretation, Derrida himself is implying a notion of 'truth' which he has elsewhere abandoned, are deluded. As I argue explicitly in my final chaper in particular, Derrida believes it would be literally non-sensical to attempt, or even to wish, to abandon truth or meaning. Deconstruction may set out to 'read between the lines', or even 'read against the grain', but it always attempts to read, and understand. The so-called 'play' of interpretation, which Derrida refers to as 'dissemination', is a play in the linguistic mechanism perhaps, but it is not the 'free play' beloved of some of Derrida's less rigorous followers. It is rather the demonstration of textual self-contradiction which is the essence of the deconstructive project. It differs from the standard philosophical technique of finding flaws in the logic of an opponent's argument in that the contradictions uncovered reveal an underlying incompatibility between what the writer believes him- or herself to be arguing and what the text itself actually says. This gap between authorial intention and textual meaning is a key focus of deconstruction.

The extraordinary acceleration of Derrida's publishing record is daunting as well as impressive. When I started thinking seriously about Derrida in 1980 he had published a dozen books, four in the 1960s and the rest in the seventies, as well, of course, as numerous articles and essays. Reading the written corpus seemed a manageable goal. By 1990, when I first considered writing a book on Derrida, he had published another twenty. Nor could I anticipate that his output would further accelerate: at least another twenty books have appeared since 1990, three in the first three months of 1997, just as I imagined I was putting the final touches to my last chapter. One of his latest works is, indeed, particularly germane to my subject, entitled *Adieu* and devoted to Levinas, and I give an account of it in my chapter on ethics and politics.

This book cannot claim to be fully comprehensive, but it is as up-to-date as publishing delays permit, and indeed takes account of *L'Animal autobiographique*, the ten-day 'Colloque de Cerisy' devoted to Derrida's work in July 1997, which I was lucky enough to be able to attend, though its proceedings are as yet unpublished. I have not been able, however, to make room in this book for some of the texts which gave me most enjoyment, such as *Donner le temps* (1991), devoted, at least in part, to 'La fausse monnaie', one of Baudelaire's prose poems, and to Marcel Mauss's theory of the gift. Nor is much time spent on the love letters of *La Carte postale* (1980), or on the wonderful study of painterly self-portraiture in *Mémoires d'aveugle* (1990). I say little about Nietzsche, less than I would like about Hegel, and very little about Derrida's relationship to negative theology, which is an abiding concern. On the other hand, this book returns at several points to Derrida's relation to Sartre, more frequently, perhaps, than some readers may like, but 'Derrideans' and 'Sartreans' have tended to inhabit very different, even opposed camps, either side of the structuralist divide, and I wanted to take this opportunity to bring them together through my delight in, and admiration for, both philosophers. I remember a similar experience of secretly longing for Sartre to stop publishing twenty years ago, in the 1970s, as I was trying to finish my thesis and, to my dismay, a third 600-page volume of *L'Idiot de la famille*, his study of Flaubert, appeared. It is my joint interest in Sartre and Derrida that motivates my interest in the various theories of the subject, which, in their implications for ethics and politics in particular, are among the most fruitful aspects of Derrida's thinking.

But if this study cannot claim to be comprehensive, I know full well that no other study could either. How to convey more than a fraction of such an extraordinary output? A restriction of scope and a rigorous, if sometimes painful, policy of exclusion of certain texts was the only possible way forward. I have, however, tried to be clear, analytic, objective and jargon-free, not imitating Derrida's style and not shunning explanation and paraphrase. This, of course, will be deeply unfashionable among many Derrida scholars, who might judge such an approach as a betrayal of Derrida or as evidence of a lack of understanding of his whole enterprise. What is more, I know that it is bound to fail. There is no way I can make some of Derrida's more difficult ideas clear without simplification, no way I can avoid 'jargon' entirely (though I hope I have explained Derridean terminology when I use it), and no way my own preoccupations and interests will leave my text uncoloured. But all this is *en connaissance de cause*: I will do best justice to both Derrida and my readers if I aim for an impossible clarity and an equally impossible objectivity, while confessing that I know I have no hope of achieving either.

Finally, a bit of advice on how to approach this book, what Derrida calls a 'protocole de lecture': the chapter headings are transparent, and it will be evident what each section is concerned with. But the level of difficulty is variable. Chapter 1, on phenomenology, lays the philosophical basis for much of what is to follow, dealing, for example, with the status of ideal objects, and with some of the complexities of Husserlian theory. It is the most textual and detailed of the chapters, as is required by its argument. It is also, I think, the hardest, and readers who do not have a philosophical bent might leave it aside and pass quickly on to the chapter on structuralism, or even go straight into chapter 3, on speech and writing, if they are looking for an account of the most popular aspects of Derrida's thinking. On the other hand, readers already familiar with Derrida's work may well find most to interest them in the last two chapters, which deal with the more recent texts and attempt to disentangle the relationship of deconstruction to psychoanalysis and to ethics and politics. However, I have absorbed the Derridean lesson: this book is out of my hands and my control once it has reached the public domain, so my desire to hold the reader's hand and guide her through, explaining as I go, can be no more than a nostalgic aspiration to recover the long-gone and illusory authority of the writer.

1

Phenomenology

As the twentieth century draws to its close, phenomenology is largely out of fashion in France, having been replaced by intellectual movements such as existentialism, structuralism, postmodernism and post-structuralism in increasingly rapid succession. But in the opening years of the century, and indeed up until the 1960s, phenomenology was a force to be reckoned with, and was the first sparring partner of many of the major exponents of those later philosophical movements just evoked. Sartre, Levinas, Lyotard and Derrida himself all started their publishing careers with a critique/ exposition of a certain aspect of phenomenology. Their works cannot be properly understood without some knowledge of what they are criticizing or refining. This chapter will attempt to elucidate the phenomenological enterprise itself and Derrida's own engagement with it. It will necessarily be somewhat technical: phenomenology had radical ambitions, it set out to revolutionize epistemology, psychology and ultimately science, and its terminology may present some difficulties to those unfamiliar with it.

Phenomenology is a philosophy of consciousness which attempts to avoid the reefs of dualistic views such as empiricism and idealism by putting aside all preconceptions about the relationship between mind and world. It sets out to rethink the fundamental distinction between subject and object, and to go beyond naturalist epistemology to describe afresh how consciousness relates to the world of phenomena. Consciousness, according to phenomenology, is always directed outside itself to the world, and this relationship is referred to as one of 'intentionality'. Husserl, the major founder of phenomenology, described it as 'the true positivism' (*ED*, 229), aiming to return 'to things themselves' ('zu den Sachen selbst'). Its specificity lies not so much in its object – after all, as Husserl commented, other sciences also treat of 'phenomena', be they psychological, scientific, cultural or historical (*Ideas*, 42) – as in its method. Phenomenology entails 'a new way of looking at things . . . one that contrasts at every point with the natural attitude of experience and thought' (p. 43). This method is that of 'phenomenological reduction', a set of procedures which involve purifying the natural outlook of the contingencies of psychology and empiricism. To use its own terminology, phenomenology aims to describe transcendental consciousness through an intuition of essences. More simply, phenomenology describes consciousness stripped of its personal, empirical irrelevancies. Its object is *transcendental* in so far as it is not identified with any particular individual. Phenomenological reduction, also known as the *epoche*, puts aside, or 'brackets off' the contingent and personal to reveal the underlying universal structures of, for example, imagination or perception. It abandons the 'natural attitude' in an effort to describe, without preconception, what appears to consciousness, that is, phenomena as they are 'intended' by consciousness. But this is, as we shall see, easier said than done.

Derrida studied phenomenology in Paris with Emmanuel Levinas and Paul Ricoeur. He considers Husserl to have been one of the major influences on his philosophical formation, along with Heidegger and Hegel. Indeed, Derrida's whole philosophical programme seems to spring from his tussle with phenomenology. It is the phenomenological attempt to ground knowledge in experience, evidence and self-presence, and its apparent failure, that leads him to the conclusion that the attempt itself is fundamentally misconceived. Phenomenology does not fail, as Husserl believed, because it is still only in its infancy and success has so far eluded it, but because it is engaged in a project based on false, though ineluctably seductive, premises. As Derrida explains in an interview published in 1984, 'I never shared Husserl's pathos for, and commitment to, a phenomenology of presence. In fact, it was Husserl's method that helped me to suspect the very notion of presence and the fundamental role it played in all philosophies.'[1] This is, of course, a retrospective interpretation of his own attitude to Husserl, and by examining the three major texts Derrida devotes to the phenomenologist we will be able to assess the development of 'suspicion' as a dominant feature in his analyses.

Derrida's first and second published books both deal with Husserl: he translates and introduces *The Origin of Geometry* in 1962, producing a 170-page Introduction to a work of forty pages; and in 1967 *La Voix et le phénomène* is subtitled *Introduction au problème du signe dans la phénoménologie de Husserl*. Earlier still, as a research student in 1954, Derrida devoted his MA dissertation to *Le Problème de la genèse dans la philosophie de Husserl* (not published until 1990). Derrida's first published paper on Husserl, ' "Genèse et structure" et la phénoménologie',[2] was delivered at the invitation of Maurice de Gandillac at a conference in Cerisy la Salle in 1959 dedicated to *Genesis and Structure*. It opens with a warning: the attempt to apply the polarized concepts of 'genesis' and 'structure' to Husserl's work involves doing violence to the nature of his thought. The use of antagonistic and antithetical terms is out of keeping with Husserl's own dislike of debate, aporias and dilemmas. Husserl shunned efforts to find decisive solutions to philosophical questions, and associated such attempts with the 'speculative' or dialectical method which he rejected. In Husserl's view, both metaphysicians and empiricists are guilty of similar oversimplifications. However, Derrida accepts the challenge of the conference topic, and agrees to engage in what he describes as an 'aggression' and an 'infidelity' towards Husserl (*ED*, 228). Husserl himself, argues Derrida, would have rejected the opposition between genesis and structure as false: some areas of investigation invite a structural approach, some a genetic one; some layers of meaning appear in the form of systems and static configurations, others reveal their origins and development and demand a genetic interpretation. Husserl's objective is faithful description rather than rigid categorization. Derrida demonstrates how consistent Husserl is in this respect, combining and moving between analyses of genetic constitution and descriptions of formal, static structures in works as diverse as *Philosophie der Arithmetik* (1891), *Logical Investigations* (1900–1), and *Ideas* (1913). Indeed, Husserl's analyses frequently pass from an account of structures precisely to an investigation of the production of those structures, which in turn leads to a further exploration of the forms (what Husserl refers to as the 'structural *a prioris*') of that very genesis. Husserl, then, is 'serene' in his unified conception of the phenomenological endeavour (*ED*, 232).

Derrida, however, is less convinced. The tensions implicit in a mode of thinking that is simultaneously an exploration of intangible, *a priori* essences *and* a philosophy of experience, becoming and temporal flux cannot be so easily overcome. Derrida envisages two main problematic areas. Firstly, he considers that an unfinished debate underlies the apparent 'serenity' of all the major phases of phenomenological reduction, with the consequence that there is an indefinite need for a further reduction, however far the process has gone already. Secondly, this same debate appears to imperil the very principles of the phenomenological method, and to compel Husserl to transgress the supposedly descriptive nature of his work and its transcendental aims, and to enter into the metaphysics of history, the teleology of which becomes increasingly incompatible with *a priorism* or transcendental idealism.

In fact, Derrida maintains, it was an initial failure to reconcile the demands of structure with those of genesis that founded the phenomenological project. Husserl's investigations began with his *Philosophy of Arithmetic* (1891), intended to lay the foundations of a philosophy of mathematics, in which he analyses the concept of number from both a logical and a psychological point of view, relating the objectivity of arithmetical series and numbers to their concrete genesis. In the first place, he refuses to envisage the 'universal structure' of numbers as an eternal truth produced by an infinite reason. On the contrary, he insists on seeking its roots in subjectivity and acts of perception, and thereby lays himself open to accusations of 'psychologism', though he never falls into the trap of confusing factual constitution with epistemological validation. Indeed, Husserl's respect for what Derrida calls the 'ideal' and 'normative' nature of 'arithmetical meaning' (*ED*, 234) ultimately prevents him from espousing a psychological theory of the origin of arithmetic and forces him to accept Frege's criticism: the essence of number is no more dependent on consciousness than the existence of the North Sea. Logicism (the theory that all mathematics can be deduced from logic), however, is equally insufficient as an explanatory system: Husserl is determined to maintain simultaneously the autonomy of logic or mathematics with respect to individual consciousnesses *and* their originary dependence on subjectivity *in general*. It is this need for a concrete, but non-empirical, transcendental form of intentional consciousness that leads Husserl to his series of 'reductions'. His search for a common root for the objective structures of mathematics involves the wholesale rejection of causalism, naturalism and historicism, but *not* (in the long term) the abandonment of genetic description. Nor will Husserl consent to solve the problems he encounters by simply distinguishing between the natural and the human sciences: this very distinction begs all the questions it sets out to resolve.

Interestingly, Derrida points out, phenomenology and structuralism are born almost simultaneously: at the same time as Husserl is developing his earliest phenomenological theories, the first structuralist projects are being produced. And what is even more intriguing is that Husserl's objections to these – as they are exemplified by *Gestalt*[3] psychology and by Dilthey's critique of historical reason – are identical with his objections to geneticism. In his view, Dilthey's hermeneutic structuralism is historicist and, despite Dilthey's protests, relativist and sceptical (*ED*, 237). Husserl is positive about Dilthey's notion of *compréhension* (*verstehen*),[4] about his conception of unified, totalized structures, and about the distinction he draws between physical and mental structures, but he believes that these modifications are not radical, and in fact increase the threat of historicism by making it more seductive. History does not stop being an empirical science simply by reforming its methods.

In reaction, Derrida surmises, against historicist and psychologist forms of geneticism, the first phase of Husserl's elaboration of the phenomenological method entails a radical rejection of all geneticism and is resolutely static and structuralist. At this stage, Husserl distinguishes between empirical and eidetic or transcendental structures, but has not yet made a similar distinction regarding genesis. Derrida here engages directly with the very specialized argumentation of phenomenology in terms of noetico-noematic structures on the one hand and morphe-hyletic structures on the other (very broadly speaking, form and matter, but I do not propose to enter into these complex, technical issues) and argues that matter itself, for Husserl, necessarily implies temporality. The implications of this are immense: if the *hyle* (matter) is intrinsically temporal, then Husserl's attempt to eschew geneticism is undermined from within. If the transcendental structure of consciousness necessitates a passage to its genetic constitution, then Husserl's determination to remain in the domain of pure structure has brought about its own downfall. As Derrida will argue time and again, the basic premises of phenomenology, that is to say, originary evidence and the unmediated *presence* of the thing itself to consciousness, are radically put in question by the logic of phenomenology itself (*ED*, 244).

These problems arise from the attempt to determine the 'objectivity' of the object. A similar set of problems is attached to phenomenological psychology: if structuralist psychology claims to be independent of transcendental phenomenology, can it escape accusations of psychologism? Husserl himself recommended the establishment of a phenomenological psychology in parallel to transcendental phenomenology. However, the notion of a parallel implies the impossibility of moving from one plane to the other, and Husserl's criticisms of *Gestalt* psychology concern precisely its attempt to make such a move. In a sense, psychology and transcendental phenomenology are separated by *nothing*, but, like a good negative theologian, Derrida claims that it is this very 'nothing' that makes the transcendental reduction possible (*ED*, 246. See also *VP*, 12).

Derrida concludes his essay on 'Genèse et structure' with a brief examination of some of the later concerns of genetic phenomenology. He describes it as diffracted, after *Ideas 1*, in three different directions: firstly, towards the domain of logic, in which the 'reduction' is applied not merely to scientific idealizations but also to those of cultural life and lived experience. Secondly, towards a description of the ego: Husserl recognized explicitly that his accounts of the relationship between consciousness and its objects presupposed an ego whose constitution he should in due course account for (*ED*, 247. See the *Cartesian Meditations*). And thirdly, in the direction of history and teleology: indeed, history and teleology are not separable for Husserl, since he describes the *eidos* or essence of historicity as its *telos*. What is more, Derrida argues, the *eidos* of history is for Husserl not merely one essence amongst others, it implies the whole of existing beings in so far as these are part of human, animal or natural life. Here, Derrida suggests, Husserl has surely gone beyond phenomenological description into the domain of metaphysics. Reason, Husserl maintains, is the *Logos* as it is produced in history. It is speech as *auto-affection*, self-presence mediated through language only to return once more to its original self-identity. The deconstruction of this position is one of Derrida's major concerns in *La Voix et le phénomène*. *The Origin of Geometry* describes the exposition of reason in the world as both indispensable to the constitution of truth yet threatened by the exteriority of the sign. This text was to be the subject of Derrida's first book and we shall examine it shortly.

Phenomenology, then, in Derrida's first account of it, is both a critique of metaphysics and also a participant in the metaphysical enterprise. It cannot avoid entrapment in the system it is setting out to criticize.[5] Husserl himself recognizes and indeed asserts this relationship in his *Cartesian Meditations* when he claims that phenomenology is indeed metaphysical in so far as the term implies the deepest knowledge of being. He envisages phenomenology as the final phase in a process that has led from pre-theoretical culture through philosophy to the phenomenological project itself. And it is this project that finally reconciles structure and genesis in so far as it may be described *structurally* as *genesis* itself. These descriptions, Derrida maintains, have depended on a series of fundamental distinctions between different kinds of genesis (worldly and transcendental) and different kinds of structure (empirical, eidetic and transcendental). Ultimately, it makes no sense to ask what the notions of structure and genesis *in general* mean, or even mean for Husserl. Husserl himself did not overlook or neglect these general questions; rather he recognized that answering them would involve moving into a domain prior to the transcendental reduction itself. And this domain would be that of the very possibility of questioning, of interrogation itself. It would be the domain therefore of meaninglessness and death, and as such prior to philosophical investigation.[6]

Derrida's first account, then, takes phenomenology on its own terms, at the same time as teasing out the contradictions and tensions which are implicit in the project and which Husserl himself believed to be symptoms of its immaturity rather than aporias lying at its very heart. Derrida does not declare himself on the vexed question of genesis *versus* structure, but reveals the disturbing paradoxes raised both by an attempt to reconcile them and by an attempt to opt for one at the expense of the other. For the moment genesis and structure appear in an uneasy and unstable symbiosis.

Derrida's translation and Introduction to *The Origin of Geometry* was published in 1962, three years after his Cerisy paper was delivered, though a couple of years before it appeared in print in Gandillac's collection of the conference proceedings (*Genèse et structure*, Paris, Mouton, 1964). As a first book from a now major figure it is notable as providing a clear foretaste of Derrida's later procedures: it is an exceptionally close reading of a text he knows inside out having undertaken its translation, in which, under the guise of exposition, he unravels and unpicks all the stitchings and patchings that have gone towards making an apparently seamless surface from a tangled web of philosophical conflicts. Once again, Derrida is concerned to explore the limits of transcendental phenomenology, but this time his object is more specific and his approach more focused and less wide-ranging. Methodologically, a major difference is the emergence of what is to become one of Derrida's trade-marks: the attention to the textuality of the philosophical argument, and, concomitantly, the preoccupation with the role of linguistic expression as it figures in the argument itself. In other words, Derrida is concerned with both the language of Husserl's thesis and the role played by questions of language in that thesis.

In *The Origin of Geometry*, a version of which was first published in 1939, though the full text had to wait until 1954, Husserl returns to the realm of mathematics and sets out to demonstrate the nature of the historicity of ideal objects[7] such as the concepts of geometry. In his account, ideal objects have their origin in human thought rather than in nature, they are not located in space or time, they are universally available and objective, and they possess what Derrida terms an 'ideal omnitemporality' (*OG*, 65–6). They do not depend for their constitution on any particular human subject, but emerge from a process of idealization and imagination in which features of the perceptual field are 'subtracted' and intuited in a kind of leap of intellectual progress. Husserl is concerned to rebut both historicism and objectivism: neither empirical transmission nor ahistorical idealism can properly explain the origin of what appears to be the privileged object of Husserl's reflexion – mathematical objects. Fifty years earlier, in *The Philosophy of Arithmetic* (1891), Husserl had accounted for the originary meaning of the ideal unities of arithmetic by returning to the structures of perception. Already at that stage he had attempted to explain both the ideal normativity of number *and* its foundation in and through an act of production. The origin of arithmetic was described in terms of 'psychological genesis'. Half a century later, *The Origin of Geometry* returns to the same project in terms of 'phenomenological history' (*OG*, 6–7). Derrida points out that the continuity is all the more remarkable in that, in the meantime, Husserl has rejected psychological and historical genesis, and that, when he does discover the genetic aspect of phenomenology, he still does not relate it to historicity. It is not until *Die Krisis* in 1935–7,[8] that history irrupts finally into phenomenology, and even there it is not explicitly problematized. Husserl still has the triple task of demonstrating that history, as an empirical science, depends, like all empiricism, on phenomenology to reveal its presuppositions; that history, despite its irreversibility, is still susceptible to imaginary variations; and finally, that the empirical content of certain eidetic structures such as geometry has itself been produced in history. It is these three ambitions which, in Derrida's view, motivate *The Origin of Geometry*. What is more, Husserl's brief text audaciously transgresses the limits of its specific and ostensible subject – geometry – to explore the conditions of possibility of the history of science in general, and, beyond even that, to consider universal historicity as the ultimate horizon of meaning and objectivity (*OG*, 13–14).

Unlike Dilthey, Husserl is not really interested in the specifics of the historical transmission of the realm of ideas but rather in the conditions of possibility for the constitution of that realm. Husserl's phenomenology of history is concerned not with empirical origins but rather with the very notion of origin. None the less, as Derrida insists, constitution and transmission, origin and *telos*, cannot be radically separated from each other. Derrida is fascinated by the implications of a phenomenology of historicity in so far as it necessarily implies a 'phenomenology of phenomenology' of which phenomenology itself is ultimately incapable (*OG*, 155 and *ED*, 248).

In 1980 Derrida refers to Husserlian phenomenology as 'a discipline of incomparable rigour', but goes on to describe his own Introduction to *The Origin of Geometry* as an opportunity to explore its 'un-thought-out axiomatics', and in particular 'the lack of attention paid to the problem of its own phenomenological enunciation, to transcendental discourse itself . . . to the necessity of recourse . . . to a language that could not itself be submitted to the *epoche* . . . thus to a language which remained naive'.[9] Husserl explores the problematics of writing in the constitution of ideal objects with a rigour that Derrida describes as 'unprecedented in the history of philosophy', but does not consider the logical implications of this for the phenomenological enterprise itself. This lack of philosophical reflexivity is the weak spot in Husserl's thinking, and one that will, in Derrida's view, ultimately prove the undoing of his project.

Husserl describes his technique of historical questioning as a *Rückfrage*, translated by Derrida as 'question en retour', in English as 'return inquiry'. Its method is that of a 'zigzag': a to-and-fro procedure between understanding and investigation, in a kind of hermeneutic circle which proceeds retrospectively from the state of contemporary science to an understanding of its development and origins. Husserl examines 'what must have been the case' (*OG*, 35). Where Derrida parts company with him is over the question of the status of the failures and misunderstandings which dog the transmission of knowledge and understanding. Even apparently fundamental axioms are surrounded, in Husserl's view, by a 'sedimentation of meaning' that separates him from their 'origin', to which he is attempting to return (*OG*, 42). Sometimes Husserl considers geometry and science in general as cultural forms amongst others (*OG*, 44), at other times he describes science as unique: an exemplary cultural form which transcends specific cultures through its universal truth-value. This contradiction underlies his hesitations concerning the significance of historical errors: for example, what he calls Galileo's 'fatal negligence', i.e. his failure to reflect on the origin of geometry (*OG*, 17; *Krisis*, 49), is interpreted variously as an empirical necessity, that is to say as a contingent matter of individual psychology; as a moral failure involving an abdication of philosophical responsibility; and as an eidetic necessity. This last interpretation would threaten Husserl's thesis if it were allowed to prevail. Derrida refutes Husserl's contention that non-communication and misunderstanding are inessential, maintaining on the contrary that they are part of a finitude which can never be entirely overcome (*OG*, 77). Forgetfulness of truth, Derrida argues, is not merely empirical weakness, it is essential to the nature of historical transmission, and may be radical (*OG*, 98).

The disagreement between Derrida and Husserl is particularly apparent where language is concerned. Husserl describes linguistic objectivation and mathematical symbolization as an occasion for alienation and degradation. In certain kinds of education, for example, signs may be used without any understanding of their original meaning, which is hidden beneath layers of sedimentation (*OG*, 99). But it is none the less writing which creates an autonomous transcendental field, an ideal objective meaning, independent of a singular speaking subject in the first place (*OG*, 83–4). Writing is a condition of what Hyppolite called 'a transcendental field without a subject', it is the locus of 'absolute objectivity' (*OG*, 85). However, the absence of subjectivity from the transcendental field may guarantee its objectivity, but such an absence can only ever be artificial (*factice*). Writing may be independent of any actual reader, but its essence as intelligibility requires a transcendental subject if it is to retain its transcendental function. It is this 'pure juridical possibility of intelligibility' that leads Husserl to describe the linguistic or graphic text as a 'spiritual body' or flesh. Writing is not simply the vehicle for a meaning which is independent of it, not a mere 'mnémotechnique', auxiliary to the truth which has no need of it. It is the act of writing that constitutes its very objectivity; the grapheme is not just the clothing of the idea, but its incarnation (*OG*, 86). Paradoxically, the possibility of writing permits the liberation of 'ideality'. But the embodiment of truth in the grapheme is necessarily double-edged: while it may make possible the persistence of truth over time, it also makes possible its loss. The illegibility of the documents of ancient civilizations is not a simple misfortune, it is a potential feature of all inscription, and reveals the transcendental meaning of death and failure (*OG*, 85). In Husserl's account, writing has a very special status: neither purely sensible nor purely intelligible, it is the locus of a whole series of ambiguities centred on the movement between essence and contingency, pure potential and the empirical, dependence and independence (*OG*, 90). Husserl, in Derrida's view, never satisfactorily resolves the problems raised in his transcendental philosophy by the possibility of the loss of meaning and truth. He can deal with the notion of the destruction of inscribed meaning only as a contingent accident. While acknowledging that the risk of destruction is real, he denies it all philosophical significance. Truth, for Husserl, cannot be seen to depend on its embodiment, even if it is that embodiment that guarantees its durability and objectivity. Derrida puts this attitude in parallel with a similar analysis in *Ideas* concerning the intangibility of pure consciousness, and the fortunes of consciousness in a hypothetical situation where the existing world would be destroyed. While recognizing that in this extreme scenario all consciousnesses would in fact be annihilated, Husserl still insists that this would not eliminate transcendental consciousness in so far as it is absolutely independent of any individual consciousness (*OG*, 95). Similarly, the truths of geometry are deemed independent of all facticity, and Husserl maintains that they could not be threatened even by a world-wide catastrophe. This position, Derrida argues, is radically incompatible with Husserl's view of writing as the incarnation of truth rather than a mere sensible phenomenon.

Derrida, then, shows Husserl unable to resolve the internal contradictions of his own theses: language and symbolization are necessary to science and truth but, by the same token, the occasion of their alienation and degradation. The notion of the 'sedimentation' of truth implies simultaneously the possibility of its rediscovery and reactivation after a period of loss, but also, and less desirably, the danger that it may be permanently forgotten (*OG*, 100). Transcendental phenomenology appears unable to deal properly with the implications of human finitude and historicity.

This weakness in Husserlian phenomenology characterizes not only his reflections on language but also on imagination, reason and temporality. Imagination, Derrida points out, is ambiguous in status: derivative and reproductive on the one hand, the manifestation of radical freedom on the other. In what is (probably) his first published reflection on Sartre, Derrida correctly pinpoints this dual aspect of the imagination as the key to Sartre's disruption and later abandonment of the phenomenological project (*OG*, 135. See also p. 148). We shall return to the complex interrelationship of the thought of Sartre, Derrida and Husserl when we examine *La Voix et le phénomène*. So far as *The Origin of Geometry* is concerned, the idealizing procedure which results in geometrical truths is never fully grounded in the morphology of the physical world: 'sensible idealities' provide a support for 'ideal essences' but these always result ultimately from an intellectual leap, the product of radical liberty and discontinuity which defies a genealogical account (*OG*, 145). Similarly, the phenomenological privileging of the present moment, maintained as an absolute origin, is undermined by the selfsame phenomenological account which displays the imbrication of the present in structures of retention and protention which ultimately reveal the relationship of temporality to historicity, facticity and death (*OG*, 149–50). Finally, the notions of the historicity of reason and a teleologically determined rationality are explored by Derrida in an analysis which once again brings to light the contradictions and paradoxes contained in Husserl's account. The historicity of reason and the rationality of history sit ill with the absolute transcendence of the Logos. But the ambiguities in his account are never recognized by Husserl as a 'dilemma' in the phenomenological scheme. The impossibility of maintaining the plenitude of the present, the purity of the origin, or the self-identity of the absolute in the face of 'delay', 'postponement' and 'originary Difference' is the focus of Derrida's final paragraph in his Introduction to *The Origin of Geometry*. It will be one of his major preoccupations in *La Voix et le phénomène*.

Husserl's *Logical Investigations* of 1900 founded his phenomenological critique of metaphysics and set forth the key concepts which dominate his writing right up until the *Krisis*, in particular the theory and practice of phenomenological and eidetic reduction and the belief in the unmediated presence to consciousness of the structures to which reduction gives access. Derrida's aim, in *La Voix et le phénomène* (1967), as also in his short essay of the same year, 'La

forme et le vouloir-dire: note sur la phénoménologie du langage'
(collected in *Marges*), is, through a study of the role of the sign in
Husserl's thinking, to show that rather than producing a critique of
metaphysics, Husserl is, in fact, himself a metaphysical thinker.
Husserl's criticisms of metaphysics are really attacks on its degradation or perversion and arise precisely from a desire to create a purer
or more 'authentic' version of metaphysics. Derrida is not simply
claiming (as he will do for certain other philosophers such as
Heidegger) that there are metaphysical residues still clinging to
Husserl's thought, but, rather more radically, that metaphysical
presuppositions of a dogmatic and speculative nature constitute
phenomenology at its deepest level, and are merely masked by the
rigour and subtlety of Husserl's analyses (*VP*, 4). Husserl's critique
of metaphysical and speculative systems cannot save his own
project to create a theory of knowledge from being itself metaphysical, 'precisely in what it will recognize as the source and guarantee
of all value, the "principle of principles", that is, originary given
evidence, the *present* or the *presence* of meaning to a full and
originary intuition' (*VP*, 3).

Husserl's argument about signification, as proposed in the *Logical Investigations*, depends on the distinction he draws between two
different meanings of the term 'sign' (*Zeichen*), that is, expression
(*Ausdruck*) and indication (*indice, Anzeichen*). Derrida describes
Husserl as carrying out a kind of phenomenological reduction *avant
la lettre*: Husserl proposes to put aside all pre-constituted knowledge, insists on the need to abandon all presuppositions, be they
metaphysical, psychological or scientific, and emphasizes that in
taking the 'fact' of language as a starting-point its contingency must
be borne in mind. In other words, Husserl maintains, his analyses
would be equally valid from an epistemological point of view
whether or not languages really existed, or speaking subjects, or
indeed nature itself. One of the major themes of Husserl's proclaimed critique of metaphysics is his denunciation of its blindness
to the 'authentic mode of ideality', that is to say, to the potential
of an ideal object for unlimited repetition in its true presence and
self-identity, precisely because it does not exist, and is unreal, not in
the sense of a fiction, but rather in the sense of being an essence or
a *noeme*. And the ultimate form of ideality is that of self-presence.
Presence has always been the form in which the infinite diversity of
contents is produced. The opposition between form and content,
which Derrida sees as inaugurating metaphysics, finds its radical
justification in the concrete ideality of the 'living present' (*VP*, 5).

Derrida proposes to destroy the self-sufficiency of this phenomeno-logical notion through his analyses of temporality and intersub-jectivity, and to demonstrate that the fissures that prevent pure presence in both cases are implicit in the phenomenological descrip-tion itself (*VP*, 5).

The sign, Derrida argues, is the privileged concept in Husserl's thinking: this means that the essence of the sign is never fully interrogated and that Husserl is compelled to defer indefi-nitely any explicit meditation on the nature of language in general. Moreover, Husserl never poses the question of the 'transcendental Logos', never questions the language in which phenomenology produces and expresses the results of its reductions. There is a continuum between the 'ordinary' language of traditional meta-physics and that of phenomenology, despite all Husserl's precau-tions, innovations and 'scare-quotes'. A metaphorical language usage cannot take the place of a proper consideration of the presuppositions of the language of phenomenology. However, in 'La forme et le vouloir-dire' of 1967, Derrida shows Husserl blaming metaphor for the inconsistencies in his own account of language: is language reflective and representative (*Abbildung*), or is it imaginative and creative (*Einbildung*) (*Marges*, 198)? Husserl does not investigate the contradiction, or analyse its common root, but simply warns against the seductions of metaphor. And when Husserl is concerned to establish the relationship between pure grammar and pure logic, to understand the rules determining whether an utterance is meaningful or not, he does not consider the whole domain of language, only its logical *a priori*, which he refers to as 'pure logical grammar' (*VP*, 7). But the singling out of logic within the domain of language is not seen by Husserl as the selection of a region, but rather as the designation of the essence or *telos* of language. And each time that self-presence might be under threat, Husserl saves it in the form of a *telos*: it is as an ideality that the presence of an object may be indefinitely repeated as one and the same. The ideality of meaning is the guarantee that its presence to (ideal or transcendental) consciousness can always be repeated. Language is the locus of this play of presence and absence. And it is spoken language that seems best to preserve simultaneously ideality and living presence, just as phenomeno-logy, a metaphysics of presence in the form of ideality, is also a philosophy of *life*. But Derrida sees this salvation of presence through ideality as indicating also the relationship of existence to death. Presence in its pure sense is not the presence of anything that *exists* in the world; the movement of idealization implies the death of the 'existent'.

Derrida's account of the sign starts with an explanation of what might be termed a problem of translation: the *Anzeichen* (indication) is a sign without *Bedeutung* or *Sinn*, that is, in French, without *signification*, and the *Ausdruck* is a sign with *signification*. Now a sign with or without signification implies a paradox not present in the German, and Derrida suggests *vouloir dire* as a better equivalent for *Bedeutung*. In English both *signification* and *vouloir dire* may be rendered 'meaning' and the problem is somewhat displaced. But the main point is that *Bedeutung* involves intention, intended meaning, and language is the major medium of such expressivity (*VP*, 20). Husserl's aim is to show that pure expression is radically separable from communication and indication; he is determined to preserve the theoretical distinction between the two domains even if, in practice, the two are almost always found together. Husserl is bent on contesting the view that language, and in particular speech, is a subset of indication; he therefore relegates the non-expressive features of language (such as its physical aspect and its communicative potential) to the domain of contingent accidents. To this end he needs to find a phenomenological situation in which indication is not present, in order to study pure expressivity. His chosen domain is that of interior monologue, and Derrida points out the paradox of focusing on *ex*pressivity in a domain where all relationship to an 'outside' is suspended. However, Derrida maintains, what he has called a paradox in fact constitutes the essence of the phenomenological project: to go beyond 'idealism' and 'realism', beyond 'subjectivism' and 'objectivism', and to describe the 'objectivity' of the object and the 'presence' of the present starting from a position of pure interiority – hence the necessity for the 'reduction' of the external world (*VP*, 23).

Husserl's analyses attempt, then, to explore 'expression' freed from the contingent additions of both indication and communication. Both, he contends, depend on the incomplete presence of the intention animating the utterance: to communicate with another I am necessarily dependent on some kind of physical mediation which comes between my intended meaning and its reception, and which keeps my *vécu* (lived experience) from being fully present. The relation to the other must be suspended in order to observe expression in its pure state. Interior monologue is the privileged domain of pure expression: Husserl claims that when I speak to myself I learn nothing, and my words have no indicative or communicative function (*VP*, 46). Indeed, in Husserl's view, in interior monologue my words do not have any real existence, they are rather represented or imagined. And in Husserl's theory of imagination, unlike the classical psychology of imagination, images do not exist, they cannot be identified with the imagined objects they may represent (*VP*, 52).

Derrida will contest the claim that in interior monologue I learn nothing by turning Husserl's own arguments against him. Husserl, he says, has himself given us the means of refuting him. The nature of the sign, as Husserl demonstrated, is to be repeatable – if it were unique it could not function as a sign. The nature of the sign is also to be representative: ideality itself depends on repeatability. In the domain of interior monologue, Husserl has to engage in some disconcerting arguments: firstly, that pure expressivity is to be found only in the imaginary realm; secondly, that within this realm any communication a subject may engage in with himself can only ever be fictive; thirdly, that a rigorous distinction may be drawn between fictive and effective, ideal and real; and fourthly, that within interior monologue some discourses may be effectively representative (expressive language uses) and others purely fictive (communicative and indicative uses). Now if it is agreed that all signs are necessarily repeatable, then the distinction between fictive and effective uses of a sign is threatened: the sign is originally fictive. The implications of this are immense for Husserl's argument: there is now no criterion for distinguishing between exterior and interior language or between effective and fictive language. But such distinctions are vital for Husserl's attempt to demonstrate the exteriority of indication to expression, and if they are illegitimate, the consequences for the whole phenomenological enterprise are formidable (*VP*, 63). What is more, the consequences can be extended from the domain of the sign to that of the speaking subject: the distinction between effective communication and a simple representation of the self as speaking subject cannot be sustained if the subject cannot speak without representing itself as so doing. The link between discourse and self-representation is not an accident: discourse and representation are intrinsically linked; discourse *is* the representation of self. Husserl maintains that consciousness is deluded when it imagines that it can communicate with itself; Derrida's argument is the exact reverse of this: it is Husserl who is deluded when he imagines that consciousness is pure unmediated self-presence and that it has no need of any kind of representation (*VP*, 64–5). For Husserl, the sign is alien to consciousness which, in

its full self-presence, has no need of mediation; representation of the
self is impossible because it is unnecessary. It would be pointless,
zwecklos, in Husserl's term. For Derrida, this is precisely the point
where Husserl's argument destroys itself.

The notion of the self-presence of consciousness necessarily has
temporal implications. In his *Logical Investigations* Husserl does not
explore the question of the temporality of experience, but a notion
of the 'now' as a punctual instant, a point in time, underlies his
whole system of 'essential distinctions'. And this is, in Derrida's
view, the stumbling block of the whole phenomenological project:
'If the punctuality of the instant is a myth, a spatial or mechanical
metaphor, an inherited metaphysical concept . . . if the present of
self-presence is not *simple*, if it is constituted in an originary and
irreducible synthesis, then all Husserl's argument is threatened at
its roots' (*VP*, 68). Consciousness is, Husserl maintains, identical to
itself in the undivided unity of the present moment. However this is
quite incompatible with his account of perception as involving
memory and anticipation, retention and protention, not as mere
accompanying features but as indispensable to the very possibility
of perception. Indeed, Husserl vacillates between describing
memory as a mode of perception in which the past is made present
and not merely represented, and describing it as the opposite of
perception. At times, perception is shown in perpetual commerce
with non-perception, and the pure moment of 'now' deemed an
ideal and abstract limit. The continuity between the 'now' and the
'not-now' introduces alterity into the self-identity of the present
moment, and this alterity is the paradoxical condition of presence.
All possibility of simple self-identity is thereby undone (*VP*, 73).
Husserl's insistence on erecting firm barriers between first-degree
and second-degree memory, and his attempt to maintain the former
(retention) as a form of originary perception, reveal both his determination and his anxiety. But even if we concede this distinction,
Derrida argues, the damage is still done: the possibility of repetition
and trace do not simply inhabit the present, they constitute it in the
movement of difference which they introduce into it.[10] The 'trace'
of retention is more 'originary' than phenomenological originarity
itself. The ideality of the form of presence means that it is susceptible of infinite repetition, and that originary truth is rooted in the
finitude of retention. It is, Derrida maintains, the non-self-identity
of so-called originary presence that explains the possibility of reflection and representation which is essential to all lived experience. So
the fissuring of the present moment fissures in its turn the self-

identity of the inner self of phenomenological reduction, and opens it up to the very alterity it was intended to exclude. Husserl himself draws the comparison between the relationship of the ego to an *alter ego* and the relationship between the present and the 'other present' which is the past (*VP*, 77. See *Cartesian Meditations*, §52). The dialectic that has been uncovered has spelt the end of Husserl's cherished distinction between expression and indication; it will also go further – into the most intimate reaches of the self, which Husserl will strive in vain to maintain are originally free from all linguistic contamination, even that of expressivity, in the absolute silence of self-presence.

In Husserl's account of interior monologue Derrida perceives a fundamental self-contradiction. Husserl takes interior monologue as the prime example of unmediated self-presence: when I hear myself speak I simultaneously understand what I am saying. In French, this is embodied in the double meaning of *entendre* as both 'hear' and 'understand', so *s'entendre parler* means both to hear and to understand oneself speak. There is an absolute proximity between signifier and signified. In this sense Husserl can, and does, argue that the speaking itself is redundant: I understand myself perfectly without the need for language or speech (*VP*, 90). Indeed, he argues that there is a *pre*-expressive level of meaning, an originary level of pre-linguistic self-understanding. This coheres, in Derrida's view, with Husserl's desire to contain the power of the sign, but not with his contention that scientific truth, and therefore ideal objects, depend for their constitution on language, and indeed not just on speech but ultimately on inscription or writing. The problem here is the one Derrida explored in his study of *The Origin of Geometry*: Husserl tries to maintain simultaneously two mutually exclusive positions with respect to language, a recognition of the essential embodiment of language and a desire to minimize, perhaps even neutralize, the role of the signifier. However, self-understanding and *auto-affection* themselves indicate, through their very reflexivity, the divided nature of self-presence: division does not enter consciousness *après coup*, it is division and difference that *constitute* the transcendental subject. Subjectivity is constituted rather than constitutive (*VP*, 92–4). In a wordplay reminiscent of Sartre's *L'Être et le Néant*, Derrida argues that the *pour-soi* (for itself) of self-presence is not unitary, it is *for*-itself in the sense that it is in place of itself, it is divided at its origin, originally divided (*VP*, 99). We will return to this similarity shortly.

The notion of replacement or substitution allows Derrida to introduce his notion of the *supplement*. The supplement has a 'strange structure': 'a possibility produces belatedly that which it is deemed to be adding to' (*VP*, 99). And Derrida describes signification, meaning, perception and presence in terms of the logic of supplementarity. In all these cases, as we have already seen, Husserl has struggled to show the pure, self-present origin to which extraneous elements such as indication, retention and division or absence are retrospectively added. Derrida, however, argues for a reversal of priorities. The additional or 'supplementary' features are in fact nothing of the sort, they are essential to the very constitution that they have been deemed to contaminate. Truth and subjectivity do not exist in a realm prior to language, they depend on language for their very existence. Husserl's desire to preserve the immediacy of presence has been thwarted by the logic of his own arguments: there is no original presence, only representation; no direct intuition, only mediated knowledge; no pure present moment, only a contamination of past and future; no self-identity, only irremediable self-division and difference. The phenomenological enterprise is doomed to failure for there can be no return to 'things themselves', because 'the thing itself is always concealed' (*VP*, 117). Self-presence and ideality have been infinitely deferred.

Husserlian phenomenology has been used by Derrida to show that presence cannot preserve itself against absence, division and difference. Difference and non-identity lie at the heart of even the most apparently unproblematic moments of plenitude. Indeed, difference is, for Derrida, precisely what prevents and replaces self-identity. It is a key term which will need exploration in its own right, especially in its gerundive formation as *différance* with an 'a'.[11]

In 1964 Derrida published an essay entitled 'Violence et métaphysique: essai sur la pensée d'Emmanuel Levinas', later collected in *L'Écriture et la différence*. In it he considers Levinas's critique of Western philosophy, carried out from the point of view of a Jewish philosopher and theologian. The essay is prefaced with an epigraph from Matthew Arnold: 'Hebraism and Hellenism – between these two points of influence moves our world' (*ED*, 117). The text is probably of most interest from an ethical perspective, but it is also illuminating in its analysis of Levinas's ambivalent relationship to phenomenology. Levinas's thought is originally phenomenological; he defines himself initially in relation and opposition to Husserl, using Heidegger as an aid to his critique, and later in opposition to Heidegger. Derrida's focus in the essay is very much on this three-way interrelationship, in which he unravels many of the knotty disagreements and misunderstandings between the thinkers in order to concentrate more clearly on the most significant points of difference between them.

The starting-point is the so-called 'death of philosophy', variously dated from Hegel, Marx, Nietzsche or Heidegger, and Derrida argues that it is through the very question of whether philosophy is dying that thought itself has a future: it can and must found a community that questions.[12] It is precisely this reflection on its own position that marks out philosophy today, in the characteristic reflexivity of twentieth-century thought. In the case of Husserlian phenomenology and Heideggerian ontology, despite their differences, this reflection on the nature and future of philosophy may be seen in three major, shared preoccupations. Both thinkers view the source of all philosophy as Greek, both believe in the subordination or reduction of metaphysics, and both dissociate ethics from metaphysics and envisage ethics as dependent on some prior, more radical, authority ('instance'). Husserl and Heidegger, Derrida argues, represent the two major paths philosophy has taken since Hegel, but Levinas contests all three of their areas of agreement: firstly the domination of Greece, secondly the relegation of metaphysics, and thirdly the subordination of ethics, which he sees rather as self-grounding and as the potential liberator of transcendence and metaphysics.

What Derrida sets out to do is complex. He starts off by defending Husserl and Heidegger against Levinas's over-literal interpretation of them, only to use Levinas as a means of embarking on his own critique of phenomenology, and to conclude with a plea for reflection on precisely those issues Levinas has raised concerning the relationship between Greek and Jewish thought, albeit from a better-grounded theoretical position. We will return to the essay in the final chapter on ethics. For the moment the aim is to disentangle Derrida's argument about Levinas's misreading of Husserlian phenomenology.

Levinas knew Husserl's work intimately: he studied under him in Freiburg in 1928–9, in 1930 he published the first work on Husserl in French, *Théorie de l'intuition dans la phénoménologie de Husserl*, and he collaborated on the French translation of the *Cartesian Meditations* (1931).[13] But even in his first work Levinas is not uncritical of

Husserlian theory, maintaining, for example, that in privileging light as a key metaphor for phenomenological understanding, Husserl predetermines *being* as an object. Derrida is unsympathetic to both aspects of this criticism, contending firstly that Levinas himself will not find it easy to do without metaphors of light when he elaborates his ethics of the face,[14] and secondly that Husserl is so far from determining *being* as an object that in *Ideas 1* only pure consciousness is deemed to have absolute existence. None the less, Derrida acknowledges the subtlety of Levinas's critique and comments on the ways in which it becomes more nuanced in later works; Levinas is described as oscillating between the letter and the spirit of Husserl's thinking, using the latter to contest the former, in a way that may sound to the reader a little similar to Derrida's own methods. But Derrida's account of Levinas's analysis of phenomenology is predominantly critical. In the first place Levinas is shown as falling into the trap of believing he can take over the phenomenological method without subscribing to its premises; and furthermore, while attempting to preserve the key notion of intentionality, Levinas misrepresents Husserl on both the question of adequation and that of the relationship of the *cogito* to the infinite. For Husserl, Derrida argues, full adequation is impossible, and it is precisely the notion of the infinite that protects against the closure of totalization. Finally, Derrida contests Levinas's interpretation of the phenomenological *alter ego*, arguing that it is a manifest misreading of Husserl to focus on the ego as some kind of alienating hypostasis and to ignore the genuine alterity implied by the *alter*. In other words, Levinas is far closer to Husserl than he acknowledges, and this will have significant implications in the domain of ethics.

In his account of Levinas's critique of phenomenology, Derrida is careful, patient, yet remorselessly critical of what he sees as misrepresentations of Husserl and Heidegger. He returns to the question of misrepresentations of Husserl and Heidegger a few years later, this time in the context not of Jewish theology and ethics, but rather of existential and humanist interpretations. Here his criticisms will be just as radical, but his reading less careful and less patient.

The critique of Husserl is continued in a paper given in New York in 1968 entitled 'Les Fins de l'homme' and collected in *Marges: de la philosophie* (1972). One of the questions the paper addresses is why the 'anthropologizing' readings of Hegel, Heidegger and Husserl, promulgated by Sartre, held sway for so long. The question is more rhetorical than real, for Derrida goes on to show what he considers to be the metaphysical and humanist underpinnings lying beneath even the most concerted attempt to escape from metaphysics and anthropology. As far as Husserl is concerned, the essay adds little to what we have already seen, but it provides fascinating evidence of Derrida's influential and arguably wilful misreading of Sartre. Sartre's 'phenomenological ontology' (the subtitle of L'Être et le Néant), is, in Derrida's view, a form of philosophical anthropology. Sartre sets out to describe the structures of 'human reality': 'human reality' is Corbin's translation for Heidegger's Dasein, and Derrida refers to it as 'monstrous' in its humanizing of the neutral Heideggerian term. Sartre is accused of never questioning the history of the concept of 'Man': 'It is as if the sign "man" had no origin, no historical, cultural or lingustic limit. Nor even any metaphysical limit' (Marges, 137). Sartre, Derrida contends, views both the en-soi (in-itself) and the pour-soi (for-itself) as Being, and their reunification as the fundamental human project. It is true that this conception is to be found in L'Être et le Néant, but it is part of a brief concluding section of metaphysical speculation which Sartre declares he will not attempt to resolve. Derrida's choice of an untypical passage of 'as if' thinking is intriguing, for it serves to minimize aspects of Sartre's philosophy which have close affinities with Derrida's own. In two lengthy footnotes Derrida discusses Sartre's ironic dismantling of humanism in the person of the Autodidacte in La Nausée, as well as the importance of the notions of lack, negativity and non-self-identity in both L'Être et le Néant and the Critique de la raison dialectique. It is clear from these discussions that Derrida is very familiar with the detail of Sartre's texts, and his relegation to footnotes of major notions which contravene his principal thesis indicates a certain scholarly scruple, not without an element of bad conscience.

Like Derrida, Sartre's first published work, La Transcendance de l'ego (1936), was also a critique of Husserl. In it Sartre argues against Husserl that the ego is transcendent not transcendental. A transcendental ego would be a personal core of consciousness, an original unitary subject, interior foundation for the self. It would, by the same token, be a 'centre of opacity' which would entail 'the death of consciousness' (TE, 23–5). For Sartre the ego or self is a synthetic and imaginary product of consciousness. In L'Être et le Néant (1943), he describes consciousness as 'a transcendental field without a subject' (EN, 291);[15] it is the reflexivity of consciousness which

brings the subject into being. The term *pour-soi* is an indication of
this reflexivity: the subject can never *be soi* or there would be no
reflexivity and the *soi* would disappear in self-identity and self-
coincidence. The for-itself is fundamentally riven, or fissured (*EN*,
120). Its self-presence is the precise opposite of 'plenitude'; on the
contrary, presence is what prevents identity: 'If it is present to itself,
that means it is not completely itself' (*EN*, 120). Conversely, the
en-soi is not present at all in Sartre's view: 'the *en-soi* cannot be
present' (*EN*, 165), 'to be *there* is not to be present' (*EN*, 165). The
term *en-soi* itself, which Sartre says he borrowed from 'tradition', is,
he maintains, misleading precisely in so far as there can be no *soi* for
a self-identical being (*EN*, 118). We will not explore Sartre's discussion of the *en-soi* in this context, but focus rather on the nature of the
pour-soi. Sartre's analysis of the self-presence of the for-itself anticipates by over twenty years Derrida's own analysis in *La Voix et le
phénomène*. The first chapter of part II of *L'Être et le Néant* cites
Husserl as evidence that even the most determined philosopher
of presence cannot escape entirely the reflexivity implicit in all
consciousness. And, again like Derrida, Sartre discusses the nature
of temporality, rejecting the Aristotelian notion of time as a series
of instants, and arguing that it is a misunderstanding of the nature
of the *pour-soi* which lies at the heart of the 'common-sense' view of
time: 'The present moment emanates from a realizing and reifying
conception of the for-itself' (*EN*, 168). The *pour-soi* in fact 'is always
in suspense because its being is a perpetual postponement [*sursis*,
deferral]' (*EN*, 771).

La Voix et le phénomène is an extended, patient and exciting reading of Husserl. In 'Les Fins de l'homme', Derrida admits that he is
only sketching out the 'dominant features' of a period. Sartre is a
vampire, rather than a careful exegete, taking what he wants from
other philosophers and using it for his own purposes. None the less,
Derrida attributes to him positions diametrically opposed to those
he in fact holds. In the case of Husserl, Derrida's own analyses are
strikingly close to Sartre's, and the foundations of his critique of
phenomenology almost identical.[16] I have argued elsewhere the case
for viewing attitudes to Sartre in the 1960s as parricidal.[17] The case
is all the stronger here as Derrida appears to be repeating the broad
lines of an analysis he is unwilling to recognize as constituting a
precursor text. Thirty years later, Derrida adopted a markedly more
generous attitude towards Sartre, as he explored with evident
pleasure some aspects of their political/philosophical common
ground.[18]

2

Structuralism

Although he is sometimes referred to as a post-structuralist, and despite his indebtedness to the structural linguistics of Saussure (discussed in chapter 3), Derrida's engagement with structuralism is nothing like as detailed, extensive and far-reaching as his engagement with phenomenology. None the less, despite this disparity of treatment, structuralism and phenomenology are envisaged by Derrida as the twin poles of twentieth-century philosophical thought, as is clear in his 1959 paper on '"Genèse et structure" et la phénoménologie' discussed in the previous chapter. Phenomenology is engaged in an attempt to describe the structures of transcendental consciousness, freed from its empirical irrelevancies; structuralism in an attempt to describe the structures of signifying systems independently of notions such as 'consciousness' or 'subject'. The two philosophical programmes may appear to be opposed, but they are arguably collusive in their incoherences and contradictions. 'Force et signification' (1963), a critique of literary structuralism as practised by Jean Rousset, and 'La Structure, le signe et le jeu dans le discours des sciences humaines' (1966), a study of structural anthropology in Lévi-Strauss's work in particular, both collected in *L'Écriture et la différence*, are striking examples of Derrida's concern with the impact of structuralism on twentieth-century thought. His critical evaluation of one of the major fathers of structuralism, the linguist Ferdinand de Saussure, is developed in *De la grammatologie* (1967), which also contains further analysis of Lévi-Strauss and of the proto-structuralist leanings detectable in Jean-Jacques Rousseau.

An early footnote to 'Force et signification' deals with the common criticism that the notion of 'structure' is nothing new: the word itself has a long history, and there are many other terms with similar meanings that have served quite satisfactorily up till now. Derrida refutes this criticism on the grounds that a proper understanding of 'structure' entails an appreciation of precisely *why* terms such as *eidos*, essence, form, *Gestalt*, *ensemble*, composition, complex, construction, correlation, totality, Idea, organism, state, system, etc. are insufficient, and to what extent the term 'structure' differs from and overlaps with them. He does not produce a detailed analysis at this point, but is content to argue that structuralism cannot be dismissed out of hand as a new name for an old theory. Derrida discusses elsewhere the specific problems of new/old nomenclature for old/new phenomena (see *Pos*, 93–4 and *Diss*, 24 on paleonymy). He describes the influx of structuralist theories as an 'invasion' which is not a mere moment in the history of ideas, but rather corresponds to a fundamental shift in theoretical reflection, a shift inextricably linked to a new perception of the role of language and of the sign in general within theory itself. Structuralism thus represents a step forward in the reflexivity of philosophical thinking, but Derrida is as relentless in his exposition of its theoretical weaknesses and internal contradictions as he was in the case of phenomenology.

'Force et signification' is clearly a reference to Rousset's *Forme et signification*, and in it Derrida pits force against form in a discussion of the inadequacies of the formalist/structuralist position. Form is traditionally associated with analysis, force with creativity. In this sense, Derrida provocatively remarks, literary criticism is, and always has been, essentially structuralist. This may explain the element of pathos underlying even the most technically brilliant critical productions – the sense that criticism is failed creativity, and reflection a substitute for strength. But in fact, by what Sartre would call the process of *qui perd gagne* (loser wins), it is precisely this impotence which liberates and emancipates criticism. Structure is more than simply form and figure, it involves totalization, schematization and perspective. Structure, in Derrida's description of it, is the *formal* unity of form and meaning (*ED*, 13). It is none the less negative terminology which dominates Derrida's account of the conditions that best enable a clear view of structural topography: catastrophe, destruction, threat, peril and dislocation. His analogy is the ease with which one perceives the architecture of a deserted town which has been laid waste. Structure is most apparent when content, 'the living energy of meaning', is neutralized. The 'disengagement' of Rousset's work from content may be liberating, but its openness paradoxically occults certain aspects of the works it describes, not merely in so far as it overlooks them, but in the very brilliance of the light it sheds, which blinds as much as it illuminates.[1]

Rousset's conception of the imagination is compared to that of Kant in its mediation between, and synthesis of, meaning and letter, singular and universal, *forme* and *fond* (form and content). The imagination 'schematizes without concept' (Kant, *Critique of Judgement*, §37), and the origin of the work of art as an indissoluble structural unity should be the first focus of critical attention according to both Kant and Rousset. However, in this view, the imagination is necessarily inaccessible outside its expression in language, and the 'determination' of the work in written form is conceived as a moment of anguish which ensures simultaneously the durability of imagination and its inevitable betrayal. In this way we encounter again, from a slightly different angle, the paradoxical problematics of 'writing', inherent in so many aesthetic and linguistic theories. Only Divine Writing could adequately convey Truth. Once God's Word has become a 'lost certainty' (*ED*, 21), meaning becomes unreliable, an insufficient echo of what might have been intended; writing itself, on the other hand, is raised in status: it inaugurates rather than simply reflects meaning. The similarity between Rousset's view of language and Husserl's in *The Origin of Geometry* is unmistakable, and Derrida draws attention to it (*ED*, 22), as well as to the further analogy with the ideas of the French phenomenologist Maurice Merleau-Ponty. Both phenomenology and structuralism would seem to share a conception of language and meaning which reverses (albeit sometimes reluctantly) the traditional critical commonplace of the work of art expressing a pre-existing Idea or plan, dismissed by Rousset as an idealist prejudice. None the less, Rousset is not prepared to relinquish the notion of expression entirely, and maintains that writing necessarily involves revelation as well as creation. His aim, he maintains, is to reconcile the 'old' and 'new' aesthetics. This vacillation or internal tension, the attempt of structuralism to have its new cake without abandoning the old one completely, is one of the most significant and recurrent features in Derrida's critique of Rousset.

The idea that language creates meaning is not, of course, applicable only in the domain of literature, but Rousset is determined to maintain the specificity of the aesthetic realm, and his concern for the formal autonomy of the work of art as a self-sufficient totality is the major defining characteristic of his version of structuralism. It provides Derrida with another example of the precariousness with which structuralism maintains its balance: Rousset attempts, like many before him, to avoid the pitfalls of both objectivism and subjectivism. He refuses the objectivist stance which would identify structure with form and ignore authorial intention, and he strives to avoid subjectivism by describing the creation of the work of art in terms of form: 'I will call them "structures", these formal constants, these links which reveal a mental universe and that every artist reinvents according to his needs' (*ED*, 25). But the attempt to avoid both Scylla and Charybdis ironically makes Rousset doubly vulnerable, for he is unable to escape the binary polarities which he resists without ever recognizing them as distorting. He insists on the importance of the work's history, but writes as though it did not have one. His opposition to historicism, biographism and psychologism – already an uneasy position for a critic interested in the writer's 'mental universe' (*ED*, 26) – risks blinding him to the internal historicity of the work. His relegation of literary history to the role of mere 'garde fou', that is to say 'safeguard', a kind of safety barrier to ward off the potential excesses of structuralism, makes it difficult for him to pay adequate attention to the history of the meaning of the text itself. Derrida comments that if literary history may be described as the *garde-fou* of structuralist criticism, he would be tempted to describe structuralism as the *garde-fou* of an internal *genetic* criticism that would focus on the historicity and temporality of meaning and value.

Rousset, it would seem, cannot live up to his own best insights. His aim is to avoid the stasis of formalist criticism, to recognize the totality of form and intention, of morphology and imagination, in a unifying critique. However, as he himself points out, his only means of working towards this totalizing understanding will frequently involve sequential analysis, the alternation between an account of form and an account of authorial imagination. It is this acceptance of the necessity of analysing form without content, even as a temporary phase in criticism, which will be the downfall of Rousset's structuralism. As Derrida's analysis of phenomenology demonstrated, genesis and structure may well be deemed inseparable in theory; in practice it proves hard, if not impossible, to give adequate room to both simultaneously.

Contemporary literary structuralism has radically transformed the role and significance of structure. On the one hand, Derrida maintains, structure has become itself the main object of study: no longer a mere heuristic tool, a method of reading, or even a system of objective relations, structure has become the end point of critical analysis. Derrida calls this tendency *ultra-structuralism*. But in Rousset's case, it goes hand in hand with a remarkably literal understanding of what structure is: Rousset focuses on spatial and formal relationships, but fails to recognize that the use of the term 'structure', when referring to literature rather than architecture or geometry, is itself intrinsically metaphorical. Despite defining structure as the union of formal structure and intention, Rousset in fact privileges spatial and mathematical models and produces a one-dimensional analysis where space dominates over time. Because he does not acknowledge the essentially metaphoric nature of his own 'structural' analysis of literature, Rousset's accounts of the texts he considers are dominated by a preoccupation with the pseudo-objectivity of the 'geometric'. Beauty, value and force are not susceptible to geometric analysis and so are necessarily excluded. Derrida's example is Rousset's analysis of Corneille's *Polyeucte*, where no mention is made of either 'passion' or 'heroic enthusiasm', for the whole of the critic's attention is occupied by the play's 'geometry', and furthermore a strange teleology dominates the analysis, so that all Corneille's earlier plays – including *Le Cid* and *Cinna* – are reduced to a prefiguration of the eventual schema of *Polyeucte*.

Derrida is keen to explain that he is not proposing a simple reversal of structuralist preoccupations in which the balance would be redressed by focusing on time rather than space, on quality rather than quantity, on force rather than form, and on value or depth of meaning rather than the surface of figures. This would merely perpetuate the inadequacies of the binary model. His aim is far more radical: to evolve new concepts or models that would escape the traditional system of metaphysical oppositions. The critique of Rousset is carried out from within the very system Derrida is seeking to overturn, in a strategy designed to expose the implicit privileging of one pole of the series of oppositions above the other.

Rousset, then, has been taken as a counter-example, as an example of the flaws inherent in structuralist criticism. Derrida's analysis is intended to dislocate and fissure the system within which he is temporarily operating (*ED*, 34). Etymologically, form and beauty are linked, but it is precisely the *formosus* (beautiful) which formalism is singularly ill-equipped to deal with, since it can describe forms but lacks any criteria for evaluating them. In consequence, structuralism privileges texts where form seems to dominate: Marivaux's plays, for example, share evident structural patterns which make them ideal objects of study; in the case of Proust and Claudel, a teleological approach is adopted in which the texts are explored as primitive models for a final version which they were striving to achieve. The comments of Proust and Claudel on their own work appear to confirm this aesthetics of 'structural monotony', which Derrida traces to their metaphysics of intemporality or eternity, and which he provocatively describes as the underlying metaphysics or theology of structuralism itself (*ED*, 41). Structuralist criticism is concerned with spatial relations, but its terminology for these is often temporal: it describes structures in terms of their 'simultaneity', for example; time is not so much forgotten as concentrated; depth, duration and volume are intolerable because structurally inexplicable.

However, Derrida insists, it is no mere coincidence that the literary work is above all a *volume*, and that the meaning of meaning is indefinitely deferred, as signifiers refer ever onwards, never coming to rest in the self-identical structures proffered by structural analysis. In this sense, he argues, 'ultra-structuralism' has lost touch with structuralism's own original intentions. Significantly enough, Derrida's views are shared by one of the major founders of modern structuralism, Lévi-Strauss, who had no time for the literary uses of structural analysis. Lévi-Strauss's main objection to literary structuralism was to its attempt to apply the techniques of, for example, the anthropological analysis of myths to individual texts. Structuralism is essentially comparative: different versions of myths are brought together and their variations analysed. Literary structuralism thus attempts a task fundamentally incompatible with structuralism proper when it describes single works.[2] Derrida's objection is not identical to Lévi-Strauss's but has much in common with it. Biological and linguistic structuralists, he maintains, examine each totality as a complete entity. They never describe a particular configuration as somehow unsatisfactory or unfinished, or as an anticipation of a superior version. Biology, linguistics and anthropology all have an indefinite number of versions of the same phenomenon to draw on and compare. Literary critics can only do something similar by imposing a finalistic interpretation on an author's production. Derrida does concede, however, that this is an acute version of a problem endemic in all structuralism: according to its theory, structuralism is descriptive not teleological, but in practice it has difficulty in describing an organized totality without taking its end into account, and this inevitably introduces notions of intention and purpose. In short, temporality and genesis cannot be kept from contaminating structuralism despite its best intentions, but while these notions may liberate structuralism from the stranglehold of its own theoretical purity, they thereby risk losing their own specificity and energy. Form cannot avoid considerations of force entirely, but it can mask and muzzle them. Development and evolution risk being treated as a mere means to an end which is the final, Apollonian form. Like phenomenology, then, on which it depends historically, however reluctant it may be to acknowledge the relationship, structuralism has no real way of accounting for intensity or force (*ED*, 45–6). Its notion of the transparency of consciousness prevents phenomenology from recognizing the possibility, indeed the inevitability, of failed intentions. Husserl could, for a long time, account for loss and forgetting only in terms of accidents extrinsic to the nature of thought. The language of both phenomenology and structuralism occults the real nature of force by seeing it as the 'other', or the opposite of form, just as 'fact' is viewed as the opposite of 'meaning'. It is from this binary and dialectical conceptual schema that Derrida hopes literary criticism will eventually free itself by loosening its dependence on philosophy, and preferring the language of difference to that of opposition and contradiction.

Apart from the final brief discussion of Jabès in 'Ellipse', *L'Écriture et la différence* both starts and ends with essays on structuralism. The concluding piece, 'La Structure, le signe et le jeu dans le discours des sciences humaines', was first delivered as a conference paper at Johns Hopkins University in 1966, three years after the publication of 'Force et signification'. It focuses not on literary structuralism but on what Derrida sees as the weaknesses and incoherences of Lévi-Strauss's structural anthropology, starting, once again, from a discussion of the history of the concept of structure. Derrida claims that something has happened which has transformed the concept, itself as old as Western philosophy. Until recently, he maintains, the concept of structure has been neutralized, because 'structure' has been thought of as organized around a centre, a fixed origin which, by the same token, limits its 'play'. Even now, an entirely centreless structure would seem unthinkable. A kind of paradox – what Derrida calls a 'coherent contradiction' (*ED*, 410) – is entailed if we imagine a type of 'play' which is always drawn back to a fixed central point; an ideal if impossible concept is created in which the pleasure of play is freed from the anxiety and insecurity that play may produce, by being referred to a reassuring and immobile foundation. Such a conception seems to correspond to the force of a *desire*, and has analogies with the equally impossible ideal described by Sartre in *L'Être et le Néant* as the 'useless passion' of all human endeavour: the attempt to be simultaneously free and fixed, a liberty with an essential core of being. Derrida lists out a whole series of different names that have been given to the conception of founding centre: origin, end, *arche*, *telos*, *eidos*, *ousia*, consciousness, God, man, amongst others, all permutations of the notion of a self-present being, and all part of the long history of Western metaphysics. It is a mark of the modern epoch to have reflected on such notions and to have recognized in them the common desire for an originating centre behind the various series of substitutions for it. But such a reflection has brought in its wake the recognition of the centre as an unattainable object of desire rather than as a reality, and a consequent acknowledgement of the endless process of substitution which attempts to put something where there is in fact nothing. It is no coincidence that this critical reflection has occurred at the historical moment when language has come into its own as an object of theoretical attention; for it is in and through language, indeed it is because of the nature of language, that the effect of perpetual substitution can take place. Language is precisely the differential system which masks absence with an illusion of presence, and whose mobility depends on its very lack of centre. Signs have no meaning except by distinction or difference from other signs, and 'the absence of a transcendental signified extends infinitely the field and play of meaning' (*ED*, 411).

The process of decentring that has occurred in Western thought cannot easily be attributed to a single event, doctrine or author. It is rather a sign of the times, but Derrida is prepared to name a few names among the most radical decentralizing thinkers. He cites Nietzsche's critique of metaphysics, and his substitution of the concepts of play, interpretation and sign for those of being and truth; the critique of presence and self-identity implied in Freud's distinction between conscious and unconscious; and Heidegger's more radical destruction of metaphysics, 'onto-theology' and presence. However, all these radical thinkers remain trapped in an inescapable linguistic circle: there is no way of attacking metaphysics without using metaphysical concepts; we have no language free from metaphysical presuppositions and are bound to use the very terms, concepts and logic we are contesting. The notion of the sign, for example, has been used to disturb the metaphysics of presence, but to demonstrate that there is no 'transcendental signified' would logically entail abandoning the concept of 'sign' itself, founded as it is on the metaphysical opposition between 'signifier' and 'signified'. When Lévi-Strauss proposes in *Le Cru et le cuit* to 'transcend the opposition between sensible and intelligible' (*ED*, 412) by remaining at the level of signs, the legitimacy of his intentions cannot save him from the paradox of his position: the concept of the sign can never transcend the opposition between sensible and intelligible because it is itself constituted by that very opposition. None the less, we cannot simply abandon the concept of sign without giving up our critique of the presuppositions it embodies. Derrida sketches two ways of effacing the difference between signifier and signified: the one, classical, which reduces the signifier by subordinating the sign to thought; and the other, Derrida's own, which questions the very system in which that reduction operates. All attempts to question a system within which one is caught generate this kind of paradox, but there are still, Derrida contends, different ways of being trapped in the circle, all variously naive, empirical or systematic. Hence the multiplicity of different contestatory discourses, each accusing the others of complicity with the object of attack, as when Heidegger, for example, describes Nietzsche as the 'last metaphysician' or the 'last Platonist'.

Derrida turns from these theoretical and historical considerations to the specific question of structuralism in the human sciences, and in particular ethnology. He argues that it is no accident that the birth of ethnology as a science coincided with the *decentring* of European culture, and the destruction of its metaphysics. Ethnology necessarily shares the same ambivalent position with respect to the language and concepts it has inherited and within which it is attempting to work as any other contemporary discourse. Ethnology is born precisely from the dislocation of European culture, no longer privileged as the central cultural reference point; ethnology rejects ethnocentrism but it cannot escape the ethnocentric presuppositions of its own language. There have been various ways of attempting to deal with this inevitable ambivalence, but they are not all equally cogent: a systematic thematization and theorization of the status of the inherited discourse are essential for its eventual deconstruction (*ED*, 414).

Lévi-Strauss is an example of an anthropologist who has faced the issues raised by a linguistic critique explicitly, and Derrida takes him to task for not living up to his own potentially radical epistemology. Derrida starts from the nature/culture opposition, since this is central not only to Lévi-Strauss's own work but to the whole history of Western philosophy: *physis/nomos* and *physis/techne* pre-date even Plato. Indeed, Lévi-Strauss finds it both essential to use the nature/culture opposition and impossible to believe in it. His attempts to redefine the opposition inevitably run into constant problems: for example, having set up the standard definitions of nature as what is universal and spontaneous, and culture as what is varied and socially determined, he is immediately faced with the anomalous situation of the incest taboo. The incest taboo creates what Lévi-Strauss calls a 'scandal' for it cannot be confined within the category of either nature or culture: in so far as it is universal it appears part of nature, but in so far as it depends on prohibition it appears part of culture. The 'scandal', as Derrida points out, is only scandalous with respect to the binary system it appears to transgress, for it cannot be thought or theorized within that system: language carries within it the necessity of its own critique. So the limitations of the nature/culture opposition may lead to a fundamental questioning of the history of those concepts. Such an inquiry into the founding concepts of the history of philosophy is neither philological nor philosophical in the usual sense, but is, Derrida maintains, a step outside philosophy.

Lévi-Strauss's own reaction to the conceptual problem of binary oppositions is theoretically less radical, but runs less risk of producing empirical sterility: he retains the old concepts, such as nature and culture, at the same time as he proclaims their limitations. The concepts are no longer given the status of Truth, but rather that of still useful tools which will be abandoned when better ones can be evolved. In the meantime, such concepts can be used to undermine from within the old system of which they are part, in a self-reflexive critique. Lévi-Strauss, in Derrida's account of him, attempts to separate methodology and truth by retaining conceptual tools of whose truth value he is sceptical. We know already, from Derrida's comments on Levinas's attempts to use the methods of phenomenology without believing in its premises, that he does not consider such a *démarche* to be a real possibility (nor did Levinas, in his more critical moments. See *ED*, 174). Lévi-Strauss himself refers to this use of whatever tools may be to hand as *bricolage* (tinkering, 'making do'), and Gérard Genette has described it – somewhat provocatively – as the essential task of the literary critic, who has no conceptual tools tailor-made but who rather makes use of whatever comes to hand conveniently from other disciplines. If 'making do' with the concepts of an invalidated heritage is *bricolage*, then all discourse may be thus described, Derrida maintains. So the 'engineer', who is for Lévi-Strauss the alternative to the *bricoleur*, and who works within a tailor-made, coherent system, is a myth, an impossible ideal. But the undermining of the status of the engineer simultaneously undermines the specificity of the *bricoleur* who is no longer able to differentiate himself from any other language user.

The second thread which Derrida follows through in Lévi-Strauss's work is that of the status the anthropologist accords to his own *bricolage*. Lévi-Strauss describes his own discourse on myth, for example, as itself 'mythological', and submits it to a reflexive critique. Its nature as *bricolage* means that it is not part of a unified and centralized system. Nor do his analyses of myths have the kind of truth-value an empiricist might recognize: the so-called 'reference myth' of the Bororos is no more than a convenient convention; it has no special status to merit the privileged position accorded to it, it is simply a transformation of other myths and no more central than any other (*ED*, 419). There is, then, in Lévi-Strauss's view, no real unity or source to myths. They are not centred; neither is the discourse which analyses them: rather than making epistemological claims at odds with the nature of the material described, the structural analysis of myths explicitly recognizes its own mythological and mythomorphic nature. As Lévi-Strauss explains in *Le Cru et le cuit*, there can be no final term to myth analysis; its unity is imaginary, an effect of the interpretative process itself (*ED*, 420). And the absence of a centre brings in its wake the absence of a subject and the absence of an author: myths have no authors. However, Lévi-Strauss does not succeed in living up to the radically anti-empirical implications of his epistemological position, and in parallel to his stringent critique of empiricism we find a will to justify his conclusions in empirical terms. The mutual incompatibility of these aims is the price he pays for his scientific pretensions. His structural schemas are presented as hypotheses which can always be put to the test of further experimental evidence. They cannot be subject to a final totalization, for two epistemologically incompatible reasons: the one, classical and empirical, which is the never-ending potential for accumulating more data – 'the infinite richness of the field' (*ED*, 423); the other, closer to Derrida's own thinking, which recognizes that language itself excludes totalization, it is the domain of play, a field of infinite substitutions, centreless and therefore always open. In this latter, more radical, view the mobility permitted by the absence of a centre may be described in terms of supplementarity.

The supplement, as became clear in Derrida's work on Husserl, is a fruitfully 'dangerous' concept whose potential for disruption is usually masked. What is scandalous about the supplement is that what is presented as a complement in fact covers up an absence. The supplement conceals the absence it supposedly completes. The very movement of signification is that of supplementarity: the signifier masks a lack at the heart of the signified, the absence of presence, so to speak. It is no coincidence, remarks Derrida, that Lévi-Strauss uses the term 'supplement' twice in his account of Mauss when he is discussing the excess of signifier over signified. On the first occasion the linguistic excess is referred to as a 'supplementary ration' which is 'absolutely necessary'; and on the second, in the context of self-contradictory terms such as *mana*, Lévi-Strauss suggests that such terms permit us to continue to think despite the antinomies of our thought, and maintains that they have a 'zero symbolic value' which reveals the need for a 'supplementary symbolic content'. Such terms have no particular meaning, but their function is to 'oppose the absence of meaning' (*ED*, 424–5). Awareness of supplementarity explains the importance of the notion of play (*jeu*) in Lévi-Strauss's work, and the series of tensions this involves. In the first place, there is a tension with the notion of history: Lévi-Strauss's reduction of the role of history represents a critique of the twin notion with which it has a paradoxical complicity, that of presence, for the opposition between history and the present moment is apparent rather than real. History is viewed by Lévi-Strauss as the transition between two moments of presence. But suspicion of the notion of history must be theorized, according to Derrida, if it is not to become a mere classical ahistoricism. In Lévi-Strauss's case, for example, structuralism has neutralized history, so that new structures are never seen as gradually evolving, but rather as representing a break with the past. History is put into parentheses and the concepts of chance (*hasard*) and discontinuity take on the role of explanatory tools. Despite his explicit recognition, in *Race et histoire*, for example, of the inevitable processes of long maturation and development, Lévi-Strauss still, like Rousseau, envisages the origin of a new structure in terms of some catastrophe. The second notion in tension with 'jeu' in Lévi-Strauss's work is presence. For 'play' is the disruption of presence; the presence of an element is only a substitutive reference inscribed in a differential system; play is a play of absence and presence. In Lévi-Strauss's work, alongside the recognition of play, there is always a nostalgia for presence, for origins, for archaic, natural innocence, and for the self-presence of speech. This is the negative, guilty and nostalgic side of the 'pensée du jeu', whose positive, joyous aspect is compared to a Nietzschean 'affirmation of a world of signs . . . without truth or origin, offered up to active interpretation' (*ED*, 427). The latter affirmative attitude envisages the absence of centre as liberation rather than loss.

In short, Derrida uncovers two very different interpretations of interpretation, of structure, sign and play. The one dreams of deciphering a truth or origin which would escape the play of the sign, and views the necessity of interpretation as a form of exile. The other no longer turns back towards an origin, but rather affirms play and strives to go beyond man and humanism, in so far as 'man' represents the yearning for full presence, reassuring foundations, and origins. This Nietzschean version of interpretation, unlike that of Lévi-Strauss, does not see ethnography as 'inspiring a new humanism'. The two interpretations of interpretation are, Derrida claims, absolutely incompatible, even though we may live within both of them simultaneously. They mark out between them the contemporary field of the so-called 'human sciences'. But there is no question of *choosing* between them, firstly because the notion of 'choice' is not pertinent here, and secondly because what is important is rather to determine what they have in common, and their *différance* rather than simply their difference.[3] Such a task is both impossible and essential, for it involves thinking what has not yet been thought, and what can still only begin to be thought or shown, in the terrifying and unformulated form of the monstrous. This rather threatening image, which may remind us of Yeats's 'strange beast, slouching towards Bethlehem to be born', appears to be Derrida's own evocation of the enterprise of deconstruction.[4]

The third major text dealing with questions relating to structuralism is *De la grammatologie* of 1967, and is concerned primarily with the writings of Rousseau and Lévi-Strauss and their common interest in the question of the origin of language and in associated areas such as the boundary between speech and writing, nature and culture. For this reason, discussion of *De la grammatologie* is best deferred to the next chapter, which will also look at the phenomenological and other theories of language collected in *Marges* (1972). But *De la grammatologie* touches on areas which throw light on Derrida's attitude to structuralism in general, and continues the deconstruction of some of the major oppositional structures informing anthropological analysis such as the ubiquitous but untenable attempt to discriminate between literal and metaphoric language.[5] Many of the problems which Derrida reveals in Lévi-Strauss's work have already been dealt with, sometimes briefly, in the Johns Hopkins conference paper, written around the same time as *De la grammatologie*. The question of the nature/culture opposition and its relationship to the incest taboo is reopened; as is the question of *bricolage*, and the ideal or unreal status of the 'engineer' (see *Gram*, 200). Lévi-Strauss is shown as lacking the theoretical power to deal adequately with the notion of progress: like Rousseau (and again like Husserl) he envisages 'progress' as involving inevitable degradation, and his analyses are shot through with nostalgia for the past and for the small communities which have managed to resist the 'corruption' of modern society. Contemporary society is envisaged as a fall from the state of grace of these imaginary, prelapsarian Edens. Closely related to this nostalgia is Lévi-Strauss's endeavour to overhaul the common ethnological distinction between societies with and without history, a distinction which he considers ethnocentric because based on the implicit assumption that all history must resemble our own. His attempts to replace it depend, however, on what Derrida considers an equally suspect distinction between societies with and without writing (*Gram*, 177–8).

There is arguably little in *De la grammatologie* to add to what Derrida has already shown to be the inherent and self-destructive contradictions of structuralist theory, apart, of course, from the central question around which the whole text is organized: that of language, and in particular speech and writing. We can no longer postpone discussion of these issues.

3

Language: Speech and Writing

In 1973 Derrida published *L'Archéologie du frivole*, a lengthy introduction to Condillac's *Essai sur l'origine des connaissances humaines* which displays succinctly many of the major preoccupations of Derrida's writings about language. Condillac's aim in his *Essai* is to construct a theory of human knowledge which would take proper account of the origins of language and its crucial role in the constitution and transmission of thought. He is content to describe his philosophy as metaphysical, provided this is understood not in the sense of being a philosophy of hidden causes and essences, but rather in the sense of a more empirical and limited description of 'things as they really are' (*Essai*, 99). Condillac expresses admiration for Locke's empiricism but wants to go further than Locke; his theory of language is set up in part as a response to Locke's argument that 'ideas' originate in sensation and reflection and are only secondarily expressed in language. Condillac maintains rather that language is vital to the construction and linking of ideas (*Essai*, 101), that reason and understanding crucially involve language, and that 'une langue bien faite', a clear and well-constructed language, is essential to all human thought. In his rejection of the notion of a progression from pre-linguistic thought to its expression in language, Condillac is arguing in the same direction as Derrida does in *La Voix et le phénomène*, but where Derrida parts company with him is over what he sees as Condillac's inability to maintain his position consistently, and his implicit prioritizing of speech over writing. Condillac sets out to differentiate between epistemologically fruitful and fruitless methods of inquiry. To this end he attempts to determine the conditions of the 'frivolous', that is the *futile* (useless) as opposed to the *utile* (useful). He defines frivolity as the mere repetition of the self-identical, for example, the statement 'a stone is a stone', which teaches nothing and employs words for their own sake, devoid of use or purpose. The more closely Derrida examines Condillac's argument the clearer its salient features become: the villain of the piece is not the self-identity of the idea itself, but rather the words used to express it: 'It is not the identity in ideas which is frivolous, it is the identity in terms' (Condillac, quoted by Derrida, p. 88). Language is the root of frivolity, especially philosophical language with its mania for tautological definitions. Orators and poets on the whole escape frivolity, Condillac maintains, for they can observe the effects of their speech on their listeners and quickly learn the importance of method and clarity; philosophers write in the dark, and risk becoming esoteric, unintelligible and vacuous (p. 89). Philosophers have no immediate audience to keep them to the point, they have no real object for their words, and their writings are endemically trivial and frivolous. Philosophy corresponds to no need and to no desire (pp. 89–95).

Despite his stress on the decisive role of language in the constitution of thought, Condillac's critique of the futility of written (philosophical) language contains many of the features Derrida finds in the various accounts of writing that he analyses in his seminal account of theories of signification, *De la grammatologie*, in 1967. It was already evident in *La Voix et le phénomène* that Derrida was fascinated by Husserl's self-contradictory efforts to maintain the immediacy of the spoken word as a direct expression of inner thoughts, uncontaminated by the deferral and distortion inherent in their translation into writing. Derrida's response was to show that such 'contamination' is not a later addition to the pure self-presence of consciousness, but rather constitutive of consciousness from the outset. His work in *De la grammatologie* focuses even more closely on signification and its history. The sign, Derrida argues, is not a neutral linguistic concept, it is intimately bound up with metaphysics and theology. The very notion of sign is inseparable from its division into signifier and signified (the medieval *signans* and *signatum*), and within this system the signified has necessary priority in so far as it is what the sign itself points to. The concept of sign is part of the age-old distinction between sensible and intelligible, and it is the intelligible (the signified) which is associated theologically with the divine Logos, from which the sensible signifier represents a fall (*Gram*, 25).

Derrida makes clear that his programme of deconstruction does not set out to 'reject' these notions; they are unavoidable, he maintains, for there is, today, no way we can even 'think' without employing them (p. 25). Nor does he propose a simple inversion of the priority of signified over signifier: the inversion would be absurd and meaningless, while still remaining (however illogically) within the logic it was attempting to overthrow (p. 32). What deconstruction attempts is rather an 'oblique' and 'perilous' movement to unsettle from within the heritage to which such terms belong, borrowing its strategies and resources from the structure it is aiming to subvert (p. 39). Derrida proposes therefore a 'prudent and minute' exploration of the critical concepts of signification which may eventually produce a chink ('faille') through which a glimmer of 'outre-clôture' (what lies beyond closure) may be glimpsed (p. 25).

The *Exergue* to *De la grammatologie* begins with three quotations about writing of which the third is an extract from Hegel's article in his *Encyclopaedia* arguing for the superiority of Western modes of transcription: 'Alphabetical writing is in itself and for itself the most intelligent' (p. 11). Derrida argues that theories of writing from Aristotle and Plato through Rousseau to Saussure and Jakobson always give priority to the spoken word, not simply in the temporal sense but also by viewing writing as a mere transcription of speech. These theories therefore privilege phonetic ('alphabetical') writing which appears 'naturally' superior to other forms, even though it is necessarily secondary, being merely 'signs of signs' (p. 39). Moreover, theorists of language are on the whole reluctant to admit the significance of elements in writing that go against the grain of the teleology of phonetic transcription, so that features of writing such as punctuation, spacing and other non-phonetic elements are frequently interpreted as accidents (p. 59). Rather than being used to demonstrate that purely phonetic writing can only be a myth, the non-phonetic evidence is relegated to a non-essential role and disregarded. However, Derrida maintains, it is paradoxically today, when phonetic writing seems to have extended its domain to all possible areas of culture, that its limits are becoming manifest, as IT and cybernetics use a radically different kind of communication process, with no relation to speech or indeed writing as usually understood (p. 21).

Phonetic writing is clearly the ground on which some philosophically significant battles are being fought, the importance of which goes far beyond linguistics in the narrow technical sense. The desire to maintain both the superiority of phonetic writing and its subsidiarity to speech is too widespread and too powerful to be understood merely as a 'querelle de clercs'. The stakes are clearly much higher than academic laurels. Derrida's demonstration of what is ultimately at issue in the wilful demoting of writing involves a dazzling display and critique of the misplaced ingenuity that can be mustered by even the most responsible thinkers when questions of philosophical self-preservation are at stake. Saussure's discussion of the many different systems of writing, for example, contrives to reduce these to two, depending on their relation to speech: the ideographic and the phonetic, both of which are envisaged as a form of transcription of the oral, ideographic writing being interpreted as a transcription which represents the whole word rather than its phonetic elements. Saussure excludes pictographic systems from the domain of writing proper on the grounds that writing is the domain of signification, not of representation. Contemporary linguistics has shown the distortions involved in this oversimple binary division (p. 49), and furthermore Saussure's own analysis is limited to phonetic writing deriving from the Greek alphabet.

In Derrida's essay on Hegel, 'Le Puits et la pyramide' ('The Pit and the Pyramid', 1968), collected in *Marges*, we are shown a very similar process of exclusion operating in Hegel's linguistic speculations. Derrida's essay explores further the implications of Hegel's belief in the superiority of alphabetic writing. In Hegel's dialectical system, semiology is a branch of psychology which is in turn a branch of the (subjective) philosophy of mind (*Marges*, 84–5). Semiology therefore forms part of his theory of imagination, and suffers from the same contradictions as that theory. The sign is described as being part of the 'productive' rather than merely repetitive imagination, but this 'productivity' involves little more than the externalization of a prior inner content. The sign is both 'productive' and 'intuitive', and carries with it a whole set of concomitant contradictions: both (or neither) interior and exterior, spontaneous and receptive, intelligible and sensible etc. The sign is both an essential moment of the dialectic *and* a mere accident; necessary to the development of rationality *and* inessential to truth. It is at one moment the incarnation of meaning, at another the tomb of meaning. Hence the metaphors of *puits* (pit or well) and pyramid: the well contains the precious liquid of images, as the pyramid preserves the body and soul of the dead. The pyramid is Hegel's own metaphor for the sign itself, sign of the sign. Unlike the symbol, the sign is arbitrary and bears no resemblance to its meaning. It is an external envelope, that can be cast off in the movement towards the Idea. Phonetic writing is Hegel's model here of course, as ideograms and hieroglyphs have a more evident independence and cannot be viewed as simple transcriptions of speech. Hieroglyphs are simultaneously too natural (empirical) and too abstract (formal) (p. 120). So alphabetic writing necessarily comes at the top of the teleological hierarchy which aims at the emancipation of the Idea. Hegel's arguments, Derrida shows, become increasingly entangled in his own self-contradictions, and in his efforts to maintain an untenable position, that of the innate superiority of speech and therefore of phonetic writing.

The history of theories of writing turns out, in Derrida's account of it, to be the history of a repression. Empirical linguistics has managed to repress philosophical and archaeological questions about the essence and origin of writing which might have risked paralysing historical inquiry. The most fundamental questions about the origins of writing and of language are relegated by linguisticians to brief, speculative reconstructions, by way of introduction to other philological issues (*Gram*, 43). Saussure, for example, maintains that speech is a self-contained system, with no need of writing, which is entirely external to it, but he none the less feels obliged to take account of writing in his discussion of spoken language despite its secondary, reflective status (p. 51). It is not possible, he argues, to ignore writing: it is necessary to be aware of its 'uses', its 'drawbacks' and its 'dangers'. Saussure shares with Plato the belief that writing is an external contaminant of speech, an artificial clothing, or worse, a *travestissement*, a distortion or travesty, which masks meaning. The problem seems to lie in part in the way in which writing refuses to accommodate the theories which make it subservient; rather than obligingly represent speech, writing has the tendency to take over from it. The graphic image, Saussure complains, imposes itself at the expense of the phonetic, and the 'natural' relationship is reversed (p. 53). The solidity and permanence of the graphic image is artificial in Saussure's view, and tends to 'usurp' the spoken word. Rousseau too shares these apprehensions about the expansionist tendencies of writing, whose dominance he describes as bizarre and unnatural. Like Plato, Rousseau and Saussure envisage writing as an *aide-mémoire* which backfires: intended to assist in the recall of the spoken word, writing in their view brings about an enfeebling of memory which ultimately entails forgetfulness of the 'natural' hierarchy of speech and writing. The prestige of writing is a trap (*piège*, p. 56) which blinds us to its artifice.

Theorists of language are evidently far from neutral on the question of writing, and the debate is often couched in moral terms. Not only 'artificial' and a 'trap', the power of writing is, in Saussure's words, 'deceptive', tyrannical, *vicieuse* (corrupt), and potentially 'pathological'. It is not writing itself which is so dangerous, but rather its effects. But, in Derrida's view, the undesirable effects are precisely *not* the accidents that Saussure and others would have us believe: it is they that demonstrate most clearly the flaws inherent in phonocentric theories of language, and this is of course what underlies the passion of Saussure's denunciation of them. The alleged tyranny and usurpation perpetrated by writing would not be possible if writing did not somehow have the very significance that Saussure wishes to deny it. Writing tells us truths about language that we may not want to hear. If writing rather than speech is taken as a linguistic model, then the answers to questions concerning, for example, absence – absence both of writer and of referent – will be very different from those obtained when speech is taken as the paradigm. As was clear in Derrida's critique of Husserl in *La Voix et le phénomène*, speech itself is not the pure self-present representation of unmediated thought, but this does not prevent us from imagining it to be so. The mediated nature of speech, even interior monologue, and indeed of thought itself, permeated by division and deferral, is masked by the common-sense view of the hierarchy of thought, speech and writing. When the hierarchy is questioned, more is at issue than just the status of Western alphabetic writing; the whole of Western metaphysics, described by Derrida as 'logocentric', is at stake (p. 64).

Logocentrism is Derrida's term for a philosophy of presence, that is to say a world-view which understands being in terms of presence: the unmediated presence to consciousness of the world, and the self-presence of consciousness. Logocentrism is a form of 'onto-theology', or religion of being; in other words it subordinates all difference to the plenitude of presence resumed in the Logos, and determines the archaeological and eschatological meaning of being in terms of presence or Parousia (p. 104). Logocentrism has evident implications for theories of language: it supports those theories which see a direct relationship between thought and language, words and things, speech and writing. It implies a chain of representations which leads in uninterrupted fashion from experiences and ideas to their expression in speech, and later, perhaps, writing. In the other direction words can be traced back through their meaning to their object; the signifier is always the representation of an original signified. Sometimes Derrida refers to this as the myth of the transcendental signified. He sees the alternative to this closed system as a form of play (*jeu*) which is marked precisely by the absence of any transcendental signified. Logocentrism enshrines a reassuringly stable and hierarchical view of the world, and one which Derrida subjects to relentless scrutiny in whatever form he finds it.

In Saussure's case, as so often in Derrida's work, it is Saussure himself who provides the tools for his own undoing. His two major theories, that of the arbitrary nature of the sign and that of the differential nature of signification, prove to have implications that run entirely counter to his theses about the priority and independence of speech. Saussure maintains simultaneously that there is a 'natural' relationship between signifiers (phonic not graphic) and signifieds in general, but that it is unmotivated in any particular case. The lack of motivation for the individual sign points necessarily to the conventional nature of signification: for communication to be possible, meanings must be instituted. This is precisely the feature that Derrida associates with writing. Writing implies inscription, the possibility of repetition, and a range of conventional differentiating features. All these elements run counter to the myth of pure presence, and all are to be found in speech. It is not possible to maintain that speech is free of them if the signifier/signified relationship is recognized to be arbitrary. Signs are precisely not images. Nor can writing itself really be described as an 'image' of speech; there are too many elements in speech (tone, accent etc.) which are not transcribed, and too many elements in writing (spaces between words, punctuation etc.) which do not translate speech. Writing and speech are too dissimilar for writing to 'derive' from speech. But conversely, as we have just seen, writing and speech both share many of the characteristics usually associated only with writing, in particular the inscription and lasting institution of the sign (p. 65). Derrida coins the term *archi-écriture* to refer to this aspect of signification: it does not mean writin in the narrow sense but rather connotes those aspects of writing shared with speech which are denied and repressed in theories that have an investment in maintaining the natural and unmediated nature of the spoken word. Derrida is of course well aware of the provocative impact of choosing the term 'writing' to refer to a structure of signification which underlies both writing (proper) and speech: he intends to force his readers away from their habits of prioritizing speech by this semantic aggressivity. He is not so much trying to reverse the order of priority of speech and writing as to bring about a reconsideration of the nature of speech: 'It is not a matter here of rehabilitating writing in the narrow sense, nor of reversing the order of dependence when it is evident' (p. 82). None the less, as the linguist Hjelmslev reminds us, Bertrand Russell maintained that it was impossible to know for certain whether the first form of human expression was written or oral (p. 85). In any case, Derrida argues, writing in the narrow sense is able to be so powerful only because so-called 'original', 'natural' language, intact and untouched by writing, never really existed.

Just as *archi-écriture* is not to be identified with writing, but is rather common to both speech and writing, so too Derrida's other key term, the *trace*, is not just a matter of letters on a page, any more than *différance* is simply a matter of difference. *Différance* is Derrida's way of referring to the trace of difference; or, less obliquely, *différance* is a gerundive formation implying not only difference but also differentiation, differing and deferring. It is one of Derrida's major levers in the destabilization of the metaphysics of presence and identity, though it cannot itself escape metaphysics (*Marges*, 28). *Différance* is, Derrida maintains, not a word like other words, for it is what makes the meaning of words possible: neither a word nor a concept, neither active nor passive, neither cause nor effect, but productive of division and differences (*Pos* 17–19, *Marges*, 8–15). Its difference from 'difference' is silent, detectable only in written form, and inseparable from the 'trace'. Derrida discusses the trace at length in connection with Freud and the mystic writing pad ('Freud et la scène de l'écriture', *ED*), which raises the question of Derrida's relationship to psychoanalysis, but the term is also important in the present context. The trace involves the notion of an inscription of meaning, present in, but prior to, incision, engraving, drawing or letters (*Gram*, 68). In simple terms, the trace expresses the absence of full, present meaning: in so far as meaning is differential, a matter of constant referral onwards from term to term, each of which has meaning only from its necessary difference from other signifiers, it is constituted by a network of traces. In his essay on 'La Différance' of 1968 (collected in *Marges*) Derrida writes at length about the trace and its paradoxes. It is a 'simulacrum of presence', through which 'the present becomes the sign of a sign, the trace of a trace' (*Marges*,

25). In so far as it implies once again that there is no pure unmediated presence free from temporalization the trace is usually concealed in philosophical discourse which has been concerned rather with the problematic of the sign. The sign implies that it is a sign of something which precedes it; the trace, on the contrary, in Derrida's account, is not a secondary mark of a prior origin, it means rather that there was no origin before the trace. Derrida uses the terms *archi trace* and *trace originaire* to convey this destruction of a notion of origin, in the knowledge that the terms are of course self-contradictory (*Gram*, 90). We are so wedded to the notion of origin that any critique of it can only be couched in such uncomfortable terms. As Derrida showed in his account of Husserl's *Origin of Geometry*, there is no way out of the logic in which we think: our thinking about the trace can no more get outside transcendental phenomenology than it can remain within it (*Gram*, 91). The trace then is what makes the sign possible. It is difference itself (p. 92). 'The trace is in effect the absolute origin of meaning in general. This is a way of saying, once again, that there is no absolute origin of meaning in general. The trace is the *différance* which opens up appearance and meaning' (p. 95). The trace cannot be described using the concepts of metaphysics, it is neither real nor ideal, sensible nor intelligible, aural nor visual. There can be no phenomenological description of the trace because it is not explicable within a philosophy of presence (p. 99).

Derrida answers the evident but unspoken question of why he has chosen the term 'trace' to carry these meanings by saying that the term takes its meanings from the use that is made of it, and that there can be no absolute justification for such strategic choices. However he also indicates that the term can be related to the use made of it by other thinkers, such as Levinas in his critique of ontology, and especially in his essay 'La Trace de l'autre' of 1963.[1] In 'La Différance', we learn that the phrase 'a past that has never been present' is in fact Levinas's way of referring to 'the trace of absolute alterity' in the Other (*Marges*, 22). Derrida uses the trace to disturb notions of presence and continuity: 'To make enigmatic what we think we understand by the terms proximity, immediacy, presence . . . this is the ultimate aim of the present essay. This deconstruction of presence goes through that of consciousness, so through the irreducible notion of trace (*Spur*), as it appears in Nietzschean and in Freudian discourse' (*Gram*, 103). We will return to Nietzsche, Freud and Levinas later; for the moment we may simply note that what they have in common is that they have disrupted deeply held beliefs in various kinds of presence: temporal presence, through Nietzsche's notion of eternal return; the transparent self-presence of consciousness, through Freud's theory of the unconscious, in particular of the unconscious part of the ego; and the presence of the other to the self, through Levinas's critique of phenomenology. They all use the term *trace* (*Spur*, in German) to express the particular form of deconstruction of presence with which they are concerned. The trace, then, is not an easy term to grasp, precisely because it is intended to defy and elude easy grasping; in a sense it enacts what it denotes: now you see it, now you don't, to use an expression from a more familiar register. 'The trace *is nothing*, it is not a being', Derrida remarks (*Gram*, 110), using the kind of formulation which has laid him open to the accusation that his thinking is a form of laicized negative theology.

But Derrida's highly speculative and theoretical alternatives to logocentric thinking form only a small part of his work in *De la grammatologie*. The first section, which we have been considering up till now, is entitled 'L'Écriture avant la lettre', literally 'writing before the letter', but also, 'writing before it was invented', or, 'writing before writing proper', all of which lose something of the Derridean play on words. The section concludes with a chapter on 'Grammatology as a positive science' in which Derrida analyses previous theories of writing, in particular in the eighteenth century, which he sees as a turning-point in the prehistory of grammatology. His account focuses on the theories of Descartes, Leibniz and Hegel in particular, and describes the hostility and opposition aroused by Leibniz's attempt to construct what he called a 'universal characteristic'[2] which would include a far wider range of transcriptions than merely phonetic writing, and would consider hieroglyphs, algebra, musical notation and other 'visible traces' (*Gram*, 116). The chapter concludes with a discussion of a spectrum of twentieth-century linguistic theories, and with a brief discussion of the empirical structures, practices and institutions which came into being through writing, which means in effect all ideological, religious, technical and scientific systems, and all the subsystems which are part of them, such as law, politics, diplomacy, administration, economics, agriculture, military strategy, ballistics etc.

The remainder of *De la grammatologie* is devoted to an analysis and deconstruction of two thinkers in particular: Lévi-Strauss and, at far greater length, Rousseau, in particular Rousseau's *Essai sur l'origine des langues*. In a chapter entitled 'The violence of the letter:

from Lévi-Strauss to Rousseau', Derrida contests chronological teleology and traditional genealogy by using Lévi-Strauss to introduce his detailed study of Rousseau. Lévi-Strauss is shown to be working not only within the binary oppositional structures he has inherited but also at the limits of them, in a deconstructive manner. As we saw in chapter 2, the fundamental nature/culture opposition, for example, is disrupted by the incest taboo which does not fit the neat categorizations that have been erected to separate nature from culture: the incest taboo is thus a 'scandal' (p. 152), both universal and cultural, whereas the universal is defined precisely by its equation with the natural. But if the incest taboo is not so much part of the nature/culture opposition as part of what grounds that opposition, then the question of nature versus culture is radically displaced. Moreover, in *La Pensée sauvage*, Lévi-Strauss describes the opposition itself as methodological rather than foundational. These contradictions, which traditional analysis might consider as 'hesitations', are for Derrida the nodal points on which his own deconstructive strategy is able to exert pressure.

Derrida describes Lévi-Strauss's structuralism as a 'phonologism', both in its exclusion of writing and in the paradoxical authority it accords to writing. Lévi-Strauss claims that phonology (the study of linguistic sound systems) has been as significant in the social sciences as nuclear physics in the exact sciences, and, it would appear, as devastating in its effects. Like Rousseau, Lévi-Strauss associates writing with violence. Derrida acknowledges that there is plenty of evidence to support such an association, but he disagrees both with Lévi-Strauss's understanding of writing and with the conclusions he draws from it. All societies have writing, Derrida maintains, if not writing in the narrow sense none the less writing in the sense of *archi-écriture*: transcription, notation, recording. Writing *is* violent in so far as it classifies and categorizes, going against the seemingly individual specificity of the purely personal. But the prelapsarian state of immediacy and personal presence is a feature of *no* society in Derrida's view, and he uses Lévi-Strauss's own examples against him to demonstrate this. The so-called secret 'proper names' which Lévi-Strauss extracts by trickery from the little girls of the Nambikwara tribe are precisely not 'proper' (in the sense of theirs alone) any more than any other names, all of which are necessarily shared with others. What is more, Lévi-Strauss is determined to maintain the innocence of the Nambikwara, as a society, in his view, uncontaminated by writing. He is therefore led to interpret all apparent violence as accidental, and the fundamental initial 'violence' of the very act of naming is overlooked. He insists repeatedly on the 'original goodness' of the tribespeople, and even from an empirical perspective his defence is disturbingly anecdotal. It is all the more surprising from a structuralist ethnologist who claims to be a follower of two of the major theorists of human weakness, Marx and Freud.

Lévi-Strauss is being accused of a cover-up job, and Derrida continues the prosecution by comparing the narratives of the same episodes as they are recounted first in Lévi-Strauss's thesis on the Nambikwara and later in the more tendentious *Tristes tropiques*. One episode concerns the Nambikwara's interest in the writing the ethnologist shows them. In *Tristes tropiques* we are told that the Nambikwara attempt to copy it by tracing wavy lines on a piece of paper; in the thesis there are several more significant details which do not find their way into the later book. In the first place, the Nambikwara already have a word for writing; secondly, they describe it as 'pretty', from which Lévi-Strauss concludes that it has a merely aesthetic function in their eyes; and thirdly, having discounted the zigzags and dots that he observes on their gourds as neither writing nor even drawing, he fails to mention the alacrity with which they start not only to draw but also to use their pencils and paper to demonstrate genealogies and social structures. The Nambikwara would not have been able to adopt the techniques of inscription so instantaneously if they did not in a sense already possess them. What is more, when the chief pretends to his tribe to be able to write (in the ordinary sense of the term), Lévi-Strauss comments that writing has immediately brought with it deception and oppression, whereas an alternative explanation might see the chief as using writing to reinforce an already oppressive power.

Lévi-Strauss is determined, it seems, to associate writing with violence and oppression and to dissociate it from its more positive consequences such as facilitating the accumulation of knowledge. To this end he argues that although writing might be essential to the growth of science over the past two hundred years, it was not a factor in the rise of science in earlier centuries. He claims that he would like to be able to describe writing as having a positive role in the development of knowledge, but that the evidence is against this. Derrida points out that this takes no account of studies such as Husserl's on the origin of geometry and its necessary dependence on writing, nor of all the evidence for early forms of pre-alphabetical writing. Lévi-Strauss is determined to define the primary function of writing as oppressive. Derrida is at pains not simply to invert this claim; on the contrary, he acknowledges that the evidence associating writing with power structures is over-whelming. What he does contest is the assumption that all power is negative, and the concomitant assumption that writing (in the nar-row sense) is the instigator of oppressive power. Lévi-Strauss takes a lapsarian view of organized society, attributing even policies of universal education to the desire to extend propaganda and lies to the masses – as if propaganda could not be spread orally equally well. Rather than attempt to disprove these claims, whose weakness is apparent as soon as they are stripped of their rhetoric of edenic idylls preceding society as we now know it, Derrida simply shows the Rousseauist assumptions that lie behind them and proposes to explore them in more depth in the eighteenth-century context. Before moving on to Rousseau and his theories of 'progress' as inevitable degradation, Derrida allows Lévi-Strauss's nostalgia to speak for itself: *Tristes tropiques* excludes from its apologia of the good and innocent Nambikwara all the episodes of violence and intrigue recounted in the earlier thesis: wars, factions, conflicts and discontent, poisonings and murder are all omitted from the sanitized version which aims to proclaim the idyll of life in a small-scale, self-present society without writing (*Gram*, 197). The myth of a truly authentic society would seem to depend on deception and concealment.

Derrida describes Lévi-Strauss as being faithful to Rousseau in his view of the pre-eminence of the spoken word, but he maintains that Rousseau's own position is ambivalent and implies a concomitant suspicion of speech. Ideally, speech should entail full presence; in practice it disappoints, and conveys rather lack and absence. Rousseau expresses this ambiguity quite strikingly: speech attempts to capture its object, but in reality presents only a deceptive mirage. Writing is simultaneously condemned as destructive of presence, but also invoked in an attempt to capture the elusive presence that has escaped speech. Writing both destroys and restores presence. The two sides of this paradoxical attitude to writing correspond to two aspects of Rousseau's work: the condemnation of writing is part of his linguistic theory, whereas the desire that writing should somehow recapture a lost presence is part of his experience as a writer. The schism itself is part of the split expressed in Rousseau's own distinction between Rousseau and Jean-Jacques.[3] Derrida suggests that it can be best accounted for by the notion of the *supplement*. The supplement has already appeared in the context of both phenomenology and structuralism. In the discussion of the Husserlian theory of signification in *La Voix et le phénomène*, it was used to explain the way in which features of language such as indication or retention, described by Husserl as extraneous, that is, supplementary to the essence of language, turned out, on closer examination, precisely to constitute the nature of language itself.[4] In the account of Lévi-Strauss, the supplement appears in the anthropologist's own text in a discussion of Marcel Mauss's theory of the symbol, where it is used to explain how the excess of signifier over signified is a 'supplementary ration' which is 'absolutely necessary'.[5] In both cases, the supplement is a 'dangerous' concept because it shows up a fissure in the metaphysics of presence, while attempting to mask absence.

The pattern in Rousseau is identical. Writing, the *philosophe* believes, should be a support and complement to speech: in Rousseau's own account it emerges as a 'dangerous' replacement for it. But in Rousseau's texts it is not merely in the domain of signification that the disturbing (il)logic of the supplement is at work. The term is used repeatedly whenever a situation of ambivalence occurs. For example, in the case of education, the supplement of culture is essentially inferior, but it may be necessary to remedy the deficiencies of Nature. Education is both the *chance* (good fortune) of humanity, and also the source of its perversion. Similar paradoxes attach to many of Rousseau's concerns: to surrogate motherhood, to the study of botany as a supplement to society, and to the study of minerals as a supplement to botany. The supplement is a potential source of scandal and catastrophe because it shows up the *essential* (rather than merely *accidental*) insufficiencies of whatever it is supposed to complete. For this reason the supplement is never perceived in its 'true', ambiguous colours. However many times Rousseau, for example, uses the term, he remains blind to its strange logic and its effects. In a sense, Derrida maintains, 'supplement' is another word for *différance*, in so far as both are ways of referring to an unacknowledged process of substitution (p. 215).

One of the most striking instances of the supplement in Rousseau's work, perhaps because it is unexpected, is in the sphere of sexual activity. Not only do Rousseau's sexual partners (the most permanent of whom he always refers to as 'Maman') all appear as a chain of substitutions for each other, and ultimately for his lost mother, but in the domain of the sexual act itself, masturbation is described as a supplement for heterosexual intercourse. It is a refuge, a substitute, a complement, and, Rousseau feels, a dangerous perversion. It shows most clearly the power of the image to replace the so-called 'real thing'. It is seductive, and may seem natural, but it is a 'vice' arising from shame and shyness (p. 216). *Auto-affection* conjures up the presence of the other while working to keep it at bay. Not so much an evocation of presence through absence, it constitutes the mastery of a presence which is both desired and feared. 'The supplement simultaneously transgresses and respects the taboo [*l'interdit*]' (*Gram*, 223). The 'perversion' then lies not so much in the acceptance of an inferior substitute, but rather in the preference accorded to it. The sign is preferred to its absent origin and referent. The chain of supplementarity is a chain of deferred mediations aiming to (re)produce the mirage of an immediate presence and an originary perception.

Derrida uses the term *auto-affection* to represent a universal and self-reflexive structure of experience. As such it shares the ambiguities of all such structures: *auto-affection*, like Husserl's *s'entendre parler*, reveals *both* subjective self-presence *and* its fissuring. Like the self-presence of the *pour-soi*, it undermines precisely what it would most desire to promote, immediacy and presence. This is how the supplement can appear in so many different domains: wherever presence is threatened, the notion of supplement emerges in an attempt to exclude the supposed interloper from the inner sanctum. So writing is viewed as an inessential addition to the self-presence of speech, masturbation as an inessential addition to heterosexual activity, culture as an addition to nature, evil to innocence, and history to true origin etc. (*Gram*, 238). Rousseau believed passionately that what he saw as the degradation of language over time was symptomatic of a generalized social and political degeneration. The decline of language and pronunciation was viewed as inseparable from political corruption, in so far as a language embodies the whole world-view of a nation. This is the reasoning that underlies Rousseau's opposition, expressed in *Émile*, to any attempt to teach foreign languages to children.

Derrida is aware that his reading of Rousseau's use of the term 'supplement' does not correspond to Rousseau's intention when he wrote, and he gives a brief justification of his method of reading against the grain of apparent authorial intention. In particular, he argues, the writer himself is not in full control of his meaning: 'The writer writes *in* a language and *in* a logic which, by definition, his discourse cannot dominate absolutely' (p. 227). So Derrida's reading is attentive to the relationship between what Rousseau does and does not control in his text. Anticipating that he risks being viewed as uncovering 'unconscious' meanings, Derrida denies that his reading is in any way psychoanalytic, not least because psychoanalytic accounts of literature are not usually concerned with the essential relationship between signifier and signified, and tend to overlook the signifier.[6] Derrida does not claim that his own reading is complete, fully successful or capable of full justification (p. 231). Alternative paths through Rousseau's texts would certainly be possible. Derrida's choice of texts is, in his terms, *exorbitant*, i.e. external, outside any apparent totality. And for this reason it cannot be justified in terms taken from within the domain it lies beyond. From within it might be deemed empirical and wandering, but the very notion of empiricism forms part of the system of binary oppositions which Derrida believes to be self-destructive. The opposition between philosophical and empirical cannot itself be viewed as simply empirical.

Rousseau's work, Derrida contends, marks a decisive articulation in the history of logocentrism. There can be no absolute means of justifying deconstructive starting points: one can only start from where one is (p. 233). However, the theme of the supplement is not just one amongst others in a chain, it describes the very being of the chain itself, with its structure of endless substitutions and its articulation of desire and language. The supplement is an *abyssal* representation of the textuality of Rousseau's text. The paradoxical structure of the supplement is not an accident, but an indication of the way in which presence is never really fully present, only represented. The supplement cannot be properly accounted for in terms of either Rousseau's conscious or his unconscious intentions: it is a blind spot (*tache aveugle*) (p. 234) in Rousseau's texts which both opens up and limits visibility.

The second half of *De la grammatologie* adds little to the theoretical analyses of the first, but rather uses them as the basis for a detailed exploration of one of Rousseau's best-known discussions of language, the *Essai sur l'origine des langues*. Derrida's preoccupation with Rousseau does not necessarily indicate that he believes Rousseau to be an original or even a particularly significant contributor to the history of theories of language: he sees Rousseau rather as typical of a mythology of language[7] that has dominated discourses about language and the human sciences for many centuries.[8] In 'Le Cercle linguistique de Genève' (1968, collected in *Marges*), Derrida focuses specifically on Rousseau's relationship to later theories of language, in particular Saussurean linguistics, and shows how he both anticipates and founds many of the key features of modern linguistics. He explores Rousseau's conception of the circular relationship of thought and language, language and society etc., and traces in his texts early versions of Saussurean concepts such as the arbitrary nature of the sign, the role of articulation, the relationship of linguistics to semiology, as well as the primacy of speech over writing. But in *De la grammatologie* Derrida's approach is more critical, and rather than explain the vicious circles of Rousseau's theories as a valiant if doomed attempt to express the logical autonomy of the linguistic realm (see *Marges*, 175), he shows how rhetoric and repetition in Rousseau's texts constitute a vain endeavour to escape from the self-contradictions of his arguments, and how, in fact, the contradictions simply emerge the more clearly through the obsessive, protestatory quality of his speculations.

Speech and writing are not the only form of binary hierarchy explored by Derrida and undermined by the logic of the supplement. Derrida explores in detail issues such as the *philosophe*'s theory of the primacy of *amour de soi* (as distinguished from its corrupt form, *amour propre*) and pity (also to be distinguished from its corrupt form, sexual passion, pp. 248–50). We come here to an ambivalence that has, perhaps inevitably, preoccupied many writers and is theorized, for example, by Sartre – the fundamental ambivalence of imagination. Imagination activates pity, it is the condition of perfectibility and of human freedom; but it is also what makes possible representation, and so the death of presence. Imagination is representative and supplementary, 'it is the other name for *différance* as auto-affection' (p. 265). It is however also a condition of morality, in so far as respect for others depends on a certain paradoxical *non*-identification (p. 270). The question of representation leads Derrida to explore Rousseau's theory of imitation, not merely as part of the debate concerning the origin of language, where Rousseau appears caught between his desire to maintain that language is originally expressive (p. 382) and the influence of more literal conceptions of its origin (p. 389), but also in the domains of music and painting. Even in the most representational of art forms, signification is at least as important as imitation. Rousseau's aesthetics are semiological rather than sensual, and as vulnerable as his linguistic theories, so that his attempt to argue for the primacy of melody over harmony, for example, ends up by demonstrating that melody itself has an inherently harmonic element (p. 303). Rousseau describes what he does not intend, and demonstrates what he set out to deny: articulation and 'writing' are inherent in language from the outset, progress is for the better *and* for the worse; culture and nature cannot be separated in the incontrovertible and non-convertible way that he would like. In Rousseau's case too, it is the incest taboo which provides the problematic pivot around which the nature/culture debate turns. The whole question of the prohibition of incest defies the categories in which Rousseau would like to enclose it. Culture or the birth of society is not a passage which took place at a certain moment in time; it is a fictive and unstable limit which is always already degraded (p. 377).

The final chapter of *De la grammatologie* shows how Rousseau's attempt to weave together the threads of his thought is doomed to the fate of Penelope's tapestry: to be undone by the very hand that wove it. Rousseau has 'said what he did not want to say, described what he did not want to conclude' (p. 349). Language is 'originally' figurative (p. 388), 'direct' painting is already allegorical: 'There is never a painting of the thing itself, and firstly because there is no thing itself. . . . The original possibility of the image is the supplement' (p. 412). The supposed supplementarity of writing is precisely what constitutes human society. Alienation from presence is thus paradoxically originary. It is supplementarity and its attendant paradoxes that save history from 'an infinite teleology of a Hegelian kind' (p. 421). And all these propositions can be inverted. All supplements are supplements of another supplement: it is supplementarity itself which is originary. Imagination arouses desire and by the same token divides presence (p. 438). The 'evil' of the supplement loses its force when no origin is thought of as having been displaced; just as the evil of writing seen as a substitute for expressivity loses its force when the original presence of the speaking subject is put in question. The articulation of writing is not a pale substitute for the living presence of the accents of speech: it is the origin of language itself (p. 443). These are the paradoxes with which Derrida is working, and his means of deconstructing the logic from which he has to draw his armoury.

In the first chapter of *De la grammatologie* Derrida uncovers another intriguing paradox at the heart of logocentric conceptions of writing: whereas writing proper (i.e. writing in the narrow sense) is conceived of as secondary, on the side of culture, artifice and technique, writing in its metaphorical usages, for example the writing of Truth in the soul of man, or nature as the writing of God (especially in the Middle Ages), is viewed as a positive and direct expression of the Logos. So metaphorical writing is paradoxically conceived as both prior to and superior to writing in the literal sense. This reversal in the status of the figurative is not theorized in the discourse in which it appears, but the logic of the paradox would suggest an unrecognized primary sense of writing as metaphor. Derrida makes clear that he is not attempting to reverse the literal/figurative hierarchy, but rather to 'determine the "literal" [*propre*] meaning of writing as metaphoricity itself' (*Gram*, 27). To grasp some of the implications of this statement, we need to turn to the more extended reflections on metaphor in 'La Mythologie blanche', first published in 1971 and collected in *Marges*. Subtitled 'La Métaphore dans le texte philosophique', the essay analyses a vast range of theories of metaphor, as they appear in Aristotle, Nietzsche, Heidegger, Leibniz, Condillac, Bachelard, Fontanier, Genette and many others. Starting from an account of various scholarly attempts to classify and categorize the use (rather than the theory) of metaphors in philosophical texts, Derrida moves to a consideration of the possibility of distinguishing between literal and metaphorical language, and to the question of their relative priority. Some theorists view metaphor as a figurative and imaginative use of words that have a primarily literal meaning, others see 'literal' meanings as usages whose original, figurative meaning has been eroded.[9] Derrida is led to reflect on the double meaning of the French term *usure*, expressing both a wearing away (usage) and an increase in value (usury). These contradictions in theories of metaphor, both philosophical and linguistic, show up the inherent ambivalence in evaluations of the metaphor/concept dichotomy. Moreover, the tendency to envisage metaphor in purely semantic terms appears incompatible with a proper attention to its syntactic organization (*Marges*, 317), a critique Derrida elaborates further in his account of Mallarmé in 'La Double Séance' (in *La Dissémination*).[10]

'La Mythologie blanche' is exceptionally dense and difficult, but its overall purpose, to 'explode the reassuring opposition between the metaphoric and the literal' (*Marges*, 323), is what the attentive reader will by now have come to expect from Derrida. It comes as a surprise, though perhaps a comforting one, to find as competent a philosopher as Paul Ricoeur going seriously astray in the critique of

Derrida's essay which he makes in *La Métaphore vive* (1975). Ricoeur becomes entangled in Derrida's hypotheses to the extent of attributing to Derrida those very theses he is expounding and criticizing. Derrida responded to Ricoeur in a conference paper entitled, 'Le Retrait de la métaphore', given in Geneva in 1978 and collected in *Psyché*. In it Derrida is in the curious position of defending himself against Ricoeur by showing how he in fact agrees with him. 'Le Retrait de la métaphore' is particularly lucid, partly because it was originally a conference paper, and partly because Derrida is setting out to demonstrate as unequivocally as possible how Ricoeur has misread him. Ricoeur sees Derrida as a follower rather than as an expositor and critic of Heidegger, and therefore attributes to him the Heideggerian interpretation of metaphor as the transfer of the sensible to the intelligible (*Psyché*, 70). He understands Derrida as conceiving the relationship between metaphorical and literal meaning in terms of 'usure', in the sense of a wearing away of figurative richness, a conception which Derrida was at pains to show up as inadequate. Ignoring one of the thrusts of Derrida's critique, which is to stress the syntactic aspect of metaphor, Ricoeur goes on to accuse Derrida of attaching an unjustified importance to nouns and names, and of furthering a monolithic conception of metaphysics which is precisely the one deconstruction aims to explode. Ricoeur's reading of 'Le Retrait de la métaphore' and Derrida's reply to it point to the peculiar and characteristic difficulty of Derrida's texts, which require a constant vigilance on the part of the reader if she is not to fall into the trap of taking as an 'authorial' position hypotheses which are being advanced as part of a critical strategy. We shall examine another example of this shortly in the Derrida/Searle debate.

Like 'La Mythologie blanche', another essay from *Marges* entitled 'Le Supplément de copule – la philosophie devant la linguistique', is also directly concerned with language. It analyses various discussions from both philosophy and linguistics of the relationship between 'Being' in its ontological sense and the verb 'to be' in its everyday uses. Derrida's point of departure is the classical question of meta-language, that is to say the problems faced by philosophy in any attempt to theorize its own language, which it can carry out only in the very language it is analysing. Derrida demonstrates the continuing dominance of nineteenth-century ways of envisaging the question, exemplified in Nietzsche's conception of philosophy being 'trapped' in the laws and grammar of its language, a language which was originally metaphoric. 'Le Supplément de copule' is primarily concerned, however, with the twentieth-century linguist, Émile Benveniste, in particular with Benveniste's attempt, through an exploration of Aristotle's theory of categories, to ascertain the extent to which philosophy is actually determined by the language in which it is written. Benveniste's basic thesis concerns the constraints by which the Greek language limits the Aristotelian system of categories; he sees the categories themselves as basically linguistic features which have been interpreted in philosophical terms. So Benveniste translates the ten major categories into their linguistic equivalents: Substance = noun; quantity and quality = adjectives; relation = comparative adjectives; when and where = adverbs of time and place; activity and passivity = active and passive verb forms, etc. 'This interpretation', he claims, 'apparently never put forward before, can be verified without long commentaries' (*Marges*, 221). With ironic acknowledgement of Benveniste's prudence, Derrida fastens onto the innocuous-looking word 'apparently'; for the theory certainly has been proposed before, though not, presumably, by anyone with whom Benveniste is familiar. Benveniste must have been looking in the wrong place, in linguistics we might surmise, but certainly not in philosophy. For his predecessors are numerous and illustrious, and the debate has been going on for two centuries at least, for example in Kant, Hegel, Prantl, Hamelin, Trendelenburg, Aubenque, Brunschvicg, Rougier, Humboldt and Cassirer.

But Derrida's main thesis concerns an afterthought of Benveniste's, a kind of footnote in which Benveniste advances the idea that the notion of the categories as a conceptual projection from the state of the Greek language can be extended to the notion of 'being'. The 'extension' is, in Derrida's view, far from evident, for 'being' is not a mere category, it is the 'transcategorial condition of categories' (p. 233). Benveniste argues that not all languages have a word for 'being', but that Greek gives the word a logical sense, making of it a copula without meaning which operates as a link between terms. Benveniste's argument is submitted to a rigorous critique on a number of scores: Derrida shows that it starts from false and self-contradictory premises, as, for example, demonstrated by Benveniste's simultaneous assertion that the verb 'to be' is absent from some languages, together with the claim that it means nothing and has a purely syntactic function. If it means nothing, how is its absence detectable, Derrida asks ingenuously. Using the example of the Ewe language of the Togo people, Benveniste attempts to show

how the 'absent' verb is supplemented by other functions, hence Derrida's title: 'Le Supplément de copule'. It is most frequently supplemented by a nominal phrase of apposition, for example, 'Rome, capital of Italy', where the copula is replaced by a pause (orally) or a comma (in its written form). So we have the paradoxical situation of a lexical absence being supplemented by another absence, a space or pause (p. 241). Like Heidegger, Benveniste takes the 'third person singular of the verb "to be"' (p. 243) as the privileged form from which notions of being derive. And like Heidegger also, Benveniste considers there to have been an erosion ('usure') of meaning of the term 'being', a fall away from an original sense, as the metaphoricity of the term became gradually lost. The linguist and the philosopher both hanker after a prelapsarian state, an original state of full meaning for 'being' before it became a mere copula. For Derrida, of course, this nostalgia for origins is part of a logocentric world-view which he will unsettle wherever he finds it. And neither philosophy nor linguistics seems equipped to deal with the questions posed by the 'supplément de copule': the answers will certainly not be found in any kind of ontology. Indeed, if there is an answer to the question of the relationship between truth, the meaning of being, and the third person singular of the present indicative of the verb 'to be', it will be found neither in philosophy nor in linguistics. It could perhaps only be sought in some 'marginal' realm, the realm where, as the title of his book indicates, Derrida wishes to situate his own enterprise.

The final essay of *Marges*, 'Signature Événement Contexte', is a discussion of Austin's speech-act theory and the first instalment of Derrida's acrimonious exchange with John Searle. Derrida meditates on the meanings of the term 'communication' in the context of the conference paper ('communication', in French) he is delivering to an International Congress on the Philosophy of Language at Montreal in 1971. The topic may sound technical and dry – *sec*, as Derrida says, referring to the acronym of his 'communication' – but, as will become clear, it is transformed by Derrida into an exciting intellectual adventure, as he pursues logocentric presuppositions in even the most unlikely linguistic corners. Derrida's paper begins with a summary of some of his major theses about language, returning once more to the question of the relationship between 'metaphorical' and 'literal' meaning; and again uses Condillac to exemplify the 'philosophical' interpretation of writing, that is to say, writing conceived as a vehicle for the communication of ideas. As we have seen, such a view envisages writing as essentially representative, and therefore marked by absence, the absence not so much of the author as of the recipient of the message. It also depends on a notion of the repeatability of the message in different contexts; Derrida's word for this is 'iterability', a term which is designed to include the notion of alterity within that of repetition. Derrida extracts what he sees as the three major defining characteristics of the classical conception of writing: writing is a 'mark that remains', it involves the possibility of a break with its context, and it is constituted by 'spacing'. He then goes on to demonstrate that all these are also features of spoken language. All signs imply absence, all signs can be cited. These arguments are already familiar from *De la grammatologie*, but what is of interest here is their implications for an analysis of Austin.

Austin's key notion in this context is that of the performative.[11] A performative utterance (as opposed to a constative utterance, which states or describes and which may be true or false) enacts what it enunciates: 'I promise' enacts a promise, 'I declare this meeting open' effectively opens the meeting, 'I declare you man and wife' validates a marriage – always depending, of course, on the context. For the performance to be fully successful, or what Austin calls 'happy', the promise has to be 'serious', the meeting must be opened by the chair, and the marriage conducted by a priest or registrar, not a child at play. Austin spends much time considering 'infelicitous' or 'unhappy' examples of performatives which, for some reason or other, fail to enact what they purport. But he explores these failures in order to exclude them. And this is the nub of Derrida's interest: Austin, he argues, recognizes the possibility that *any* performance may fail, but his distinction between happy and unhappy performatives means that such failure is a contingent, perhaps even a lurking, possibility, whereas for Derrida it is a structural element, indeed a condition of possibility of any utterance (*Marges*, 387). Furthermore, Austin excludes certain situations in which performatives do not operate normally, on the grounds that they are parasitic: fiction, play-acting, quoting, are all deemed extraneous to his analysis (*How to Do Things with Words*, 22). For Derrida, on the contrary, these cases are interesting precisely for what they have in common with the operation of ordinary performative utterances. For it is the notion of 'iterability' that underlies these excluded, 'hollow' performatives: they involve a kind of citation, and a non-presence of the intention of the speaking subject, whether this be in jest, on stage or in fiction. But this is exactly what they share with all other performatives in Derrida's account: he insists on the fact that marrying, promising, opening meetings and naming boats are all highly ritualized operations which depend not on the spontaneity or intention of the speaker but on citation and context. Austin 'excludes from consideration' precisely what might have been most interesting to analyse, and has produced a theory which cannot deal with the failure implicit in the very nature of the speech-act. Intention, Derrida argues, is never fully present, context is never perfectly defined (*Marges*, 389). The gradual collapse of Austin's constative/performative distinction from lecture V onwards, as the relevance to performatives of the truth/falsehood opposition becomes increasingly apparent, and constatives in turn appear liable to all the infelicities that haunt performatives, was, in Derrida's view, inevitable from the outset. Austin's 'patient', 'aporetic', 'open' and 'fertile' analysis starts from false premises in that it does not recognize the constitutive role of those linguistic features which Derrida has called 'graphematic', and which undermine from the start the purity of the oppositions Austin seeks to establish (*Marges*, 383).

The question of authoritative speech-acts raises in turn the question of the signature, the condition of possibility of which – that is, the singular originality of the particular signing – is also, Derrida argues, the very condition of its impossibility, at least in a pure and rigorous form. For a signature cannot be unique: to function it must be recognizable and repeatable. It is always the same and always other; it is iterable, to use Derrida's term. Derrida concludes with a brief explanation of why he chooses to retain the traditional name (*écriture*) for his deconstructive, post-logocentric view of writing. In short, this paleonymy[12] is a strategy to provoke – and to provoke thought. There is no meta-language which could get outside the metaphysical heritage; all deconstruction can do is disrupt the accepted meanings of old words and sometimes coin new ones. And Derrida signs his text with what he calls 'la plus improbable signature' (the most improbable/unprovable signature, *Marges*, 393, *Limited Inc.*, 51).

The essay enraged one of the best-known followers of Austin, the philosopher John Searle. And Searle retaliated in an article entitled 'Reiterating the Differences: A Reply to Derrida', published in vol. 1 of the periodical *Glyph* (1977),[13] which also published the English translation of Derrida's essay. Derrida in turn responded with 'Limited Inc. abc' (in *Glyph*, 2) in which he attacks Searle overtly and severely. This paper and 'Signature Événement

Contexte' are both collected in book form in *Limited Inc.*, together with a third piece which comprises a question-and-answer session on the problems raised by the debate with Searle. This interview with Gerald Graff, editor of the American edition of *Limited Inc.* (which in fact appeared a year before the French edition) is entitled 'Postface: vers une éthique de la discussion', and gives Derrida's views on the polemic more than ten years later. Searle refused to allow his 'Reply' to be reprinted in the same volume, so it was summarized by Graff and quoted *in extenso* by Derrida in his critique of it, which of course allowed him to exemplify some intriguing issues concerning citation, intellectual ownership, property and copyright.

At first sight, 'Limited Inc.' appears to take a long time to get going: Derrida explores the implications of the notions of signature and authorship, elaborating on what he said in 'Signature Événement Contexte', seeming to tease Searle by refusing to engage directly with his arguments, indeed pulling himself up short from time to time with the admonition to be serious ('soyons sérieux'). But of course all this is very much part of the polemic, part of the problematization of the serious/non-serious opposition, and an exemplification of some of the issues it raises.[14] Derrida proposes to continue the debate with Austin that, according to Searle, 'never quite [took] place', partly because Austin died too soon; Searle refers for example to an aspect of speech-act theory 'that Austin did not live long enough to develop himself' (*Limited Inc.*, 74). Derrida takes Searle's repeated references to his 'misunderstanding' of Austin and uses them to question precisely the structure of speech-acts in general. How are such misunderstandings possible? Of course, Derrida does not believe that he has misread Austin, but, on the contrary, that it is Searle who has misread them both; indeed Derrida claims to feel very close to Austin on a number of issues, hence his interest in speech-act theory.

Searle's critique of Derrida is direct and patronizing: Derrida says things 'that are obviously false'; Searle lists 'his major misundertandings and mistakes' and argues that 'Derrida's Austin is unrecognizable' (p. 83). Searle starts by remarking that Derrida's paper is in two parts; Derrida points out that it comprises, not surprisingly, three sections, on signature, event and context, and that Searle addresses none of them. Searle curiously suggests that 'Signature Événement Contexte' is attempting to distinguish between writing and speech using the criteria of iterability and absence, and proceeds to reject both as grounds for such a discrimination. It will be clear to anyone who has read thus far that we have an exact replica here of the Ricoeur phenomenon: Searle is attributing to Derrida the opposite of the views he in fact proposes, and using Derrida's own arguments to challenge him. Derrida, of course, is concerned to deconstruct the speech/writing opposition, not to propose it. Speech is indeed iterable, and absence is not the dubious prerogative of writing: as Searle himself says, 'Does one really have to point this out?' (p. 96). Derrida, clearly irritated, does not simply seek to refute Searle; he is at pains to add to his previous arguments: here, for example, he explains that, *pace* Searle, the writer and the receiver of a message one writes to oneself (say a shopping list), are not (except in a trivial sense) self-identical. If they were, the note would be unnecessary. The present self is sending a reminder to a future self who may have forgotten something. But we can only look here at the bare bones of Derrida's argument. Much of Searle's criticism may flow from a misunderstanding of some of Derrida's key notions. He accuses Derrida for example of confusing iterability and permanence, and argues that whilst iterability is common to both speech and writing, it is the relative permanence of writing that distinguishes them (p. 101). Now this is precisely the classical conception of writing that Derrida is opposing in 'Signature Événement Contexte', and the reason why he uses the term 'iterability', which implies difference rather than self-identity through time.[15] The misunderstanding may arise in part from a problem of translation: Derrida's use of a neologism, the 'restance' of writing ('remainder', in the English translation), to alert the reader to a new concept, not to be confused with 'permanence'. And 'restance' is associated with non-presence. Derrida comments that the notion may be paradoxical, but that he never promised to be orthodox.

Similar misreadings are to be found in a variety of areas: intentionality, parasitism, citation etc., and problems of translation emerge in other areas too. Searle, for example, seems to misunderstand 'grapheme' when he argues that only writing proper is graphematic. Similarly, he reads Derrida as claiming that Austin 'somehow denied the very possibility that expressions can be quoted' (p. 181). The claim, whether attributed to Austin or to Derrida, is so patently absurd that one suspects a fundamental misreading has taken place, due perhaps in this case to the fact that 'possibilité' (theoretical) and 'éventualité' (contingent and empirical) are quite distinct in French, but translated by the one term, 'possibility', in English. Derrida recognizes this problem, but considers it insufficient in the context to have caused Searle such confusion (p. 162).

In the dialogue between Gerald Graff and Derrida which occupies the final section of *Limited Inc.*, Derrida has another opportunity to explain himself, though he claims to want to open up discussion rather than close it. Searle, on the other hand, clearly had no desire to engage in further debate, and Derrida points out that Searle managed to review Jonathan Culler's book *On Deconstruction* without once referring to the exchange that had taken place between the two philosophers, and certainly without taking the opportunity to return to it (pp. 225–6). The argument in the interview is laid out clearly and in fine detail, but I wish rather to draw attention to two footnotes which lead to some general considerations about the widespread misreading of Derrida. The first footnote concerns Habermas, who, in *The Philosophical Discourse of Modernity*,[16] Derrida claims, takes Searle's side in the debate without ever quoting Derrida directly, or even referring to any of his published texts. Habermas's knowledge of the issues seems to have been gleaned primarily from Culler's work, which is quoted on the grounds that it is clearer and easier to follow than either Derrida or Searle. Culler's book is a pedagogic explanation, simpler but by the same token necessarily less refined than Derrida's writing itself, and when Habermas describes Derrida as reversing the primacy of logic over rhetoric (*Philosophical Discourse*, 187) and of deconstructing philosophical texts with the tools of literary criticism, in particular through a critique of style (pp. 188–9), it draws an untypically curt and categorical response from Derrida: 'Cela est faux' ('This is false', p. 245). Habermas claims that Derrida's arguments are circular, that Derrida believes all interpretations to be erroneous, and all understanding to be misunderstanding (*Philosophical Discourse*, 198). Derrida denies that he has ever expressed such views, and contends that he has rather emphasized the *possibility* of misinterpretation and misunderstanding in any speech-act. If Habermas had read Derrida rather than Culler (who indeed writes 'Every reading is a misreading')[17] he might at least have achieved a more subtle (mis)understanding!

This kind of dependence on secondary sources is woefully unscholarly, but typical of a debonair attitude towards 'deconstruction' on the part of certain thinkers who righteously proclaim the necessity of a classical kind of proof, while not bothering to read, or read closely, the texts they are attacking. The second footnote to which I referred makes clear the potential political significance of second-hand judgements. Searle, in his review of Culler's book, quotes Michel Foucault as having accused Derrida of 'obscurantisme terroriste': 'Michel Foucault once characterized Derrida's prose style to me as "obscurantisme terroriste". The text is written so obscurely that you can't figure out exactly what the thesis is (hence "obscurantisme") and when one criticizes it, the author says "You haven't understood me; you're an idiot" (hence "terroriste")' (p. 257). Derrida has no wish to deny that Foucault may have said such a thing – 'hélas'. But he does question the ethics of repeating cocktail-party gossip as part of what ought to be serious intellectual engagement; and he recounts how the quote was used against him by an American academic (Ruth Barcan Marcus) who petitioned a French government minister to block Derrida's appointment as director of the Collège International de Philosophie in 1984. Deconstruction finds little favour with conservatives afraid that some of their most cherished beliefs are being undermined. It is Derrida's own view that the constant reviewing of the most seemingly unquestionable assumptions is vital to any healthy intellectual life, and provides one definition at least of deconstructionist 'politics'.[18]

But Derrida's texts clearly pose problems of reading and interpretation rarely if ever encountered to the same degree in other philosophers. The reasons for this have less to do with the intelligence or good will of his readers than with certain characteristics of his writing, which is extraordinarily dense and often plurivalent. Deconstruction frequently follows first one and then another line of argument through a text, thereby bringing implicit underlying conflicts to the surface; Derrida espouses so intimately the texts he is deconstructing that only a very attentive reader can tell where his own views start and where his exposition ends. His critique often takes the form of a subtle and complex refining of positions which are true in part or up to a point, and the marking of that point is a demanding task. 'Paleonymy', the use of an old term for a new or revised concept (e.g. 'écriture', writing), requires the reader to keep the habitual sense at bay if she is to focus properly on the revised concept. When a paleonymy or neologism (like 'différance', 'trace', 'supplement', 'restance', 'iterability', 'logocentrism' etc.) has been used and explained in one place, the explanation is not repeated in other contexts where the term occurs, although an elaborate system of cross-references allows the term to gather strength and further accretions of meaning as the text moves along. But there is a further reason for the difficulty: Derrida's writing is in a sense itself 'performative', that is, it enacts what it describes; it is not merely constative and argumentative, but it exemplifies the features it is discussing. This kind of language use is alien to most philosophical traditions, and is more readily thought of as a feature of literary texts; but, as we shall see, another feature of the Derridean strategy is to undo the conventional distinction between literature and philosophy and the hierarchy which subordinates the former to the latter.

If Derrida seems inimical at first reading, it is much easier to dismiss him than to spend the immense amount of time required to learn to read and understand him. Hence even competent theorists like Habermas will resort to expository texts such as this one, or Culler's, and attack them instead of the original; or analytic philosophers like Searle will read a very limited amount of Derrida's work and assimilate all that is novel in it to some (distorting) previously existing categories; or original thinkers like Ricoeur will read him hastily and latch on to what they imagine is being argued (e.g. that literal meaning is a form of *usure* of the metaphorical) because they are more interested in their own arguments than in the correctness of their reading of others. Misrepresentation of this kind probably occurs on a large scale all the time, but it is rarely analysed and responded to with such brilliance and scholarship as Derrida seems able to muster at any moment. Derrida's intelligence is formidable: this is why it is vital to read and understand him, not merely to dismiss him as obscurantist.

4

Deconstructing the Text: Literature and Philosophy

Just as Derrida considers traditional conceptions of the relationship between speech and writing to be false and misleading, so he considers the classical opposition between literature and philosophy to be based on an erroneous view of the nature of both. The opposition is predicated on the belief that literature is concerned with aesthetic representation, style and fiction, whereas philosophy is the domain of truth, objectively presented. This familiar binary opposition is one of the most significant targets of Derrida's deconstructive analysis, in the first place because philosophy deludes itself and its adherents if it claims to present Truth, independent of the language used to express it. This has already been discussed in previous chapters with respect to fields such as geometry and phenomenology. And secondly because literature is not primarily fictional representation, clothed in a pleasing style: the last chapter demonstrated how much more complex Derrida's conception of language is than this classical model. Derrida considers both literature and philosophy as 'texts', and the implications of this will become progressively clearer. It means that philosophical texts are subject to the same kind of analysis as literary ones; to some eyes this may look suspiciously like treating the philosophical text as if it were literature, but this suspicion is based on the assumption that philosophy is 'above' questions of its language, operating in an ideal domain of pure truth which Derrida is precisely questioning. We saw Habermas accuse Derrida of approaching philosophical texts via a critique of style, and Derrida's curt retort: 'Cela est faux' (*Limited Inc.*, 245). It is false because the very term 'style' is part of the style/content opposition which Derrida contests. But it is none the less true that Derrida approaches texts traditionally viewed as 'philosophical' with the same deconstructive protocol as he approaches those traditionally viewed as 'literary', and in this sense what he has to say about literature is also pertinent to philosophy. What is certain, however, is that Derrida rejects any assimilation of philosophy to literature, as he has been forced to stress repeatedly over recent years in the face of an uncomprehending backlash from certain philosophical quarters, explaining that deconstructing and questioning an established distinction is not the same as denying its existence. The complexity of the relationship between philosophy and literature, the history, conventions and limits of the two types of text, indeed, the 'turbulence' of their relationship, are among the questions that are explored most forcefully in his own writings. (See the interview entitled 'Y a-t-il une langue philosophique?', 1988, in *Points de suspension*, 1992.)

Derrida does not, however, pose the simple question 'What is literature?' In the first place because he says it cannot but sound like an echo of Sartre's famous Qu'est-ce que la littérature? (*Diss*, 203); more seriously, because it is a question from the ontological realm which Derrida rejects: 'There is no essence of literature, no truth of literature' (*Diss*, 253). But this does not prevent him from attempting to discover 'what was represented and determined by the term – literature – and why' (*Diss*, 253). Derrida uses the past tense, and refers to the 'crisis of literature' (p. 275); the texts of writers such as Artaud, Bataille, Mallarmé and Sollers have forced us to undertake a radical review of our conception of literature: 'These texts operate . . . the demonstration and the practical deconstruction of the representation we had of literature, it being, of course, understood that long before these "modern" texts, a certain "literary" practice may have worked against that model, against that representation' (*Pos*, 93–4). Texts such as Mallarmé's, Derrida argues, resist the classificatory systems which may be applied to them in traditional criticism, rhetoric or aesthetics: 'For example, the values of meaning or content, form or signifier, metaphor/metonymy, truth, representation etc., at least in their classical form, can no longer account for certain very determinate [textual] effects' (*Pos*, 94).

In his attempt to compel his readers to rethink the speech/writing opposition, Derrida coined the term *archi-écriture* to refer to the most fundamental basis of inscription on which both speech and writing in their common usages depend. In the case of literature, Derrida sets up an opposition between notions of 'book' and 'text' to force a similar re-evaluation. The 'book' is envisaged by Derrida as a fundamentally theological notion: Nature described as the Book of God in the Middle Ages (*Diss*, 51); the totalizing project of the eighteenth-century *Encyclopédie* and of Hegel (*Diss*, 54); the ideal book imagined by Leibniz in which every detail of life on earth since Creation would be found. In all these cases the Book is conceived as a totality, a meaningful whole, referring beyond itself to the 'real world', a 'volume heavy with meaning' (*Diss*, 51). 'The idea of the book', Derrida writes, 'which always refers to a natural totality, is profoundly alien to the meaning of writing [*écriture*]. It is the encyclopaedic protection of theology and logocentrism against the disruption of writing, against its aphoristic energy and . . . against difference in general' (*Gram*, 30–1). In opposition to this view of literature as Book is the notion of text, fragmentary, partial and productive of its own meaning, which is always deferred: 'The fragment is not a style or a specific failure, it is the very form of the written. Unless God himself were writing' (*ED*, 108). Just as he considers metaphysics is dying but will never die, so Derrida believes that we are witnessing what he calls 'the closure of the book' and 'the opening of the text' (*ED*, 429). The theological encyclopaedia is giving way to a 'tissue of traces', though the text will never finally replace the book, and to maintain that it could is to betray a metaphysical conception of ends and origins. This is why Derrida argues that 'writing can no more begin than the book finish' (*Pos*, 23): there are no absolute endings. Like philosophy, the book reassures us by its assumption of meaning, purpose and unity (*Pos*, 11); it provides 'the most certain forgetfulness of death' (*ED*, 115). The text, on the other hand, makes no claims to unity; it is heterogeneous and constituted by differences (*Diss*, 111). The term 'text' itself suggests a woven texture, a cloth which is not transparent: 'A text is only a text if it hides at first sight, from the first-comer [*le premier venu*: anybody who comes along], the law of its composition and the rules of its game. . . . The dissimulation of texture may in any case take centuries to unweave its cloth' (*Diss*, 71).

Derrida's terminology – composition, game, texture, cloth – itself indicates one of the major differences between the old and new conceptions of literature: the text is not mimetic. It breaks radically with the Aristotelian conception of art: for Aristotle mimesis is the origin of poetry, it is natural to man, and, as mimesis, art is a form of truth (*Marges*, 283). But in so far as it is imitative, art is necessarily secondary: it represents rather than creates; it is guaranteed by its connection with the 'real world', but it is by the same token inessential and potentially dangerous: 'Since supplementary mimesis adds *nothing*, is it not useless . . . is not this imitative supplement dangerous for the integrity of what is represented?' (*Gram*, 290). In the mimetic view, art is necessarily subject to the same ambiguities as the sign in traditional linguistics: if nature is seen as pre-existing its expression in language (and art), language and art are in a sense inessential. But language, the sign and art are none the less prized as specifically human, as the means by which man transcends nature, so that our attitude to mimetic art is bound to be ambivalent. Moreover, if art is valued for its resemblance to the real, it thereby sets itself a goal whose achievement would entail its dissolution. In this sense, 'imitation would be at once the life and death of art' (*Gram*, 297). Ambivalence and paradox permeate the Aristotelian conception of art: art both reveals nature and constitutes a form of alienation from nature; imagination, the source of art, awakens our desire to possess the world while rendering such possession impossible (*Gram*, 438).

For Plato too art was mimetic, but it was thereby not merely secondary but at least tertiary. Given Plato's conception of the world we live in as a pale reflection of the more real world of Ideas, art necessarily becomes a mere copy of a copy: 'Plato always refuses the intuition of the thing itself to writing and painting in the "proper" sense, because they deal only in copies and copies of copies' (*Diss*, 216). However sophisticated our understanding of the mimetic nature of art may be, the work of art always remains subservient to nature. Theorists of art may stress that the work of art is not servile but creative, going beyond even the beauty of nature; it is none the less to nature that they turn for their comparisons: 'Surplus value . . . makes art a richer nature, freer, more loveable, more creative: more natural' (*Diss*, 218). Even if art is seen as providing a higher form of truth than science, it is still a truth about the world. To this extent, the artistic 'creator' of traditional criticism does not really create, he transcribes: 'He has only the illusion of creating because he is only transcribing and producing a text whose nature is itself necessarily representational, maintaining with what is called "the real" . . . an imitative and reproductive relationship' (*ED*, 346).

Derrida breaks radically with all conceptions of art as mimesis. This is necessarily entailed by his rejection of the identification of truth with a description or reflection of things as they really are, whether this be in a theory of *homoiosis, adaequatio, aletheia* or the certainty of the *cogito* (*Diss*, 219). All such theories of Truth imply an established world pre-existing perception and representation; but there is for Derrida no 'world' (in the sense of an organized totality) pre-existing the sign; the sign is constitutive of the world as we know it: 'the phenomenon presupposes its originary contamination by the sign' (*ED*, 190). *A fortiori*, then, 'there is never a painting of the thing itself, in the first place because there is no thing itself' (*Gram*, 412). This is one of the major implications of Derrida's notion of *différance*, and it is what he means when he says that Mallarmé, Artaud etc. have led us to break with the traditional conception of literature as representation. Mallarmé may appear at first glance to have a sophisticated version of a mimetic view of art, but this is an illusion; his imitation is of nothing which pre-exists it: the 'reality' revealed does not exist, it is constantly deferred, like the 'rose absente de tout bouquet'. We witness a play of mirrors, but the play is unending: 'this mirror reflects no reality', 'there is no longer a model' (*Diss*, 234). A Mallarmé poem like 'A la nue accablante tu' is strictly syntactical but does not give a single set of propositions corresponding to an aspect of the 'real world': the syntax may be read in several different and mutually exclusive ways simultaneously, thus turning the poem into its own plurivalent object. *Un coup de dés* exploits this tendency in an even more radical fashion.

Modern art, Derrida maintains, produces meaning rather than reflects truth. This is both the good fortune and the cause of anguish of modern man, and it defines the contemporary aesthetic. The impossibility of the Book in the Leibnizian sense, recognized as impossible by Mallarmé, a 'lost certainty' (*ED*, 21), opens up 'the play of meaning'. And the replacement of 'book' by 'play', Derrida argues, is most apparent in the case of theatre, which is *représentation* (performance) *par excellence*. In his vision of a Theatre of Cruelty, the playwright Antonin Artaud broke radically with the model of theatre as a spectacle repeating a pre-existing text: 'Artaud wants a theatre where repetition is impossible' (*ED*, 264). French permits a word-play here which is not possible in English: *répétition* means both repetition and rehearsal; similarly, *représentation* means both representation and performance. Artaud, Derrida argues, 'wants to finish with the imitative concept of art. With the Aristotelian aesthetics espoused by Western metaphysics' (*ED*, 344). Mimesis is part and parcel of Western metaphysics, part of the identification of Being and presence: 'another name for "la répétition représentative": Being' (*ED*, 361). However, Artaud may encourage improvisation and creativity by the actors, and may refuse to rely on the repetition of a written text, but he cannot escape representation altogether. His ideal of pure theatre is unattainable: the Theatre of Cruelty would, in its ideal form, be life itself, in its original purity, free from representation, in other words, an impossible and logocentric myth of pure presence in Derrida's eyes, as impossible on the stage as off it. 'Presenc . . . has always already begun to be represented, has always already been breached [*entamé*]' (*ED*, 366). 'Tragedy is the necessity of repetition' (*ED*, 364). Like metaphysics, and like the Book, representation will never finally end, but writers like Artaud and Mallarmé help us imagine its ending (*clôture*).

However, if art has, in Derrida's view, broken free of the tyranny of the mimetic model, this does not mean that he envisages the author as freely creating *ex nihilo*. In the first place, the writer is not totally in control of his medium: 'The writer writes in a language and a logic whose system, by definition, his discourse cannot dominate absolutely' (*Gram*, 227). Language is not mine: its meaning does not come from me. This is what Derrida means when he refers, in his essay on Artaud, to 'stolen speech' (*la parole volée*): 'As soon as I speak, the words that I have found, precisely because they are words, no longer belong to me, they are originally repeated . . . Speech . . . is always stolen. Always stolen because always open. It is never specific [*propre*] to its author or its recipient' (*ED*, 264–6). Similarly, perception itself is not original – there is no pure perception precisely to the extent that there is no 'thing itself' – the world is a structure which depends on a system of relations in which the individual plays a minor rather than a constitutive role:

> There must be several to write and even to perceive. . . . Pure perception does not exist. . . . The 'subject' of writing does not exist if one understands it to imply some sovereign solitude of the writer. The subject of writing is a system of relationships between layers . . . of the psyche, of society, of the world. Within that scene, the punctual simplicity of the classical subject cannot be found. (*ED*, 335)

Since the individual writer is not in full control of the meaning of his text, the 'joyous wandering of writing [*graphein*]' (*ED*, 429) seems to be that of language itself. This is also why Derrida maintains that the determining of an author's intended meaning, although an essential phase in textual analysis, 'the indispensable condition of any hermeneutics' (*ED*, 53), is not the final aim of criticism. Indeed, the categories of voluntary and involuntary effects have no absolute pertinence in deconstructive criticism (*Diss*, 82). Analysis of a text will reveal the 'play of a chain of meanings', but the chain is not identical with the author's intentions: 'This system is not primarily that of intended meaning [*vouloir-dire*]' (*Diss*, 108). Nor will Derrida distinguish between conscious and unconscious intentions. But if the meaning of a text does not depend on its author (*Marges*, 331), the literary text is no different in this respect from any other language use. In speech also I never communicate exactly what I intend, 'the intention animating the utterance will never be entirely present' (*Marges*, 389); however in speech we may have the illusion of a correspondence between intention and meaning. The written text can be read and reread; its different possibilities of meaning are thus more apparent. 'What must a text be', Derrida asks, 'if it is able, independently in some sense, to turn around to shine again . . . in a time which is no longer that of its productive source . . . and to repeat this resurgence again after [the death of its author]?' (*Marges*, 331).

Derrida's four essays, collected in *La Dissémination*, on Hegel and prefaces, on Plato, Mallarmé and Philippe Sollers, are all concerned with the question of textual meaning. The title term, dissemination, refers to the multiplicity of meanings spawned by the modern text. As Derrida explains in his interview with Jean-Louis Houdebine, published in *Positions*, dissemination differs from polysemy in so far as polysemic meanings can be gathered together and totalized, whereas disseminated meanings remain fragmented, multiple and dispersed (*Pos*, 61–2). Dissemination disrupts semantics in so far as it produces an indefinite number of semantic effects. Derrida plays on the illusory appearance of a relationship between 'seme' and 'semen', and uses the mirage of this link to provide a way of discussing the generation of meaning. In so far as dissemination cuts a text off from its author's intentions it can be described, he maintains, as a form of castration: 'Dissemination figures what does not come back to the father. Neither in germination nor in castration.' 'Dissemination affirms endless substitution' (*Pos*, 120).[1] We will return in the next chapter to the psychoanalytic references which form part of Derrida's intermittent dialogue with Lacan. Unlike polysemy, then, dissemination is not dominated by the author, and its multiple meanings cannot be totalized as forming part of the author's intentions. But like *différance*, dissemination is positive: it is not a loss of meaning but rather the affirmation of an indefinite number of meanings. It is anti-reductive: 'One of the theses inscribed in dissemination is precisely the impossibility of reducing a text . . . to its effects of meaning, content, thesis or theme' (*Diss*, 13). 'One has to choose between text and theme' (*Diss*, 389). Like metaphor, 'dissemination opens up the wandering of semantics' (*Marges*, 287). This was why Aristotle mistrusted metaphor, and felt polysemy should be restricted: dissemination presents us with a world of meaning out of our control.

One of the most striking features of dissemination is the occurrence of 'undecidable' terms which radically unsettle a text, and make a final decision as to its meaning impossible. Derrida did not invent or discover undecidable terms: they were discussed previously (and to different ends) by the anthropologist Marcel Mauss and the classicist J.P. Vernant (*Diss*, 150–1) as well as by Freud (*Diss*, 249), and the word itself is taken analogically from the mathematician Gödel, as Derrida pointed out in his Introduction to Husserl's *Origin of Geometry* in 1962 (p. 39).[2] In its scientific sense, the undecidable designates a proposition that is neither true nor false in relation to a certain axiomatic system: 'An undecidable proposition – Gödel showed the possibility of it in 1931 – is a proposition that, given a system of axioms which dominates a multiplicity, is neither an analytic or deductive consequence of the axioms, nor in contradiction with them, neither true nor false with respect to these axioms' (*Diss*, 248–9). Derrida uses the term 'undecidable' to designate what he defines as 'unities of simulacrum . . . "false" verbal properties, nominal or semantic, which can no longer be understood in terms of (binary) philosophical opposition, and which none the less inhabit it, resist it, and disorganize it, but without ever constituting a third term, without ever giving rise to a solution in the form of speculative dialectics' (*Pos*, 58). Undecidables are terms which mean both one thing and its opposite; neither one thing nor its opposite. In the interview in *Positions*, Derrida claims that they are 'in a rigorously Freudian sense, the unconscious of philosophical opposition' (*Pos*, 60), and we will return to the psychoanalytic aspect of this claim later. For the moment, it is its anti-Hegelianism that is important to note.

We have already seen one important example of an undecidable featuring in phenomenology and structuralism, and in particular in the writings of Lévi-Strauss and Rousseau: that of the 'supplement'. The supplement is both an unnecessary addition and an essential

complement: adding to an already complete whole and complet-
ing something unfinished. Features described as supplementary
turn out to be constitutive, and in this way the supplement is a
'dangerous' concept, because its (il)logic not only masks but also
reveals the inadequacy and failure of what it supplements. Retention and indication in Husserl's account of speech, writing, education and masturbation in Rousseau, are supplements which are
scandalous in so far as they show up the essential insufficiencies of
what they are supposed simply to complement.[3] Undecidables
appear to be commonly viewed as dangerous and, what is more, to
feature frequently in discussions of writing. Derrida's summary in
Positions lists some of the striking examples he has analysed:

> The *pharmakon* [from *Dissémination*, on Plato's *Phaedrus*] is neither
> remedy nor poison, neither good nor evil, neither inside nor outside,
> neither speech nor writing; the *supplement* is neither a more nor a less,
> neither an outside nor the complement of an inside, neither an accident
> nor an essence, etc.; the *hymen* [from Mallarmé's *Mimique*] is neither
> confusion nor distinction, neither identity nor difference, neither
> consummation nor virginity, neither the veil nor the unveiling, neither
> the inside nor the outside, etc.; the *gram* is neither a signifier nor a
> signified, neither a sign nor a thing, neither a presence nor an absence,
> neither a position nor a negation etc.; *spacing* is neither space nor
> time. . . . Neither/nor, it is *both* or *either*. (*Pos*, 59)

Derrida insists that undecidable terms are not for him a matter of
'enigmatic equivocation' or 'poetic mystery'; he is not repeating
Hegel's wonder in the face of words such as *Aufhebung*, or *Urteil*,
or *Meinen* or *Beispiel*, which were seen as naturally expressing
the speculative dialectic (*Diss*, 249). On the contrary, undecidables
witness not to lexical richness, but rather to a syntactic practice
which composes and decomposes them. In the case of the
pharmakon, which is both poison and remedy for Plato, and which
seems to express his deep-seated ambivalence towards writing, the
undecidability may appear primarily semantic and Derrida's insistence on syntax may seem a little strained, though the brilliance
of his analysis of the *Phaedrus* more than compensates for this. In
the case of the *hymen*, which signifies both marriage and virginity,
Derrida himself comments on the misleading impression that
everything in his analysis of Mallarmé's *Mimique* hinges on the
double meaning of the one word, whereas, in fact, the undecidability is ultimately a matter of syntax, as demonstrated in his
analysis of the functioning of the term 'entre' (*Diss*, 249–50). One
of the most convincing yet simplest examples of syntactic

undecidability comes from one of Lautréamont's *Chants de Maldoror* in the use of 'plus': 'Au réveil mon rasoir, se frayant un passage à travers le cou, prouvera que rien n'était, en effet, plus réel' (*Diss*, 50) ('On waking, my razor, making its way across my neck, will prove that nothing was more real', *or*, 'that nothing was real any longer']. There is no way of deciding whether reality is at its height or if it has disappeared.

But dissemination does not simply disrupt the stable signification and syntax of un/intended meaning, it disrupts the unity of the word itself. One of the myths of logocentrism, in Derrida's view, is that of the *word* as elementary unit: 'The word is experienced as the elementary and indecomposable unit of the signified' (*Gram*, 34). And this is precisely where thematic criticism[4] fails: it can cope with the totality of the book, but not the dispersion of the text. It cannot account for 'the formal, phonic or graphic "affinities" which do not have the size of the word. . . . It necessarily neglects, in so far as it is thematic, the play which disarticulates the word, breaks it up, and makes its elements work "obliquely"' (*Diss*, 287). It cannot therefore account for a text like Mallarmé's, for Mallarmé 'was interested as much in the dissection of the word as in the integrity of its own life' (*Diss*, 287). Derrida illustrates his point with a brilliant analysis of the prose poem *Or*, in which 'or' is to be found dispersed (disseminated) throughout the text – deh*or*s, fantasmag*or*iques, trés*or*, h*or*izon, maj*or*e, h*or*s – and inverted in the *ro* of zé*ro*, 'negative inverse of *or* [gold]' (*Diss*, 295) as Derrida describes it. RO as an inversion of OR is more apparent to the eye than to the ear, and is certainly not part of the meaning of the word. It is this stress on the signifier that explains Derrida's interest in versification: in rhyme, for example, words often apparently unrelated semantically are brought together by fragments of phonic and graphic resemblance. Rhyme is in a sense the counterpart, in terms of the signifier, of metaphor and metonymy, which relate words because of some element of their semantic content. This is perhaps what Derrida means when he claims that versification deconstructs the opposition between metaphor and metonymy: in so far as the opposition is purely semantic it is irrelevant to rhyme, and is ignored in the phonic relations established by versification (*Diss*, 314). To this extent, Derrida is stressing the primacy of the signifier over the signified in the modern text. But as he explains, this apparent priority is an effect of the reversal phase of deconstruction (*Pos*, 56 and 110); signifier and signified cannot be separated: their opposition remains intrinsically metaphysical (*Gram*, 228).

It is Derrida's attempt to deconstruct the binary oppositions of Western thinking that underlies much of his critique of the various different types of traditional literary criticism: all of them, in their various ways, set up a false opposition between form and content, and concentrate on one at the expense of the other:

> Criticism of content alone (thematic criticism, be it philosophical, sociological or psychoanalytic, which takes the theme – manifest or latent, full or empty – for the substance of the text, for its object or for the truth it is illustrating) can no more cope with *certain* texts . . . than can a purely formalist criticism, which is only interested in the code, in the pure play of the signifier, in the technical construction of a text-object, and which neglects the genetic effects or the ('historical', if you like) inscription of the text being read *and* of the new text that the criticism itself is writing. These two inadequacies are rigorously complementary. (*Pos*, 63–4)

Psychoanalytic criticism, for example, tends to ignore the specifically literary aspect of the text, or it may cobble together a psychoanalytic account with a weak attempt at more traditional literary criticism, with no real attempt to account for the form of the expression. Derrida cites René Laforgue as an example of this type of naive psycho-biography (*Gram*, 228–30). This is perhaps one of the reasons why Derrida insists that his own study of Plato's *Phaedrus* is not, despite certain psychoanalytic elements, psychoanalytic in the proper sense of the term (*Diss*, 150). Less rigorous psychological criticism is similarly dismissed as insufficient: the 'psychologism' of Jean-Pierre Richard's thematic criticism reduces the text to its 'meaning', and is incapable of accounting for the 'graphic' (*Diss*, 280). Derrida rejects attempts to explain the so-called 'thematic' content of a text like Mallarmé's by reference to the writer's psyche: to his *imaginaire* (imaginary world), his *intentionnalité* (intentionality) or his *vécu* (lived experience) (*Diss*, 282). In these three terms we may detect an implicit rejection of Bachelardian, existential and phenomenological criticism. All criticism which is exclusively concerned with the 'content' of a text is considered by Derrida to be a form of 'philosophy of literature' (*ED*, 47). For this reason he describes the Russian formalists with their concern for the purely literary nature of the text (its *littérarité*) as helping to liberate criticism from its reductivist tendency: 'The emergence of this question of literarity has permitted the avoidance of a certain number of reductions and failures of comprehension which will always tend to recur (thematism, sociologism, historicism, psychologism in the most disguised forms)' (*Pos*, 94).

However, thematic criticism and formalist criticism may be opposed, but in so far as they are theoretically mutually exclusive they are subject to the same insufficiencies, and may indeed both appear within the same piece of criticism. Lacan's study of Poe's 'Purloined Letter' is attacked by Derrida for being both hermeneutic and formalist (*Pos*, 118). There is in fact a necessary, if apparently paradoxical, complicity between thematic or empirical criticism on the one hand, and formalism on the other (*Diss*, 17). Formalism ultimately confirms the logocentrism it contests by its support of the metaphysical opposition between form and content. Derrida warns against what he calls a new 'idealism . . . of the text' (*Pos*, 89) which he fears may result from an unthinking abandonment of all elements of traditional criticism: 'We must avoid . . . the indispensable critique of a certain naive relationship to the signified or the referent . . . becoming fixed in a suspension, or even a pure and simple suppression, of meaning and reference' (*Pos*, 90). He stresses the necessity for the critic to take into account the historical nature of the text, be it literary or philosophical. And the author's intention forms an important part of the history of the text: it must be accurately determined before it can be transgressed in a new reading (*ED*, 54 and *Gram*, 227).

Derrida's notion of the articulation between signifier and signified is elaborated with considerable theoretical subtlety; it is related to the fundamental question of the relationship between the written text and the 'world' to which it is commonly seen as referring: '[There needs to be a] re-elaboration of the problem of "ideology", of the specific inscription of each text . . . in the fields commonly referred to as fields of "real" causality (historic, economic, political, sexual)' (*Diss*, 50). Since Derrida does not envisage the text as reflecting or referring to a pre-existing world, his thinking on the question of inscription or ideology is not easily relatable to any categorizable theory such as Marxism or structuralism. His position may be summed up elliptically in his own frequently quoted phrase: 'Il n'y a pas de hors-texte' (There is no outside-the-text) (*Gram*, 227). The notion is frequently misunderstood, and interpreted as meaning that Derrida too subscribes to an 'idealism of the text'. But Derrida's position is more subtle and more complex. Since there is no presence pre-existing the sign, 'There is nothing before the text, there is no pre-text that is not already a text. . . . If there is no "hors texte", this is because generalized graphics has always already begun' (*Diss*, 364). There is no referent in the traditional understanding of the term ('conceived as a real thing or cause, anterior and exterior to the system of general textuality', (*Diss*, 10)), no presence (in the sense of meaning, essence, form), no transcendental signified (*Diss*, 10). Just as writing proper is only one example of all-pervasive *archi-écriture*, so the written text is simply part of an *archi-texte*: it is not a closed totality as the formalists would have it, nor a reflection of a more real external world; it is necessarily open to the broader text of which it is part: 'If there is nothing outside the text, this means, with the transformation of the concept of the text in general, that the text is no longer the insulated inside of an interiority or a self-identity' (*Diss*, 42). Rather than cutting the text off from the so-called 'outside world', Derrida re-evaluates the notion of text, and establishes on different premises the complex relationship between the text in the narrow sense and the 'general text' (*Pos*, 125): 'What is happening in the current upheaval is a revaluation of the relationship between the general text and what used to be considered, in the form of reality (historical, political, economic, sexual etc.), the simple, referable exterior of language or writing, whether that exterior was envisaged as cause or simply as accident' (*Pos*, 126). The 'real world' is neither the source of art (as in the mimetic view), nor irrelevant to art (as in pure formalism). Derridean deconstruction attempts to overcome the art/world opposition, and set both on the same footing. If all is general text, then the text/*hors-texte* opposition loses its pertinence.

This chapter started with a reference to Derrida's rejection of Hegel's totalizing encyclopaedic project, which aimed at absolute knowledge (*Savoir Absolu*), and the previous chapter referred to Derrida's critique (in *Marges*) of Hegel's theory of language, which affirms the dialectical overcoming of the signifier in the process of meaning (the signified).[5] In 'Hors livre', the first essay of *Dissémination*, Derrida again returns to Hegel's overweening belief in totalization, and argues that it is difficult to reconcile with his predilection for prefaces. As Hegel himself recognizes, the philosophical preface is particularly problematic: is it part of the text it introduces, or an extraneous *hors-texte*? (And, of course, 'il n'y a pas de hors-texte.') For a philosophy of totalization, the question raises insuperable paradoxes. In this sense, Derrida argues, Hegel is simultaneously as close to and as far away as ever from the modern conception of the text. His totalizing teleology means that nothing precedes generalized textuality; however, Hegelian logic may also

be seen as a prime example of logocentrism and as directly opposed
to any theory of textual dissemination: 'Logic (is) of what returns to
the father (dead – more than ever) as to the law and the logos:
dialectical overcoming [*la relève*] itself. It is *true* and it constitutes the
truth *of* logocentrism. Of logocentric culture and of the logocentric
concept of culture' (*Diss*, 56). Hegel is a predatory philosopher,
infinitely hard to escape, as Kierkegaard discovered. A frontal
attack on him is bound to fail, because of the way the dialectic
transforms all opposition into a negative, antithetical moment in an
ongoing synthetic process. Derrida's most concerted critique of
Hegel comes in 1974, in *Glas*, where he sets up the fragmented
textual practice of the arch iconoclast and nihilist, Jean Genet,
against the all-devouring rigour of Hegel's search for *Savoir Absolu*
(absolute knowledge, abbreviated as *Sa*). *Glas* is organized in two
parallel columns which pit Hegel against Genet, thereby permitting
an extraordinary web of chiasmic interchanges, directly related
to Derrida's assault on the dialectic. In a sense it stages a battle
between literature in the modern sense of disseminated textuality,
and philosophy in the old sense of the search for ultimate truth. It
is also a battle of a more concealed sort with Sartre, another opponent of the Hegelian dialectic, and one who had already used Genet
to contest him. *Saint Genet, comédien et martyr*, published in 1951,
was familiar to Derrida, used by him as seminar material at the
École Normale, and allusions to it, both explicit and implicit,
abound in *Glas*, where Derrida reflects that trying to undo Hegel
is like trying to decapitate the hydra (*Glas*, 118). The dialectic
engulfs contradiction and recuperates subversion as error to be
transcended:

> If one thinks what the *logos* means, if one gives thought to the words of
> the *Phenomenology of Mind* and the *Logic*, for example, there is no way out
> of the absolute circle. In any case that is what the discourse of the *Sa*
> [Absolute Knowledge] means. To believe one can get out of it, or attempt
> to, is pure verbalism: one is not thinking what one is saying, one does
> not realize the meaning of the words which therefore remain empty.
> (*Glas*, 253)

How to prevent the fire in which Absolute Truth and Values are
consumed from becoming, in its turn, an Absolute? 'If you want
to burn everything, you must also consume the fire, avoid keeping
it alive like a precious presence. So you must extinguish it, keep it
in order to lose it (really) or lose it in order to keep it (really)'
(*Glas*, 269). How to interrupt the operation of the *Aufhebung*, how

to handle a negative which is more than a mere moment in an all-embracing process, how to escape the perpetual reversal entailed in any oppositional system of thought? As Derrida asks elsewhere: 'What would be the nature of a negative which could not be transcended [*relevée*]?' (*Marges*, 126). It is far from certain whether the ambiguous status of Derrida's parenthetical 'really' (*vraiment*) or the vehemence of his rejection of all originary or teleological thinking can ensure his own immunity from Hegel's transformative logic.

Glas is one of Derrida's most perverse texts. In comparison with it, his Introduction to *The Origin of Geometry*, *La Voix et le phénomène*, *De la grammatologie*, *Marges* and even *La Dissémination* seem models of clarity and argumentation. The perversity seems to have two main sources: in the first place it imitates Genet's own perverse techniques of trapping conventional bourgeois readers in positions they would never have taken unless forced by the power of the text; and secondly, it is an attempt to deal obliquely with a philosopher who positively relishes all opposition as offering grist to his mill. In the final part of this chapter I propose to allow Derrida to speak for himself in a more intricate and allusive manner than up till now, in order that readers should have a taste of the difficulty and fascination of his performative approach. I shall also thereby feel freer to take issue with him on certain points.

Glas constitutes Derrida's most intensive study of Hegel whom he opposes (literally) to Jean Genet. And the commentary on Genet is set up, in part, as a critical response to Sartre's seminal *Saint Genet*, published over twenty years earlier. Direct reference to Sartre is limited to a few relatively brief passages, but the precursor text underlies more of Derrida's writing than he acknowledges explicitly. *Glas* is an example of what Harold Bloom would call *Tessera*, a work of 'completion and antithesis',[6] in that Derrida 'misreads' *Saint Genet*, but in the process creates a most remarkable work of his own. The two main accusations levelled against Sartre's reading of Genet are that it is 'thematic' criticism (*Glas*, 36), and that it purports to provide a 'key' (p. 36) to the interpretation of Genet's works. Sartre does occasionally use the terms *thème* and *clé* (studiously eschewed by Derrida who prefers *foyer* (focus), *question*, *champ* (field), *chaîne*, etc.), but not in a sense that would make his account either 'thematic' or reductive. As an example of reductivism, Derrida cites: 'Genet is a child who has been convinced that, in his inmost depths, he is *an Other than himself*' (*SG*, 47; *Glas*, 37), and interprets this as no more than a rephrasing of Sartre's notion that the ego is synthetic and transcendent with no specific relevance to Genet: 'General enough to serve as an introduction to the transcendental structures of the ego,[7] it was as efficient and undifferentiated as a *passe-partout* [master-key], as a universal key slipping into all the lacunae of meaning' (*Glas*, 37). In fact, Sartre's point is not that Genet's 'self' is transcendent like the ego of us all, but that Genet specifically experiences it as alienated, 'Other than itself'. The accusation of reductivism might be reversed here, and one might speculate that it arises out of a desire on Derrida's part to distance himself from the precursor text.

Glas represents one of Derrida's most sustained attacks on intentional authorial meaning and textual unity; *Saint Genet* also marks the point at which Sartre comes closest to abandoning his attempt to preserve the authority of the subject. Genet is *pensé*, *parlé* (thought, spoken), his words are stolen from him, he cannot use language which belongs to the bourgeois, and so he tries to manipulate *la part du diable* ('the devil's share', that is, language as it escapes its user) in a refusal of communication which none the less risks being deviated in its turn. But Derrida is singularly unsympathetic to this discussion of Genet's language, dismissing as 'vague Mallarmeism' Sartre's analysis of the ' "vibratory disappearance" of signification' (*SG*, 564; *Glas*, 21), though the phrase is very close in sense and no more metaphoric than Derrida's own reference to 'the knell . . . [which] marks the end of meaning, sense and the signifier' (*Glas*, 39). *Glas* may be read as an unacknowledged response to Sartre's work, whether by opposing it, striking off obliquely from it, expanding it, or even imitating it. Of course, *Glas* and *Saint Genet* remain radically different in many vitally important respects. Derrida's elaborate treatment of death or flowers, for example, Sartre's exploration of the 'themes' of sainthood, evil or the Medusa-like stare of the Other undeniably establish the specificity of their respective works. And furthermore, certain similarities may be attributed not to any version of 'influence', however complex, but rather to the way in which the criticism of both philosophers appears to embrace so closely the characteristics of the text under scrutiny.

Like Sartre, Derrida is uncomfortably aware of the hostility his reading would arouse in his subject, Genet, who might be amused to be called a *machine à draguer* (pick-up machine, seducing machine) (*Glas*, 229), but who would hate to be understood, mastered or pressed into the service of a 'worthwhile' (anti-)philosophical cause. But whereas Sartre overtly betrays Genet by inter-

preting him and suggesting a possible 'good use' for his texts,
Derrida expresses the hope that his fragmentary and 'preliminary'
study (*Glas*, 229) will, by its nature, obviate the risk of seeming to
totalize the writer. He acknowledges, however, that even the least
pedantic comments the least 'hermeneutic and doctoral' comments
(*Glas*, 239–40) may still become a 'matrix' or a 'grammar' (p. 229),
and that Genet would quite rightly not be reassured by the plea of
good intentions: 'He will hate me for it. . . . And in every case. If I
support or valorise his text he will see this as a kind of approbation
or even appropriation – masterful, scholarly, paternal or maternal'
(*Glas*, 223).

Paternal or maternal: sexual difference, its elision and inversion,
forms much of the stuff of Genet's texts, and is intimately related
to the question of signification. Sartre's commentary on Genet's use
of the image of the thyrsus forms part of his discussion of
pansexualism:

> When it is a matter, for Genet, of marking the relations of a 'queen' with
> a male, a comparison always comes back to his pen: that of a spiral
> twisting around a rigid upright pole. And this image evolves to the point
> of becoming a sexual motif reproduced everywhere in Nature; here it is,
> first of all, as a spectacle: 'The queens chat and twitter around the males
> who are upright, still, vertiginous, still and silent as branches.' Then as a
> gesture: 'All the queens imparted to their bodies a spiral movement and
> tried to entwine the handsome man and wrap themselves around him.'
> Then as a metaphor: 'Around some of them, more upright and solid than
> the others, coil clematis, ivy, nasturtiums, little pimps too, entwining.'
> Finally the sexual schema flows over into perception itself: the sky in the
> midst of the palaces becomes 'the column of azure that marble entwines
> around'. (*SG*, 125)

Baudelaire's *Thyrse*, and its 'astonishing duality', is clearly the
precursor text here:

> The stick is your will, upright, strong and unshakeable: the flowers are
> the wanderings of your fantasy around your will; they are the feminine
> element executing around the male its prestigious pirouettes. Straight
> line and arabesque, intention and expression, firmness of will, sinuosity
> of the Word, unity of aim, variety of means, all-powerful and indivisible
> amalgam of genius, what analyst will have the hateful courage to divide
> and separate you?[8]

Derrida in turn takes over the metaphor to describe the way
in which 'Genet's sentences wind themselves around a direction,
like ivy along a truncated column' (*Glas*, 87), and he imagines
Genet's feeling of entrapment within *Glas*'s critical commentary

in similar terms: 'He would already feel entwined. Like a column, in a cemetery, eaten away by ivy, a parasite arriving too late' (*Glas*, 228).

The identification of 'intention' as masculine and 'expression' as feminine is common, though with varying degrees of irony and playfulness, to Baudelaire, Genet, Sartre and Derrida; and equally all four, in their different ways, strive to undermine the oversimple opposition between male and female, signified and signifier. Sartre writes of the inseparability of 'sense' and 'expression' even when he is remarking not on a successful act of communication but rather on its inevitable failure, in the 'infernal circle' (*SG*, 193). Derrida, as we have seen, announces the death of 'meaning', 'sense', and the 'signifier' (*Glas*, 39), because, in part, of the (false) oppositional system on which they are based. The title-word, 'Glas', is primarily neither signifier nor signified, not simply the death-toll of 'meaning' and 'theme', which remain to haunt any textual analysis, nor yet merely the phonetic decomposition of language into its formal elements. Derrida traces *Gl* through Genet's texts in such a way as to subvert the form/content opposition which cannot, none the less, be overthrown entirely. The proliferation of puns (Derrida denies there is a single pun in the text in the sense of gratuitous, aleatory wit) which depend on the interplay of phonic resonance and meaning, is part of the strategy of subversion. So too is the playful neo-Cratylic etymologizing, which bestows on the word an autonomy and personal history, self-destructive in the immensity of their pretensions. These seemingly idiosyncratic features of Derrida's writing in *Glas* have done much to damage his reputation as a 'serious' thinker, but they are, as I have suggested in other contexts, part of the 'performative' function of his text. *Glas* represents Derrida's most radical attempt to date to get beyond the infernal complicity and inevitable failure of semanticism and formalism (*Glas*, 165), empiricism and metaphysics (*Glas*, 252–3, 220). Sartre has a similar point to make about the complicity of realism and idealism (*SG*, 69–70). Intriguingly, but perhaps inevitably, both philosophers are led from the question of oppositions and their ultimate connivance and falsehood back to the question of sexual difference. When Sartre discusses the pederasty of Genet's texts he is not referring solely to their homosexual content, but rather to the system of inversions, illusions and betrayal which the texts establish. 'Poetry risks becoming treachery' (*SG*, 206). 'He steals a word, just one, and the reader notices that he *is spoken*. . . . Genet's poetry is the vertiginous flight of meanings towards nothingness' (*SG*, 560, 572). 'He forces others to support, in his place, the false against the true, Evil against Good, Nothingness against Being' (*SG*, 575). By a quite different route, and as part of his meditation on Hegel, Derrida comes to a similar conclusion about the relationship of difference and opposition in the sexual sphere. Infinite difference is ultimately self-negating (see *Gram*, 91). 'Non-existent and infinite difference would thus be sexual difference as *opposition*. . . . And if it transcends [*relève*] difference, opposition, conceptuality itself, is homosexual' (*Glas*, 249).

It is in their relation to Hegel that *Saint Genet* and *Glas* have most in common, for Genet serves both Sartre and Derrida as an ideal foil to Hegelian totalitarianism. But if Derrida owes much to Sartre in his choice and treatment of Genet as an opponent to Hegel, the debt is an unacknowledged irony, for Derrida has on occasions represented Sartre as some kind of neo-Hegelian interested only in synthesis and totalization. As we saw in chapter 1, Sartre, contrary to Derrida's assertions, persistently refuses to identify being and presence, maintaining that 'the in-itself cannot be present' (*EN*, 165), and rejecting the Hegelian notion that 'only the present is',[9] arguing that, precisely, 'the present is not' (*EN*, 168), it is *néant* rather than *être* (*EN*, 164–5). The whole argument of *L'Être et le Néant* is to insist 'against Hegel that being *is* and nothingness *is not*' (*EN*, 51). Hegel's transformation of negation into affirmation is vigorously resisted by both Sartre and Derrida in so far as it risks obliterating difference and reducing the power of the negative to negate. The negative moment of the dialectic is, for Hegel, precisely that: a moment which will be transcended. Hegel dissolves difference in the eventual unity of being and non-being, presence and absence. The *Aufhebung*, or speculative dialectic, is for Derrida an 'inexhaustible ruse' (*Marges*, 339) which *différance* precisely sets out to elude: 'If there were a definition of *différance* it would be precisely the limiting, the interruption, the destruction of the Hegelian dialectic *everywhere* it operates' (*Pos*, 55).

Sartre's own attack on Hegel is three-pronged – through the ontology of *L'Être et le Néant*; through Marxism in the *Critique de la raison dialectique*; and finally in 'L'Universel singulier' through the lesson of Kierkegaard who teaches that failure is a subjective reality which cannot be explained away as an objective 'relative positivity'.[10] It is through failure that human subjectivity proves inassimilable to *le savoir objectif* (objective knowledge). Derrida's response to Hegel necessarily shares similar focuses: an opposition to Hegelian ontology through *différance*; a reflection in *Glas* on Marx's *Theses on Feuerbach* and their attempt to come to terms with the dialectic (see *Glas*, 222–31); and a discussion of the struggle by Bataille and Kierkegaard to escape Hegelian totalization in their respective ways, i.e. through 'a-theology'[11] and a version of Christian mysticism. Kierkegaard faces the same danger as anyone vulnerable to the seductions of negative theology: that of falling back into precisely the trap he set out to evade and transforming negation into affirmation: 'Universal negation is equivalent to the absence of negation.'[12] Furthermore, Hegel has already confronted Kierkegaard's argument in advance: absolute singularity is, by its very absoluteness, part of the universal, ultimately sacrificed and thereby preserved: 'It is "saved" at the same time as lost as a singularity. . . . It . . . renounces its singular freedom. . . . " Singularity is absolute singularity, infinity, the immediate contrary of itself"' (*Glas*, 160, quoting Hegel). Negative theology, for Sartre and Derrida, is not truly negative; both philosophers use Eckhart to illustrate what Derrida calls onto-theology and what Sartre calls 'la sophistique du non': 'When I said that God was not a being and was above being, I was not thereby contesting his being, on the contrary I was attributing to him a higher being' (*ED*, 398. See also *SG*, 229). Their objections to negative theology are the same as their objections to Hegel: it is a sophistical reaffirmation of Being parading as negation. It also bears what they recognize to be an uncanny – but strongly resisted – resemblance to their own versions of paradoxical logic. Indeed, Derrida's forceful repudiation of the similarity might be interpreted as *dénégation* (denial): he insists that his 'description of *différance* is not theological, not even of the most negative order of negative theology. . . . *Différance* is . . . irreducible to any ontological or theological . . . reappropriation' (*Marges*, 6).

As Derrida points out, any 'misreading' of Hegel, including necessarily Sartre's and his own, is always already inscribed within absolute knowledge, or otherwise simply falls by the wayside 'as a remainder' (*Glas*, 259). Hegel, in this view, has confounded both Sartre and Derrida in advance by enclosing them within the sceptic's perennial dilemma. This perhaps in part explains their fascination with Genet, who seems to slip the net of recuperative dialectics precisely because he has no interest in Hegel, absolute knowledge, or even truth, and refuses to enter the debate except in parodic mode. For Genet is evidently familiar with the paradoxes and inversions of negative theology and perhaps also with its Hegelian resonances when he writes:

> To want to be nothing is a phrase one often hears. It is Christian. Should we understand by it that man seeks to lose, to allow to be dissolved, that which in some fashion gives him a banal singularity, that which gives him his opacity, so that, on the day of his death, he may present to God a pure transparency, not even iridescent? I don't know and I don't care.[13]

Genet may not care but Sartre and Derrida certainly do. Hence their shared anxiety that they may be 'betraying' the arch-traitor; hence too their tendency to 'idealize' him in the sense of accepting too readily his own self-portrait as villain. In *Saint Genet* Sartre seems to recognize a degree of authenticity in the simple ethical inversions he condemned five years earlier in the case of Baudelaire, and Derrida writes with apparent admiration of Genet's choice to follow a path of danger, terrorism and revolution (*Glas*, 45). Both Sartre and Derrida may *use* Genet to get outside Hegelian totality through loss, failure, fragmentation, or through consenting to be some kind of 'remainder', but it is clear that Genet has not (really) failed in the eyes of either of them. Genet's technique of inverting hierarchized oppositions – the most evident, perhaps, those of hetero- and homosexuality, good and evil, real and imaginary, original and copy, fidelity and treachery, communication and non-communication, truth and lies – fascinates Sartre by its unconventional, paradoxical, anti-bourgeois nature. It fascinates Derrida by its proximity to the reversal phase of deconstruction. In theory, Genet does not go far enough for either philosopher, he remains stuck at the level of inversion, but in practice he perhaps goes further than either. His lack of interest in either synthesis or truth saves him from falling back (or forwards) into either seriousness or metaphysics. His use as a foil to Hegel lies then not so much in a duplication of the Kierkegaardian project, but rather in the way he lends himself to both the Sartrean and the Derridean enterprises: to undermine the overweening truth-claims of the totalizing dialectic. Derrida focuses primarily on its *telos*, absolute knowledge, *le Savoir Absolu, le sa;*[14] Sartre on its *process*: thesis, antithesis, synthesis. If Genet appears to mimic a dialectical mode of procedure, it is only to undermine it in a sequence of spiralling *tourniquets* which never come to rest in synthesis or totalization. Sartre sets Genet's shot-silk textual and sexual contradictions up against the totalitarian clarity of Hegel's *Logic*, for they lead only to a dizzying repetition of the same self-destroying reversals. For Genet 'the dialectical progression . . . curves round to become a circular movement' (*SG*, 171). 'A work of Genet's, like Hegel's phenomenology, is a consciousness which sinks down into appearances, discovers itself at the peak of its alienation, recovers itself and relegates things to the rank of its objects' (*SG*, 145). Genet derealizes himself in the imaginary, in a celebration of falsehood which defies God and his 'goods', rather than Satan and his 'pomps': 'Nothing on earth belongs to this waking dreamer except lies, falsity and imitations. He is the lord of pretences, con-tricks and *trompe l'oeil*. Wherever objects appear as what they are not, do not appear as they are, he is king. Fake king, king of fakes. And what is a fake, but the counterfeiting of being?' (*SG*, 402). But Genet only *imagines* his bad taste, it is an inversion of 'real' bad taste: 'For Genet a taste for the false becomes false bad taste' (*SG*, 406). In Derrida's account, similarly, Genet's studied inversions are related to the pattern of loser-wins: 'The worst is the best, but you must not get it wrong, the worst is not the least good. . . . You need to be a connoisseur of fakes' (*Glas*, 226). Genet's preference for the fake subverts the hierarchy of original/copy, but stops short of a radical contesting of origin. For Genet, *toc* still takes its value by opposition to the 'real'.[15]

Genet, then, provides Sartre with a non-serious opponent to Hegel, for his obscene practical demonstrations of dialectical reversal cast Hegel's lofty abstract philosophical theorizing in a comic mode. Treachery, for example: 'Treachery is not a return to the good; it is Evil doing evil to itself; two negations do not make an affirmation: they are lost, coiled one with the other, in the demented night of the no' (*SG*, 195–6). And sodomy: Genet's admiration for the homosexual who takes the active role is undermined in a parody of the speculative dialectic which is also a form of self-parody: 'The Tough-Guy is, to speak like Hegel, Evil transformed into the absolute-subject' (*SG*, 135).

It is this undermining of any pretension to a stable truth by a series of reversals which refuses to privilege even its own position, that Derrida has focused on in his choice of the initial text for *Glas*, 'Ce qui est resté d'un Rembrandt déchiré en petits carrés bien réguliers, et foutu aux chiottes', in which Genet proceeds by an ostentatious rejection of definitive conclusions: 'It goes without saying that everything I have just said only has any importance if one accepts that everything was more or less false. . . . And it goes without saying that the entire works of Rembrandt have a meaning – at least for me – only if I know that what I have just written was wrong.'[16]

The 'Rembrandt' text, published in 1967, is clearly full of parodic allusions to the Hegelian/Sartrean notion of the universal singular, and one can identify verbal echoes of *La Nausée* and *Les Mots*: 'I had the revelation that every man is worth every other. . . . I was incapable of saying how I passed from the realization that every man is like every other to the idea that every man is all other men' ('Rembrandt', 21, 26); 'A whole man, made of all men and who is worth all of them and whom anyone is worth' (Sartre, *Les Mots*, 214).[17] The layout of the 'Rembrandt' text on the page also, one may assume, gave Derrida the idea of juxtaposing two contrasting but interrelated columns, a technique used previously in *Marges*. The textual interplay between Hegel, Genet, Sartre and Derrida would be too complex to unravel here.[18] Suffice it to say that *Glas* is precisely *not* Derrida's attempt to totalize Hegel, Sartre and Genet. It is intentionally fragmented and open-ended, but Derrida is not in a position to control the meaning and reception of his own text any more than any other writer. *Glas* escapes Derrida in at least two ways: first because it appears to master the texts he is decomposing, juxtaposing and deconstructing; and secondly, and perhaps more seriously, because it may in fact constitute the unreadable text he claims to have intended. As Derrida admits, 'il bande double' (*Glas*, p. 77), he wants to have it both ways, but above all to be irrecuperable. He approaches Genet in a way which is explicitly intended to alienate 'the archaeologists, philosophers, hermeneuts, semioticians, semanticists, psychoanalysts, rhetoricians, poeticians, perhaps even all readers who still believe in literature or anything' (*Glas*, 50). If *Glas* is unreadable but *not* irrecuperable, then Derrida has failed (really) on both scores. But when all else fails, magic comes into its own. If Sartre and Derrida are confounded, like Hercules, in their attempts to behead the Hegelian hydra, Genet perhaps succeeds, by dint of lateral prestidigitation, like Iolaus who decapitated the Hydra with fire not sword: 'Since that kind of operation could not succeed through dialectics, I had recourse to magic' (*Glas*, 276, quoting Genet).

My account of *Glas* is intended to give some impression of the confusing complexity of Derrida's text. It may, of course, still leave readers with a misleading illusion of readability. Derrida's writings on literature, and indeed on some philosophers (for example Nietzsche in *Éperons: les styles de Nietzsche*), in the 1970s and 1980s are frequently playful to the point of frustration, or even despair. But he does not remain permanently in this ludic mode. Psychoanalysis and ethics will, as we shall see, be treated with the seriousness they deserve.

5

Deconstruction and Psychoanalysis

Derrida's relationship to and interest in psychoanalysis have become increasingly significant since his first essay on Freud in 1966, 'Freud et la scène de l'écriture' (*ED*). Since then, *Glas* (1974) used certain psychoanalytic notions (such as the fetish) in its account of Genet and Hegel; *La Carte postale: de Socrate à Freud et au-delà* (1980) was devoted to a large extent to Freud and Lacan; several of the essays of *Psyché* (1987) are concerned with psychoanalysis; and most recently, *Mal d'archive* (1995) and *Résistances: de la psychanalyse* (1996) are entirely occupied with issues of psychoanalysis. The development of Derrida's views on psychoanalysis will be traced in the course of this chapter; suffice it to say at this point that as his interest increases it becomes less academic, more political, more ethical and, at times, more overtly critical, at least of the institutions of psychoanalysis. It also becomes increasingly preoccupied with the vexed question of the relationship between psychoanalysis and deconstruction as different modes of *analysis*.

The earliest essay, from *L'Écriture et la différence*, is also the best known. As its title indicates, it is concerned as much with 'the scene of writing' – that is, the stage where the inscription of the unconscious is performed – as with Freud. Indeed, it shares many of the concerns of *De la grammatologie*, in particular those of supplementarity, the trace and the repression of writing. Derrida introduces the essay as a fragment of a lengthy conference paper given as part of André Green's seminar at the Institut de Psychanalyse, at the opening of a debate on the issues raised by *De la grammatologie*. He summarizes the main points of the sections omitted from the published version, arguing that, contrary to appearances, deconstruction is not a psychoanalysis of philosophy. The 'appearances' which might lead us to view deconstruction as a kind of psychoanalysis are not spelled out by Derrida, but they are numerous. On the most general level they include Derrida's attention to the gap between what is claimed in a text and what is enacted or described; as in the case explored in *De la grammatologie* of Rousseau's assertion of the primacy of speech and presence, and his conflicting awareness that 'writing' is at the origin of both, interrupting their plenitude: 'Rousseau *declares* the absolute exteriority of writing, but *describes* the interiority of the principle of writing to language' (*Gram*, 441). Another example of Rousseau's 'describing what he does not wish to say' (*Gram*, 326) would be his claim that 'progress' is *either* for the good *or* for the bad, and his contradictory depiction of the ambivalence of progress, simultaneously for the worse *and* for the better. In a sense Derrida's attention to apparently insignificant details in a text may also seem akin to the psychoanalyst's awareness that what is most 'essential' may not be recounted at the centre of a discourse. Derrida takes particular account of footnotes, apparent afterthoughts, prefaces and postscripts – all the 'supplements' that turn out to be vital to the argument despite the fact that, or rather because, they may undermine or contradict it. This marginalization of the inconvenient or the painful is indeed analogous to psychoanalytic repression. And Derrida argues that *De la grammatologie* deals precisely with the repression of writing, a repression whose failure is manifested symptomatically in the metaphors of language that haunt Western discourse, but he maintains that it is logocentric repression which enables us to understand psychoanalytic repression (*refoulement*), not vice versa. This critique, and indeed attempted reversal, of the totalitarian explanatory claims of psychoanalysis are a constant in Derrida's writings for the next thirty years, and its justification will become increasingly apparent. He explains his caution with respect to Freudian categories by pointing to their complicity with the necessary 'logophoneticism' of the human sciences, in concepts such as presence, perception, reality and the conscious/unconscious opposition. What Derrida aims to do in his 1966 essay is to isolate those aspects of psychoanalytic theory which do not fit easily with its tacit logocentric premises, and to show their unsettling effect on the more 'metaphysical' of Freud's concepts.

It is with Freud's metaphors of writing as representative of the unconscious that Derrida is primarily concerned. He sets out to show how such metaphors gradually take over the whole of Freud's representation of the psyche, culminating in the image of the *bloc magique* (the mystic writing pad) of 1925. Derrida starts by maintaining that the question is not (or should not be) so much how appropriate the metaphor of the mystic writing pad is as a representation of the functioning of the psyche, but rather what Freud's metaphor of a 'writing machine' tells us about the way the psyche operates. Similarly, the question is not *whether* the psyche is a kind of text, but rather, what the psyche must be like if it may be represented by a text. The importance of these distinctions will become progressively clearer.

In 1895, in his *Project for a Scientific Psychology*, Freud's model for understanding memory is neurological. He wants to explain how experience traces a permanent impression in the psyche while leaving it intact. His explanation is in terms of permeable and impermeable neurons, grids and resistances (*ED*, 299). It is differences between forces which permit memory. Derrida draws a comparison here with Husserl's notion of *retard originaire* (originary delay), which is a matter of *différance* rather than simple lateness, in the sense that there is no full presence, belated or timely, but rather a paradoxical conception of an origin that is never original, but always already repeated. So there is no full, original experience of life, rehearsed and echoed in memory: even the 'first' experience is already represented. Of course, as Derrida points out, such notions are strictly speaking unthinkable within a traditional logic of identity; this is why they are so difficult to comprehend. None the less, something similar is implied by Freud's discussions of repetition and the pleasure principle (*ED*, 302).[1] Only a year after the *Project*, Freud's terminology for the trace left in the memory is already less neurological and more 'graphic'. He explains his theory in a letter to Fliess in 1896 in terms of 'sign', 'inscription', 'transcription' and 'mnesic traces'. And from *The Interpretation of Dreams* (1900) onwards, the metaphor of writing progressively takes over Freud's account of the structure of the psyche, as Derrida persuasively presents it. But the dream theory creates its own set of paradoxes: in the first place because Freud's conception of the individuality and originality of signs in dreams is such that it should, theoretically, make translation and interpretation impossible, whereas, as we know, Freud interprets constantly. And a further consequence of the lack of a reliable code is that the difference between signifier and signified is necessarily eroded (*ED*, 311). In effect, Derrida argues, Freud's interpretation of dreams is not a matter of translating an unconscious truth or meaning into conscious terms. This would imply a pre-existing unconscious text, whereas the unconscious is a realm not of truths, but rather of traces, differences and transcriptions. The unconscious itself is a region of reproduced and belated archives. Of course, this is what Derrida can read between the lines of Freud's writings, for Freud was too much a man of his age to possess the conceptual apparatus necessary for thinking through the full implications of his insights, in particular that of the non-originary nature of the present, which appears at times as a kind of 'supplement' (*ED*, 314).[2]

Derrida traces the development of Freud's metaphors of writing and memory: hieroglyphs, photographic images and *Bildeschrift* (figurative writing), through a selection of the *Collected Works* to the essay of 1925 on the 'Mystic Writing Pad'. At first Freud, like Plato in the *Phaedrus*, envisages writing as a tool to assist memory, but gradually writing takes over until it becomes the model for memory itself (*ED*, 328). Freud is searching for an image capable of representing both the persistence of memory and its limitless capacity. Paper becomes saturated, slate can always be used afresh, but only at the expense of what went before. Freud's answer is the *bloc magique*, probably familiar to us as a child's toy: a wax surface covered by a fine sheet of cellophane, it can be written on by any sharp implement which presses the cellophane against the wax, the inscription is erased by gently detaching the cellophane from the wax. Where the *bloc magique* wins over the slate as a model for the psyche is in the wax's ability to retain the (invisible) trace of what was written, while remaining apparently clear. And by the strange logic with which we are by now familiar, writing 'supplements' perception even before perception (is aware of what it) perceives, since perception itself has no means of retaining impressions. The wax, Derrida suggests, represents the unconscious (*ED*, 332). Its profundity is in a sense illusory: it is constituted by infinite regress with no real depth, it is 'perfectly superficial' (p. 331).

But there is a still more interesting question raised by the mystic writing pad: that of psychic spontaneity. Freud considers that the image of the writing pad fails in so far as the pad is not able to function unaided. It is precisely *not* 'magique' and in this sense does not truly resemble memory. Again like Plato, Freud envisages mechanical representation as deathly or life-denying. But in Derrida's view, Freud is not asking the right questions. He sees only the failings of the metaphor of the mystic writing pad, and does not consider what these failings might indicate about the workings of the psyche. For Derrida the sense of the metaphor is reversed: it is the limitations of the writing pad that reveal the limitations of memory. The supposed spontaneity of memory is put in doubt both by its subjection to the censor-mechanism and by its need for an external supplement. In fact, despite Freud's disenchantment with the metaphor, the mystic writing pad might indeed be seen as revealing the 'truth' of the psyche: the function of the writing pad is no more 'external' to memory than death is external to life. It founds and constitutes memory; it is necessary rather than contingent; it is a supplement to the essential finitude of the psyche (*ED*, 337). Freud confirms Derrida's own conception of the limited nature of subjectivity: the subject is not an independent sovereign power but rather part of a 'system of relations between the layers: the mystic writing pad, the psyche, society, the world. Within this scene, the punctual simplicity of the classical subject is not to be found' (*ED*, 335).

'La Différance' of 1968 (collected in *Marges*) and *La Dissémination* (1972) continue Derrida's reflections on the relationship between psychoanalysis and deconstruction in the context of a rejection of the values of presence, origin and ultimate meaning. Derrida returns to the question of the Freudian 'trace' (*Spur*) as an inscription of 'différance', and prepares the way for an analysis, which he undertook a few years later, of the Pleasure Principle and its deferral through the Reality Principle. Most significantly, he gives a strongly deconstructive and anti-phenomenological reading of the unconscious which is described in its alterity, that is as alien to any conception of presence, and specifically not 'a hidden, virtual, potential self-presence' (*Marges*, 27). The unconscious is not a reservoir of what was once present, but rather a 'past which was never present and never will be' (p. 22); it is deconstruction which helps clarify Freud's notions of the trace and the unconscious, not vice versa. Similarly, it is dissemination which helps explain castration in so far as it 'affirms endless substitution' and 'figures what cannot come back to the father' (*Pos*, 120). Dissemination is another concept which resists what Derrida calls 'the effect of subjectivity . . . and appropriation' (*Pos*, 112), as it points to the internal self-division of 'presence' and disorganizes the unity of symbolic meaning and truth (*Diss*, 336). But the play of dissemination is unending:

understanding dissemination, and acknowledging the negative fear that loss of a transcendental signifier (or signified) may unleash, may help us understand the castration complex, but castration should never become in its turn a final meaning.[3] This teleology is what Derrida cannot accept in Freud's essay on 'The Uncanny' (*Das Unheimliche*), which he believes provides an extraordinarily complex account of Hoffmann's tale of 'The Sandman', in terms of ambivalence, doubles, endless substitutions, symbolism and the play between fantasy and reality, only to find the ultimate resolution of the 'secret' in the castration complex (*Diss*, 300). Sarah Kofman, in her *Lectures de Derrida* of 1984, takes Derrida to task on this score, claiming that Freud's essay is far more nuanced (and, indeed, playful) than Derrida allows, and that rather than envisaging castration as a 'final signified', Freud presents it as the point beyond which rationality cannot go.[4] As we shall see shortly, Derrida's objections to Lacan's reading of Poe are very similar to his criticisms of Freud, and an American theorist has accused him of an identical oversimplification. Deconstructive analysis is necessarily vulnerable to its own procedures, and is always open to a still more subtle deconstructor's charge of having sinned by producing an apparently conclusive reading.

Sarah Kofman has some interesting points to make about the notion of the 'undecidable' effects of dissemination.[5] Freud acknowledged that he used the theories of the linguist Abel concerning the 'opposed meaning of primitive words' to confirm the way in which dreams represent a return to archaic modes of thought. Abel himself, says Kofman, seems to hesitate between a speculative, 'Hegelian' interpretation of this phenomenon, and a (Saussurean/Derridean) interpretation in terms of traces and differences, but decides in favour of the former. Freud, on the other hand, does not try to rationalize the archaic logic of dreams but rather resists the 'metaphysical' interpretation, preferring to argue in favour of a permanent and unresolvable trace in the psyche that no dialectic can sublimate. This means, Kofman maintains, that Freud's argument is not affected by Benveniste's claim that Abel's examples were false, both historically and linguistically. Benveniste asserted that terms which appear to manifest contradictory meanings do so only in the eyes of those whose language has two opposed terms for the single term in question; for the language containing the 'contradictory' term, the opposition is irrelevant. Kofman defends Freud against Benveniste, for if Freud's arguments use Abel's work, they do not come to the same conclusions. *A fortiori*, Derrida is immune from attack from Benveniste on this score, since, as we saw in the last chapter, his 'undecidables' are syntactic as much as semantic, and precisely *disorganize* philosophical opposition rather than embody contradiction.[6] This may be just as well for Benveniste, given Derrida's scathing critique of him which we examined in chapter 3.

From 1966 onwards it was no longer easy for Derrida to write about Freud without at least acknowledging the work of Lacan. Lacan's collected *Écrits* and Derrida's first essay on Freud were both published in that year, one of two exceptional years in terms of the production of original and ground-breaking work not only by Lacan and Derrida but also by Foucault and Lévi-Strauss. Lacan's explicit aim was a return to the letter of Freud's works, to their radical significance freed from the accretions of the moralizing and humanizing interpretations that had accumulated during the course of the century. For Lacan, Freud's insights are fundamentally linguistic: in Lacan's famous phrase 'the unconscious is structured like a language', and the implications of this are more far-reaching than might at first be apparent. The attraction for Derrida of a linguistic reading of Freud will be evident, though Lacan's major concern is with speech rather than writing, and he is therefore simultaneously a prime example of contemporary logocentric discourse. However, as Derrida explains in an interview with Jean-Louis Houdebine in 1971, prior to the publication of the collected *Écrits*, he had read only two of Lacan's essays, 'Fonction et champ de la parole et du langage en psychanalyse' and 'L'Instance de la lettre dans l'inconscient ou la raison depuis Freud'. His negative response to these, together with Lacan's persistent and aggressive criticisms of Derrida's work, did not initially encourage him to devote time to Lacan's writings as a priority, though this neglect was eventually to be followed by apparent fascination.

In his early years, Lacan was influenced by phenomenology and existentialism. His celebrated paper on the mirror phase ('le stade du miroir'), which explores the (alienating) formation of the infant's ego as a product of self-reflection, was first delivered in 1936, the same year as Sartre's essay on a very similar topic, *La Transcendance de l'ego*. Later (roughly speaking, after 1956), Lacan drew increasingly close to structuralism, and modified his notion of the dialectical relationship between subject and language in favour of one in which language is the only real agent, and human autonomy is eroded to the point where he can write that 'man is . . . a pawn in the play of the signifier' (*Écrits*, 468).[7] For Derrida, however, Lacan is never radical enough, especially in so far as traces of his phenomenological past persist in his writings. Derrida's lengthy footnote on Lacan was added to his interview with Houdebine retrospectively, as if he did not perhaps trust himself to speak of Lacan 'off the cuff', but still wanted to mark out his extensive reservations concerning Lacanian theory. These reservations concern firstly Lacan's explicit assimilation of 'full speech' to truth; secondly, what Derrida describes as Hegelianism masquerading as a return to Freud, and which he does not consider adequately explained away by Lacan's later claims that his vocabulary had a purely didactic purpose, nor indeed that it could somehow be 'bracketed off' in a pseudo-phenomenological *epoche*. Thirdly, Derrida criticizes Lacan's use of Saussurian phonology to prioritize speech over writing; and fourthly, he remarks on the total lack of any questioning by Lacan of the concept of writing itself despite his self-proclaimed attention to the 'letter' of Freud's writings. Finally, Derrida alludes briefly to Lacan's metaphysical leanings, to the persistent traces of phenomenology and existentialism in his thinking, to his overhasty style of writing, and his rhetorical sleight of hand, and indicates that in combination these factors were enough to encourage him to postpone a close study of Lacan when the *Écrits* first appeared. But between 1966 and 1971 he read the *Écrits* in their entirety, and promises a detailed reading of texts such as 'Le Séminaire sur *La Lettre volée*' which he already castigates as inadequate in its combination of semantic hermeneutics and formalism.

Those anxious to know more of Derrida's response to Lacan had to wait a further four years till 1975 when 'Le Facteur de la vérité' was first published. In this essay, later collected in *La Carte postale: de Socrate à Freud et au-delà* (1980), Derrida analyses Lacan's seminar of 1955/6 on a short story by Edgar Allan Poe, 'The Purloined Letter', translated by Baudelaire as *La Lettre volée*. Though it was not chronologically the first paper in the sequence, Lacan chose the piece to open his collected *Écrits*, and it retained pride of place in the later, paperback, Points edition, so Derrida seems justified in supposing that Lacan remained attached to it. What is more, it is precisely at the cusp of the development of Lacan's ideas on language.

Poe's story concerns a queen who has a compromising letter stolen from her by a scheming minister, and relates its ingenious recovery by the all-seeing detective, Dupin, who finds it 'hidden' in full view on the minister's mantelpiece, and manages to retrieve it for the queen. Lacan's interpretation of the tale is delightful: the letter becomes a metonym for the signifier, migrating from place to place, its meaning never revealed, and eventually returning to its original destination. Derrida's critique cannot destroy the poetic appeal of the 'migratory signifier', but it is probably already apparent that Lacan's 'happy ending' in which origin and end are reunited in teleological bliss is unlikely to meet with Derrida's approval. Lacan is shown not to be living up to his own radical intentions, and remaining trapped, almost inevitably, within metapysical discourse. The main butt of Derrida's critique is the naive nature of Lacan's belief in truth. Psychoanalysis, Derrida argues, is committed to a conception of truth revealed through an exploration of hidden meanings. Indeed, Freud's *Interpretation of Dreams* involves a series of metaphors of unveiling or uncovering, all of which refer to a hidden or disguised truth (*CP*, 443). Often, as in Nietzsche, this unveiling is related to the *pudenda* – ultimately the female genitalia or, in the notion of castration, their lack. Derrida proposes to explore this conception of Truth as revelation of the hidden, and in particular the relationship between truth and fiction, in Lacan's seminar on Poe's story.

Derrida starts by according to Lacan an interest in the text itself not shared by earlier psychoanalytic or psychological studies of literature, such as the psycho-biography of Marie Bonaparte, Bachelard's 'substantial' psychoanalysis of the ways we imagine matter, Sartre's existential psychoanalysis or Mauron's psycho-criticism.[8] Unlike these, Lacan is constantly concerned with textuality. He is not interested in the author, but in the 'pre-eminence of the signifier over the subject' (*CP*, 450). However, it is not only Poe who is eclipsed; the 'author of the letter' and, indeed, the narrator of the story also escape his attention. Lacan avoids 'semanticism' only to fall victim to formalism. What is more, the literary text is primarily illustrative, for Lacan, of the 'truths' of psychoanalysis. Derrida has three main objections to Lacan's reading: in the first place, the purloined letter appears to have a single meaning; secondly, the letter (the signifier) is deemed 'indivisible' in its materiality; and thirdly, the letter necessarily returns to its rightful place. This means that the break with semanticism and psycho-biography has not produced the theoretical sophistication that might have been expected. Lacan uses Poe to illustrate the truth of Freud: he never considers the status of the text as fiction, and its ultimate interest, for him, seems to lie in the 'message' it carries. Lacan is concerned with the story told, but never with the telling of the story. The act of narration itself is marginalized by being described as a 'commentary', and all attention is focused on the dialogues rather than on their framing within the tale. As we saw in the last chapter, 'formalism and hermeneutic semanticism support one another' (*CP*, 460). Their complicity is inescapable. Lacan may have a theory of the 'split subject', but the split is not allowed to affect the truth of psychoanalytic theory which is never fragmented (*morcelée*), but remains whole. Castration may be the truth of analytic discourse, but the phallus itself remains untouched. Indeed, and only apparently paradoxically, thanks to castration, the phallus always remains in its place: it may be represented by a lack (*manque*), but the lack has its own fixed domain as part of a 'transcendental topology' which renders it indivisible and hence indestructible (*CP*, 469). Conversely, in dissemination, Derrida remarks with deliberate ambiguity, lack has no place. Lacan may deny any hermeneutic aim, but despite this denial (*dénégation*), Derrida insists that 'the link between Femininity and Truth is the ultimate signified' (*CP*, 470), and significantly both terms will be treated to capitalization in the Points reprint of the *Écrits*.

Derrida has other objections, different in kind, to Lacan's seminar which can be dealt with briefly. In the first place, Lacan never mentions Marie Bonaparte's analysis of Poe's tale (1933), despite clear evidence of his familiarity with it,[9] nor, *a fortiori*, does he refer to her interpretation of the tale in terms of female castration. Bonaparte's essay, Derrida comments, has, moreover, the inestimable advantage of an intertextual focus, as well as paying close attention not only to the story's author but also to its narrative devices. Lacan, on the contrary, concentrates solely on the truth delivered by the 'transcendental signifier' (*CP*, 493). His distinction between truth and reality thus simply leads him to the ultimate position of viewing truth as the adequation of speech not to an object but rather to itself, in a bizarre kind of hermeneutic circle which is literally phallogocentric (*CP*, 502, 508). Derrida catches Lacan in what looks like a delightful slip when he twice misquotes Poe's story. The occasion is the text of the letter which Dupin substitutes for the purloined letter in order to conceal the retrieval of the real letter from the minister who stole it. The substitute letter contains a quotation from Crébillon:

... Un dessein si funeste,
S'il n'est digne d'Atrée, est digne de Thyeste.

Lacan quotes these lines three times, and on two occasions substitutes *destin* for *dessein* ('destiny' for 'design' or 'plan'). *Destin* appears to have suited his reading of a letter which always reaches its 'destination' irresistibly well. Derrida points out the substitution, but makes no comment other than to say, ambiguously, that it was 'exprès, sans doute' (*CP*, 524), 'doubtless, intentional'.

The postscripts to the essay on Lacan are numerous. The final section of *La Carte postale*, 'Du tout', contains a dialogue between Derrida and René Major at a conference on *Glas* in 1977. The dialogue turns to Derrida's essay on Lacan, and in particular to his comments on the *dessein/destin* substitution, all the more relevant since the publication of the book by François Roustang, *Un Destin si funeste*. Derrida's comments are biting as he throws the cat among the pigeons of the psychoanalytic community by quoting a letter attacking Roustang: 'We will simply mention the *misprint* whose adoption in the title [of Roustang's book] is a *lapsus* [i.e. a slip or parapraxis]' (*CP*, 542). Derrida restricts himself to feigning surprise that a supposed analyst should believe he had such an unfailing grasp of what constitutes a 'misprint' and what a 'slip'. Derrida clearly has the upper hand, and by a long way. Another postscript, mentioned briefly earlier, is Barbara Johnson's turning of the tables on Derrida himself in her critique of *Le Facteur de la vérité* as itself finding an ultimate meaning in Lacan's own text. In her argument, Derrida is as reductive of Lacan as Lacan was of Poe. Her essay is closely argued and a delight to read.[10] A critique of Johnson's position in its turn was undertaken by Marian Hobson in 1982.[11] Shoshana Felman takes Johnson's side and argues for the originality, flexibility and insight of Lacan in contrast to what she sees as Derrida's unsympathetic and tendentious critique of him.[12] Fredric Jameson provocatively suggests that it is Poe's text rather than Lacan's reading of it which is eliciting the panoply of conflicting interpretations;[13] and certainly the debate is a fascinating illustration of how partial even (or perhaps especially) the most convincing analyses ultimately remain. Derrida's own postscript on the subject comes, as we shall see, in *Résistances: de la psychanalyse* (1996).

The other major essay in *La Carte postale*, 'Spéculer – sur "Freud" ', puts quotation marks around Freud's name because it is concerned with autobiography and questions the relationship between 'man' and 'work'. Its main focus is Freud's *Beyond the Pleasure Principle*, and it is probably closer to what we might expect a classic text of 'deconstruction' to be like than the two essays discussed above. It explicitly tackles questions such as the gap between Freud's apparent 'intentions' and the way his essay is written, and the hesitations and false starts which may alert us to his underlying uneasiness and anxiety. 'Spéculer', on the other hand, is typically polysemic. It refers to Freud's anxieties about his relation to speculative philosophy, but also carries echoes of financial and economic 'speculation', as well as to the 'specular' or mirroring effect whereby Freud's text enacts what it describes – specifically the *fort-da* principle. In this latter sense, Freud's text has a performative function, at least in a broad, non-technical sense.[14]

Derrida is intrigued by Freud's 'anxiety of influence': his determination that his ideas should not be seen as derivative, or, more specifically, as indebted to speculative philosophy. Freud comments on his affinities with both Nietzsche (eternal recurrence) and Schopenhauer (sexuality and repression) only to deny categorically that there has been any influence, because, he claims, his ideas derive from clinical observation, not speculation (*CP*, 283). Both Nietzsche and Schopenhauer have conceptions of death as integral to life, or even as its ultimate goal, which seem close to the Freudian notion of the 'death drive' (*pulsions de mort*),[15] but Freud mentions them only to disavow any connection or debt. His denial of speculation itself is similarly problematic. It hovers uneasily between rejection, insistence on his own inability to philosophize, and the admission that he had recently given his speculative tendency a freer rein. In all these areas Freud seems engaged in a forceful but transparent form of *dénégation*, or 'denial'.

One of the major problems Freud considers is the apparent ambivalence of pleasure, in the face of which philosophers seem at a loss. On the one hand, common sense encourages us to imagine we all know what pleasure is; on the other, we encounter the puzzling psychoanalytic observations of displeasure, its origins and the way pleasure itself may be experienced as displeasure. At first sight the 'reality principle' might seem to provide the explanation for displeasure, for rather than involving an entirely different principle it may be seen as a simple deferring of pleasure to a more appropriate or less antisocial moment. But while deferral may explain the element of moderation in some sexual behaviour, for example, it cannot deal with the whole gamut of experiences of displeasure (*CP*, 301), nor with the range and extent of repression (*CP*, 308). So while insisting that the Pleasure Principle is sovereign, the 'absolute master', Freud is obliged to introduce a whole set of exceptions which make it increasingly difficult to prove the rule. And it is with the first 'exception' that the way is opened for the move from observation to speculation.

The best-known section of Freud's essay is probably that dealing with the game of 'fort-da', Freud's name for the infant's game of throwing objects away and having them retrieved for him by adults or, as in the original anecdote, retrieving them himself because they are attached to a string. The child calls 'fort' ('away' or 'gone'; in fact Freud's observed child calls 'oooo', but Freud is sure he understands what it means) when he throws the toy, and 'da' ('there') when he retrieves it. Freud determinedly interprets the game in accordance with the Pleasure Principle: the pleasure is one of control and mastery, both of the infant's environment and, by extension, of the mother. The mother is often absent for hours on end, and although the baby is very 'good', and never cries for her, he none the less reassures himself by his repetitive game that she will return eventually (*CP*, 328). Derrida observes in Freud's text several tell-tale signs of a very personal involvement: the child, he is sure, is Freud's grandchild, son of his daughter Sophie who died shortly before the essay was completed. There are traces of affect apparently irrelevant to the anecdote: a note of regret that the boy does not play with his toys in a more traditional way, and the insistence that he does love his mother despite his apparent indifference to her absence, almost a tone of reproach. Freud himself denied that the death of his daughter had affected his essay, and pointed out that it was very nearly finished when she died. Indeed, he found time to complete it before he allowed himself to mourn in earnest.

Derrida makes no explicit comments on these biographical details, which he describes without analysis. If Freud's text is autobiographical, he remarks, it is so in a far from conventional sense; and the fact that the 'author' should tell us something of his life does nothing to undermine the 'truth-value' of his text (*CP*, 343). The question of autobiography and subjectivity will be relevant in the closing chapter of this study, which is concerned with the ethics of deconstruction; for the moment we may simply note that it arises necessarily from Derrida's insistence that nothing lies 'outside the text', and also, indeed, from his definition of 'the subject of writing' as 'a system of relations' (*ED*, 335). In this connection,

Derrida has recently referred to *La Carte postale* as a 'performative problematization of the public/private distinction'.[16] But however much Freud may deny it, the death of his daughter is, Derrida maintains, inscribed in his text, in the very game of 'fort-da' itself. Freud insists that the Pleasure Principle alone is involved, but the principle would have to be stretched considerably to cover the complex nature of the 'fort-da' game which entails mastery and displeasure rather than pleasure in any simple sense. Intended to be a pure example of the Pleasure Principle, the game manifests loss and ultimately death. Indeed, many readers believe this to be Freud's own interpretation of the game, but Derrida argues that such readers have 'read between the lines' of the essay and uncovered what the text itself appears to imply rather than what Freud himself intended. When we remember that the anecdote was introduced for purely illustrative purposes – not something Freud is struggling gamely to reconcile with his theory of the Pleasure Principle, but rather a simple example of it – and when we remember that an eighteen-month-old baby is involved, not an adult with all the complex and confusing history involved in achieving maturity, we may agree with Derrida that the Pleasure Principle has been stretched to breaking point. Freud is clearly uncomfortably aware of the tenuousness of his theory, for he sketches in a whole series of alternative explanations such as vengeance on the mother for her absence, but only to return to an insistence on their ultimate subordination, however apparently counter-intuitive, to the Pleasure Principle. Freud's own complex feelings about his daughter's death may be deduced from his ambiguous reference to the way in which, within a week – for her death was swift – it was as if she had never existed (*CP*, 350). In Derrida's view, jealousy and resentment are not contingent accidents which befall the 'fort-da' game, they are constitutive of it from the outset, and this has implications for the Pleasure Principle itself.

The nature of Derrida's deconstruction of Freud's text will be clear by now: Freud's explicit intention is to explore the Pleasure Principle, but in Derrida's view he is unwilling to accept what he uncovers; every time a negative element seems to dominate or underlie the Pleasure Principle, Freud attempts to explain it away. His text is marked by self-doubt and anxiety as he finds himself going from one dead-end to the next in a series of blind-alleys which serve to mask the unthinkable.[17] By the third of the seven chapters of his essay, Freud is apparently ready to make another move in his attempt to go 'beyond the Pleasure Principle', not yet to acknowledge the death drive, but simply to put forward the hypothesis of a 'repetition compulsion', and to examine its relation to the Pleasure Principle. The repetition compulsion does not seem to produce pleasure, on the contrary it tends to involve the reliving of displeasure, and Freud describes such compulsive and neurotic repetition as 'devilish' (*CP*, 363). His recognition of it is what releases the pent-up speculation that he has been trying to control: the primary process of repetition is acknowledged to be prior to the Pleasure Principle, but is brought under control precisely by that principle. The Pleasure Principle is still dominant, and it is only as a result of some traumatism that it appears to retreat, whereas it is in fact attempting to master the psychic processes which have been unleashed (*CP*, 370). So the exception to the law still does not contradict it in Freud's account, it rather precedes it and is brought under its control.

At this point Derrida gives a brief but fascinating deconstruction of the classical conception of repetition as a secondary rehearsal of something original that precedes it, and shows how repetition both confirms the mastery of the Pleasure Principle and at the same time undermines it by apparently seeking displeasure. The child's game again provides a puzzling case in so far as repetition seems, in Freud's account, to give pleasure to the child, whereas it is rather novelty that an adult seeks in order to experience pleasure. Compulsive repetitive behaviour in an adult is regressive and not a source of pleasure. Freud goes not so much 'beyond' as back before the Pleasure Principle. What is more, the compulsion to repeat is arguably both a condition of analysis in so far as it facilitates transference, but also an obstacle to analysis if it persists and prevents the liquidation of transference.

Half way through Freud's text, Derrida points out, the death drive has still not been explicitly mentioned. It is about to appear, in connection with Freud's hypothesis about the general nature of *pulsions* ('drives') as aiming for the restoration of some prior state in the organism they inhabit, or, in other words, for a state of inertia (*CP*, 376). This means that the ultimate aim of the living creature is paradoxically a return to the inorganic; it means that death is not so much an accident of life as an internal law, and indeed it is life which seems to be the accident. Hence the connection with Schopenhauer, and, Derrida adds, Nietzsche and Heidegger, in particular with the notion of *Dasein* and its authentic 'being-for-death'.

But if we imagine that Freud has now finally gone 'beyond the

Pleasure Principle', and has formulated a more fundamental drive (the death drive), we are mistaken. He struggles in the web of contradictions and tensions which beset his theory, moving, for example, into the realm of biology and attempting (somewhat bizarrely) to use contemporary genetic theories to reconcile the drives towards life and death by looking at the history of 'germ-cells' and multi-cellular organisms. Yet Freud remains unsatisfied. He still wants to take another step in his argument. He moves further within the biological model by politicizing it: within each cell the two drives (life and death) may neutralize each other, and may sacrifice the life of one cell in the interests of another. Heroism and narcissism are now on the micro scale (*CP*, 388). But this in turn creates further problems: the notion of narcissism, which involves a libido turned in on itself, has the effect of annulling the distinction between 'ego instincts' (deathly) and 'sexual instincts' (procreative). And this raises again the danger of monism: it would mean that all drives were ultimately libidinal, the Jungian position which Freud is determined to avoid. He is stubborn beneath the mantle of a passionate scientist in search of truth. Indeed, he now acknowledges that he cannot prove the dualism he believes in, but that he is certain his hypothesis is correct. He tries a variety of other avenues hoping for a breakthrough: sadism looks promising, but has to be abandoned in turn in case it too backfires in favour of monism.

As Derrida presents it, *Beyond the Pleasure Principle* seems to enact in itself the processes it describes: the compulsion to repeat *and* the 'Fort-da' game, as Freud advances only to retreat, takes a step beyond the Pleasure Principle only to withdraw again. Each time Freud appears at last to have taken a decisive step, a *pas au-delà* (a step beyond), he seems to lose his nerve, 'pas au-delà' (not beyond), always returning to the reassurance of the Pleasure Principle, apparently afraid of the implications of his own speculation.[18] If it is simply the death drive which lies beyond the Pleasure Principle, perhaps Freud cannot bring himself to say so. Or worse, if Jung's monism were right, but the one overwhelming drive were that of death rather than libido or life? Whatever Freud's allies and opponents claim, Derrida maintains, he is never able to decide definitively in favour of the Pleasure Principle or of the death drive or simply of an inner limit to the Pleasure Principle.

In the last analysis, Freud admits that he cannot prove his point, indeed he claims not to wish to convince others and not even to know to what extent he believes his own theories (*CP*, 404). Intriguingly for Derrida, Freud blames language for his own inability to conclude; one of the major problems as Freud sees it lies in the linguistic expression of what has been observed: simple empirical observation appears somehow distorted by its 'translation' into words, the more particularly when the terms are inevitably metaphorical (*CP*, 406). Observation seems to undergo a whole series of transmutations: first it is described, then it is theorized, and the schemas for this theory come from other sciences, and finally there is the problem of the images used by theoretical discourse. Derrida notices Freud's hesitation between the prioritizing of intuition, observation and description on the one hand, and on the other his awareness that there is no original, pre-verbal truth, the observations themselves are inhabited by language from the outset, indeed, they would not otherwise ever be possible in the first place (*CP*, 408). Similarly, Freud oscillates in his view of the *metaphoricity* of scientific language: is it a provisional, contingent stage prior to a more accurate terminology, or is it the inevitable condition of all language, scientific or other? And speculative theories themselves may have no firmer grounding: the 'artificial structure of hypotheses' may be blown away in time by the findings of biology, like a 'château de cartes' (a house of cards), as the French translation has it (*CP*, 411). Freud seems uncertain of the status of his own theorizing, or, perhaps, simply to recoil from its consequences.

A series of articles collected in *Psyché: inventions de l'autre* (1987) touch more tangentially on psychoanalysis. They explore Freud's speculations on telepathy, as well as the implications of translating terminology such as 'Ich' / 'Ego' / 'Moi' or, indeed, 'Pleasure'; and, in 'Géopsychanalyse "and the rest of the world" ', call on the psychoanalytic movement to acknowledge more explicitly its ethical and political responsibilities. But it is in *Mal d'archive: une impression freudienne* (1995) that Derrida returns substantially to Freud and to the subject matter of his own early essay, 'Freud et la scène de l'écriture'. *Mal d'archive* is concerned with the relationship between memory and inscription, between the postulated 'origin' of memory and its necessary registering and repetition. The problematics of 'origins' and their inscription are suggested in the elliptical title (*Archive Fever*, in English), which refers not merely to the 'ills' of the archive but more significantly to the desire or passion (in the double sense of the word) for the archive. The *Arkhe* is itself both beginning and commandment, a dual principle which is simultaneously a matter of chronology and law. Its relationship to law leads Derrida to explore the political implications of the archive: its control, the limits of access to it, and its significance for democracy. The repression of the archive is common, and nicely named by Derrida 'the patriarchive' in so far as it is often restricted, in fact if not in theory, to male historians (p. 16). It is awareness of the death drive and its destructive power which lies beneath the desire to construct an archive, a desire which thus manifests radical finitude, but the death drive works to destroy its own traces, and indeed is not readily detectable except in an eroticized form (pp. 25, 38). Moreover, the desire to produce an archive is related to the repetition compulsion, itself indissociable from the death drive.

One of the questions that fascinates Derrida in his meditations on the archive is the effect that changing modes of inscription must have not only on the storing of what is communicated but also on its content. (Lyotard looked at this in another context in *La Condition post-moderne*.)[19] The mystic writing pad might now be replaced by the word-processor; and the effect of the telephone, or more significant still, perhaps, of e-mail, on the exchanges between Freud and Fliess can only be imagined. The archives of psychoanalysis itself would be very different (*Mal d'archive*, 31–4).

A large part of *Mal d'archive* is concerned, as might be expected, with another text; in this case a book on Freud by Yosef Hayim Yerushalmi, *Freud's Moses: Judaism Terminable and Interminable*, which argues that psychoanalysis is a Jewish science. This is a question which seems to fascinate Derrida himself, and is the starting-point of a series of reflections on his own Jewish family background, his relationship with his ancestors and with his sons, and on ritual circumcision as a form of bodily archive, or inscription. The construction of the essay is unusual, but not untypical in its apparent deferral of its thesis: *Exergue* (twenty-five pages), Preamble (ten pages), *Avant-Propos* (seventy-four pages), *Thèses* (twenty pages) and Post-Scriptum (six pages). In the brief Preamble Derrida expounds the three meanings of 'Impression' in his subtitle, *Une impression freudienne*: these are inscription, notion and the impression or effect made by Freud on someone else. The *Avant-Propos* constituting the bulk of the text develops the question of Freud's Jewishness, already announced in the *Exergue*, and explores the paradoxically 'messianic' nature of the archive, which records the past whilst being envisaged as pointing to the future. The tense of the archive is thus the future perfect, (pp. 61, 72), which Derrida explores further in his discussion of Lacan in *Résistances*.

The aspect of Yerushalmi's book which captivates Derrida's interest is the final section, the 'Monologue with Freud', where Freud is addressed directly in a series of questions about the Jewishness of psychoanalysis, following a technique similar to Freud's own in the fourth chapter of *The Future of an Illusion*. Freud, of course, cannot reply, but Yerushalmi explores the many places in Freud's writings where answers, direct and indirect, may be found, including all the *dénégations* or 'denials' of Jewishness. Freud seems haunted by the spectre of Jewishness, and Derrida returns to the motif of the ghost as it is to be found for example in *Hamlet*, and which he has already discussed in some detail in *Spectres de Marx*. By using 'we' to speak of the Jews, Yerushalmi drags Freud, willy-nilly, into the Jewish camp which he resisted. Freud is invited to admit 'in secret' that psychoanalysis is at root a Jewish science, though a science 'without God' (p. 78). The structure of the monologue itself resembles a psychoanalytic dialogue, and Derrida examines what he sees as Yerushalmi's equivocal claim to an (impossible) degree of scholarly objectivity, precisely at the moment when he is most personally implicated. It is, in Derrida's view, Yerushalmi who is engaged in 'denial' rather than Freud, for he both claims not to be a psychoanalyst and also excuses himself for not being one. The paradox is clearer in French: 'L'historien se défend d'être un psychanalyste mais il se défend aussi de *ne pas* être un psychanalyste' (p. 89). Yerushalmi, in Derrida's account, further enacts what he describes when he discusses Freud's 'deferred obedience' to his father, the patriarch, in his writing of *Moses and Monotheism*: Yerushalmi is similarly 'obedient' to Freud, belatedly and whilst apparently 'preserving his independence' (p. 97).

One of the subjects of Yerushalmi's one-sided debate with Freud concerns Freud's suggestion that the Jews in fact killed Moses but repressed their memory of the murder. Yerushalmi claims that this repression is impossible, and that the murder would have been recorded as an extreme example of Israel's 'disobedience'. The claim, Derrida argues, separates memory or archivation on the one hand and repression on the other, whereas in fact the two are interlinked and repression is precisely a form of archivation. Yerushalmi can prove nothing against Freud from the lack of explicit biblical archive, for Freud's whole endeavour was to analyse signs, symptoms, figures, metaphors, lapses and lacunae which might constitute the kind of archive an 'ordinary historian' would overlook. So we are led back to the initial question of the nature of the archive, and to Derrida's argument that the archive is inescapable because there is no 'meta-archive': all discussions of the archive are fated to form part of it at a future date (in the 'future perfect'). Yerushalmi is himself contributing to the archive when, for example, he raises three questions at the end of his monologue which all concern the future: What is the role of the secret to a historian? What is the definition of 'Jewish' and of 'science'? And finally, what is the future of Judaism? Derrida is dismayed by Yerushalmi's suggestion that only Israel holds hope for the future, for it is the fear and erosion of *différence* in the Other which, as Levinas showed, is the source of all violence.

Thèses, in *Mal d'archive*, contains a series of statements of Freudian positions, all marked by their thoroughgoing self-contradiction. Derrida's own primary thesis is precisely this: 'All the Freudian theses are riven, divided, contradictory, like the concepts, starting with the concept of archive' (p. 132); his phrase for this internal division is the potentially explosive notion of 'disseminatory fission' (*fission disséminante*). Freud's discourse on the archive, and his concept of archive itself, is explosively divided. This is the sense of what Derrida now calls the 'trouble d'archive', not so much the 'trouble with the archive' as the 'disturbance in the archive' (p. 141). And Derrida considers Freudian psychoanalysis to be partly responsible for this form of 'mal', in so far as it expresses a desire for origins, a nostalgia for an impossible return to an absolute beginning, prior to division and repetition.

Just as Derrida has many more pages of preambles than of theses, so his theses themselves defy classical counting. They number three plus one, rather like the essay on Sollers's *Nombres* in *La Dissémination*, thereby defying not only the closure of the dialectic but also that of the Oedipal triangle. They constitute a series of paradoxes. First: on the one hand, through his topology of the mind, Freud rendered the concept of a psychic archive thinkable; on the other hand, as was demonstrated in 'Freud et la scène de l'écriture', as a classical metaphysician, Freud considered technical aids to memory as secondary, and maintained the primacy of living memory. Second: on the one hand, the archive is made possible by the death drive and by radically destructive aggressivity; on the other hand, as an Enlightenment thinker, Freud does not want to dwell on death, and especially not on any spectral forms of it. Third: on the one hand, no one has given a better deconstruction than Freud of patriarchal authority (the 'archontic principle') and its destruction in parricide; on the other hand, in his life as well as his works, Freud repeated the logic of patriarchy and indeed described it as marking the progress of civilization (p. 148).

The final thesis is, of course, a supplementary one, the Post-Scriptum, with its implicit promise of divulging a repressed truth. This is Derrida's postulation of Freud's desire to trace the archive back to the moment of its inception, that is to say to the moment just prior to the separation of origin and representation, or of impression and trace. This would be the irreplaceable and unique moment of truth before its repetition and loss of originality. Freud's essay on Jensen's story of *Gradiva*, from which Derrida has already taken several illustrations concerning archaeology and archive, illustrates how Freud's thinking contains its own undoing. Freud, Derrida argues, missed a vital element in Jensen's story: when the young archaeologist hero, Norbert Hanold, travels to Pompeii in search of the bas-relief of a young woman (Gradiva) that has bewitched him, it is precisely her *traces* that he hopes to find. Her presence, if he discovers it, will lie in the trace of her footsteps in the ashes of Pompeii. The original that he is seeking is already itself divided and repeated. Norbert is haunted by a spectre, but the spectre itself had no original plenitude, it was always fissured. This, Derrida suggests, may be the secret Freud is trying to protect. The archive itself does not record an original experience which can be returned to. This is what psychoanalysis is burning simultaneously to reveal and to conceal.

Résistances: de la psychanalyse was published in 1996 and contains three essays on psychoanalytic topics, all first delivered as conference papers in the early 1990s, and dealing respectively with Freud, Lacan and Foucault. The ironically titled, 'Pour l'amour de Lacan', presented at the conference *Lacan avec les philosophes* organized by Derrida's own Collège International de Philosophie in May 1992, may be seen in part as Derrida's personal postscript to the discussion that followed 'Le Facteur de la vérité' in 1975. Derrida situates himself somewhat ambivalently with respect to Lacan, indicating clearly none the less his fascination with the psychoanalyst. Public homage to Lacan is, he suggests, an act of cultural resistance (p. 64) in so far as it recognizes the necessary difficulty of Lacan's thought, not easily recuperable by academic or editorial 'normalization'. Derrida's essay is permeated by partially unexplained allusions to in-fighting within the psychoanalytic community, in particular in connection with Derrida himself and his participation at the conference, but also with the false claim (made by Serge Doubrovsky, but also, it seems, by Lacan) that Derrida was undergoing analysis. Derrida takes the opportunity to set the record straight.

'Pour l'amour de Lacan' is both anecdotal and theoretical: in it Derrida recounts his two or three meetings with Lacan and their discussions about death; he returns to his critique of Lacan's 'Séminaire sur *La Lettre volée*' in 'Le Facteur de la vérité' and denies that it was 'totalizing', 'homogenizing' or 'critical' (p. 81), while again using the 'Séminaire' as a means of reiterating his fundamental objections to Lacan. It is precisely *because* Lacan is a more philosophical thinker than Freud that he is so vulnerable to criticism. Freud, as Derrida has shown elsewhere, undertakes an implicit deconstruction of the privilege of presence, at least in the forms of consciousness and the ego. In Lacan, on the other hand, Derrida finds at least eight motifs which call out to be deconstructed: a militant phonocentrism, i.e. belief in full, self-present speech and the disqualification of the mechanical recording of speech as alienating; a view of truth as adequation; the transcendental position of the phallus as meeting place of logos and desire; a misunderstanding of the literary structure of narration; a conception of the circular path of the letter which returns to its destination; and finally, a failure to take into account the effects of the double in Poe's narrative (pp. 77–8). Although Derrida recognizes Lacan's move away from an emphasis on speech towards 'writing' after 1968, in accordance with the theoretical mood of the times (and indeed as part of a generalized misunderstanding of what Derrida meant by *écriture*), he points to the problems inherent in any real attempt to give an account of Lacan after the *Écrits*. Lacan's later *Séminaires* were all transcribed from tape recordings and actively 'edited' by his followers in a way which left considerable room for debate as to 'what Lacan might or might not have said', especially in view of the essential preciosity and refinement of Lacan's style (p. 81). Furthermore, a final assessment of Lacan is virtually impossible because the future of psychoanalysis is not calculable so long as it appears to be in the process of its own interminable deconstruction (p. 88).

The essay on Foucault also returns to the battlegrounds of thirty years earlier, as well as to Derrida's favourite Freudian text, *Beyond the Pleasure Principle*. Like the paper on Lacan, it was delivered at a posthumous conference, this time to celebrate the thirtieth anniversary of the publication of *Histoire de la folie à l'âge classique* in 1961, and its tone is consequently less virulent than Derrida's original essay on Foucault. '"Être juste avec Freud": l'histoire de la folie à l'âge de la psychanalyse' traces a fascinating and unexpected path from the Cartesian *cogito* to the death drive. As was the case with the paper on Lacan, Derrida sketches briefly the record of his relations with Foucault, and in particular the shift from friendship to hostility. In 1972, in a 'postface' to the new edition of *Histoire de la folie*, Foucault took the opportunity to reply publicly to Derrida's critique in *L'Écriture et la différence* of his analysis of Descartes's *cogito*. Derrida promises that on this occasion he will not return to the old debate, and will concentrate not on Foucault's account of Descartes but rather on Freud, largely absent from the 1964 article. The essay traces what Derrida calls the *fort-da* of Foucault's account of Freud throughout his writings, the change from positive to negative even within *Histoire de la folie*, in which Freud is initially portrayed as a 'liberator' of madness along with Nietzsche and Blanchot, but ends up on the side of law and order as an accomplice to the non-physical incarceration of the mad. Foucault is uncertain whether Freud belongs to the old psychology or to the new psychoanalysis; the uncertainty, Derrida points out, is not simply a 'failing' in Foucault, it is quite possibly indicative of a contradiction in Freud himself, or 'in things themselves' (p. 124), but Foucault is none the less evidently undecided where to place himself with respect to these contradictions. Freud is described both as a 'malin génie' and as a 'bon génie', but it is paradoxically the latter which seems to be the most harmful in Foucault's eyes, because it stands on the side of authority.

The two sides of Freud are reflected as pendulum swings in Foucault's attitude to psychoanalysis. In *Maladie mentale et psychologie* of 1962 the picture is more subtle and positive than in *Histoire de la folie*, in so far as Freud is seen as enabling communication in a common language between 'reason' and 'unreason' (p. 127). Later, in *Les Mots et les choses* (1966), Freud becomes a hinge ('charnière') or pivot for an understanding of human finitude, with respect to death, desire and the law. However, Foucault remains dubious about the role of psychoanalysis, and indeed the only forms of madness he truly recognizes are schizophrenia and psychosis, both of which are untreatable and even unapproachable by psychoanalysis. But at the same time, Foucault defends psychoanalysis against the very accusations of mythologizing that he had himself previously levelled against it. Violence and alienation are no longer 'constitutive' of psychoanalysis as Foucault now sees it.

In the last swing of the pendulum, *Histoire de la sexualité* (1976–84) presents the final stage of Foucault's views on Freud, in which psychoanalysis is incriminated not just for the reification and alienation of the mad, but for attempting to master sexuality. It is not the popular denunciation of Freud's alleged 'pansexualism' that is most erroneous, claims Foucault, so much as the illusory belief in his emancipation of sexuality (p. 139). However, despite all these changes of emphasis, Foucault's Freud is limited, Derrida suggests, by the extent of Foucault's reading. He rarely, if ever, refers specifically to any of Freud's texts, and remains throughout deaf to the contemporary dialogue with Lacan, whom he does not seem to recognize as part of the 'age' or 'episteme' he is describing. A serious reading of *Beyond the Pleasure Principle*, and a better understanding of the death drive, would radically undermine Foucault's assurance of Freudian 'mastery'. Foucault's power/pleasure duality, Derrida suggests, could perhaps have been fruitfully related to Freud's attempted duality of the death drive and the Pleasure Principle. It is none the less his own internal dividedness, as well as his awareness of the divisions in Freud himself, that makes Foucault such a modern and intriguing figure.

The remaining piece in *Résistances: de la psychanalyse* gives its title to the collection. It is concerned not with the classic 'resistance' to psychoanalysis manifested by analysands, though this will also be discussed, but rather with resistances internal to psychoanalysis itself. Derrida's strategy is to reverse the usual (reductive) claims of psychoanalysis to be able to explain even apparent objections to analysis in analytic terms. He will, in the process, reclaim some of the terminology of psychoanalysis: for example replacing the term 'resistance' in its political context, and replacing 'analysis' in the context of its very long philosophical history, as well as restoring to it some of its etymological complexity: untying, freeing, delivering, dissolving, solving and acquitting (p. 15). However, Derrida's essay is primarily concerned with Freudian epistemology, and in particular with Freud's conception of the extent of the interpretative power of psychoanalysis. The issue at stake is the allegedly uninterpretable 'navel' or nodal point (*Nabel, nombril*) of dreams, the core which will not give up a meaning to the analyst. Derrida spends some time exploring the paradoxes contained in Freud's way of writing about this 'navel': Freud refers, for example, to the necessity of untying a knot, when, in a sense, the navel is not so much a knot as a scar where a cord has been severed (p. 24). Is Freud an epistemological optimist or a pessimist: is the 'navel' uninterpretable in a provisional or a permanent sense? And if it is permanently resistant to interpretation, is this because some aspects of the psyche will always lie too deep for conscious access, or, more fundamentally, because they in fact have no meaning? This latter sense is not just fatalistic about the ultimate impotence of psychoanalytic investigation, it is nihilistic about signification itself. Perhaps the 'hidden truth' is that not all psychic phenomena are, after all, meaningful (p. 29)? Truth and meaning are radically at stake here.

When Derrida turns to the relationship between philosophical and psychoanalytic analysis, he argues that, in fact, psychoanalysis is heterogeneous rather than unified. On the one hand it is archaeological, seeking explanation in terms of a simple, undecomposable element which would constitute an 'origin'. On the other hand, analysis is always seeking an ultimate dissolution, which Derrida terms eschatological, as opposed to archaeological. For example, if resistance to analysis is not unified in its source, this is because analysis itself is not unified. Derrida disentangles at least five different types of resistance to analysis: three emanating from the ego (from repression, from transference, and from the benefit derived from illness); one from the id, in the compulsion to repeat; and one from the superego which opposes guilt to the possibility of cure. The most irreducible of these seems to come from the id in the compulsion to repeat; and significantly, Derrida points out, this is a resistance devoid of 'meaning', linked to the death drive, and paradoxically itself 'analytic' in the eschatalogical sense of an ultimate dissolution.

Ultimately, resistance to analysis emanates from analysis itself. The double bind of two mutually contradictory imperatives which Derrida has located in the psychoanalytic notion of analysis is also to be felt in deconstruction. On the one hand, deconstruction is critical and analytic, decomposing and deconstituting what it explores; on the other, it involves disjunction and a belief in ultimate *ir*reducibility. In this sense, it shares with psychoanalysis the double motif of a search for the origin, combined with a perpetual deferring and dissociation. It puts in question not simply the possibility of origin but even the desire for origin (p. 42). The 'hyperanalysis' of deconstruction is thus a necessarily endless drama, like the drama of psychoanalysis. And this is why deconstruction has to resort to those very laws that are being deconstructed, employing impossible concepts like *archi-trace* or *archi-écriture*, in an attempt to show up the non-originarity of the 'origin'. This double bind, argues Derrida, is what underlies all the 'undecidable' figures that he has explored in their internal self-contradiction.

Derrida's account of *Beyond the Pleasure Principle* showed how the paradoxes of Freud's contradictory concepts led to an interminable analysis from which Freud himself was unable to escape. Similarly, Derrida's account of Lacan's 'Séminaire sur *La Lettre volée*' aimed to show the interminable divisibility of the letter, against Lacan's claims for its indivisibility. Both these cases illustrate the most powerful and persistent *thesis*, even the sole thesis, of deconstruction: that of *différance* as divisibility (p. 48). Deconstruction analyses what ultimately refuses analysis. But the paradox is only apparent, for it is precisely because there is no indivisible element or simple origin that the analysis is interminable. Derrida calls deconstruction a 'hyperanalytisme', subject to the double bind of being a post-Enlightenment (rationalist) mode of thought, yet opposed to any notion of simple origin or end. This paradox is uncomfortable, a tense antinomy that has to be endured, for analysing the desire for origin and end does not make the analyst immune from it. The double bind is not, however, pathological, Derrida claims, it is rather the condition of all analysis, 'a transcendental sickness of the analytic'; nor is it simple, it is multiple and disseminated, in infinitely divisible knots (p. 52). In *Résistances*, Derrida has given his fullest account yet of the relationship between psychoanalysis and deconstruction, both caught in the aporias and double binds of their own projects, but with radically differing degrees of consciousness of the effects of this entrapment.

6

The Ethics and Politics of Deconstruction and the Deconstruction of Ethics and Politics

The ethics and politics of deconstruction have aroused considerable controversy. Accused by the right of iconoclasm and dangerous irresponsibility, and by the left of fostering inactivity by rendering political action unjustifiable, Derrida's work is certainly far too difficult of access to find favour with the common-sense anti-obscurantism of centrist liberal thinkers. The links between deconstruction and the philosophy of Martin Heidegger, who for a period was a member and supporter of the Nazi party, and the case of the (Belgian) Yale deconstructionist, Paul de Man, whose youthful writings were discovered after his death to be arguably sympathetic to fascist anti-Semitism, have clouded the issue still further.

The question is by no means a simple one. In the first place, of course, Derrida's own (left-wing) politics must not be confused with the politics of deconstruction. And secondly, the questions of whether deconstruction itself suggests or entails a particular ethics or politics, whether it is even compatible with any, or whether it is ethically and politically neutral, are complex. Since deconstruction is an approach to texts ('un protocole de lecture') rather than a philosophy, theory or set method of analysis, we will evidently not find any ethical or political theory or methodology in deconstructive writings. But deconstruction does frequently deal with ethical and political issues and raise ethical questions. And despite an initial intuition that it will eschew dogmatic or prescriptive ethics in favour of some kind of open-ended questioning which undermines ethical certainties, the texts examined in this chapter prove more coherent, specific and precise than one might expect. However, the move from ethics to politics is itself not an easy one: a deconstructive ethical position, if there were one, would be unlikely to provide easy answers to concrete political questions, any more than do Kantian or existentialist ethics, for example.

Ethics

Derrida's first major discussion of ethical issues comes in his lengthy assessment of Levinas, 'Violence et métaphysique', of 1964. We looked at this from the perspective of phenomenology in chapter 1. Here again, Derrida's sympathetic/critical entering into the thought processes and textual intricacies of the writers he analyses makes it difficult to disentangle his own views from those he is exploring. There are many examples of critics attributing to Derrida views which he is merely describing prior to, or in the process of, deconstructing them. Derrida's hypotheses and conditional tenses may get lost in the reader's desire to follow the detail of his argument. Derrida comments on this in his interview with Julia Kristeva in 1971 (see *Pos*, 67). In the case of Levinas, however, the position is somewhat different, as Derrida makes clear an unusually large degree of sympathy with the views of the Jewish philosopher and theologian. Levinas may not, in Derrida's view, give an entirely accurate account of some aspects of Husserl's thinking, but his ethical views are evidently attractive.

'Violence et métaphysique' starts with the large issue of the 'death of philosophy', envisaged not as the end of serious reflection but rather as, potentially, the beginning of another, less limited kind of (philosophical) questioning. Derrida describes the preservation and necessity of free questioning as being itself ethical, not in the sense that it belongs to the ethical domain, but rather in that it 'authorizes' ethics (*ED*, 118–19). The relationship between laws and commandments on the one hand and freedom and questioning on the other is fundamental. Philosophy has entered the reflexive phase of explicit meditation on its own existence and origins. Husserlian phenomenology and Heideggerian ontology, despite their differences, both participate in this attempt to return to the origins of philosophical questioning, and share certain major areas of agreement. For both, philosophy is originally Greek; metaphysics is to be relegated or transgressed; and ethics is dissociated from metaphysics and subordinated to a more fundamental domain.[1]

These themes are, Derrida argues, common to philosophy as it is traditionally understood: they are generally presupposed in an unquestioning identification of philosophy with Greek thought. So when Husserl speaks of the 'crisis' of philosophy, he is assured in his own mind that it can only be a temporary phase in the maturing of philosophy as 'science'; and when Heidegger describes contemporary philosophy as arid, his solution is for it to reimmerse itself in its Greek origins.

Levinas breaks with all three aspects of this traditional Hellenist understanding of philosophy. He comes from a different pole of cultural activity, the Hebraic, and rejects the domination of Greek thought; he sets out to undo the relegation of metaphysics and restore to it its rightful priority; and most importantly in this context, he refuses the subordination of ethics which he sees rather as the potential liberator of transcendence and metaphysics (*ED*,123). For Levinas, ethics has priority over ontology. That is to say, ethics is not a secondary subsection of philosophy, dealing with the question of how human beings should relate to each other and the world about them; human beings do not pre-exist their relations with each other, they are rather constituted by them.

In *The Ethics of Deconstruction* (1992), Simon Critchley makes a strong case, perhaps too strong a case, for the Levinasian quality of Derrida's ethics. He contends that 'Derridean deconstruction can, and indeed should, be understood as an ethical demand, provided that ethics is understood in the particular sense given to it in the work of Emmanuel Levinas' (p. xi). In Critchley's view, deconstruction *is* ethical, but it is not the case that an ethics can be derived from deconstruction. The present chapter takes issue with the second of these claims. Following Levinas, Critchley understands by ethics something prior to moral questions, and *a fortiori* to moral law, and concerned rather with a primordial ethical experience from which moral questions may derive (p. 3). This experience, as Levinas describes it, is of the otherness of the Other, the encounter with his or her face as expressive of his or her subjectivity; and it is an experience which puts in question my own self-sufficient subjecthood, my self as ego or as subject with inalienable priority. The notion of the 'face' in Levinas is crucial. It is not, Levinas insists, part of the body as object, nor is it 'just' a metaphor for the otherness of the other; it refers in the first place literally to the primacy of the face-to-face experience in any encounter. Perhaps it could be seen as a positive version of the Sartrean 'look' ('le regard'), though Sartre of course stresses rather the alienating power of the other over me, the way she or he objectifies me and denies my freedom. Unlike the 'look', the 'face' is also related to language.[2] In putting my primacy as subject into question, the face of the other frees me from reification, and grounds the ethical. In *Totalité et infini* Levinas defines ethics as precisely 'the questioning of my spontaneity by the presence of the other' (*TI*, 14. See Critchley, *Ethics of Deconstruction*, p. 5). He conceives the questioning of the priority of the self as a means of refuting the alienating effect, as he sees it, of the Husserlian transcendental ego, a view of Husserl very similar to Sartre's in *La Transcendance de l'ego*. Derrida of course does not consider that Levinas is doing justice to Husserl when he reproaches him with reifying the ego, and argues that Levinas has misrepresented the phenomenological *alter ego* by a sleight of hand which permits him to focus on the *ego* and ignore the genuine alterity of the *alter* (*ED*, 178–82, *passim*). For Levinas, it is the 'same', *le même*, that alienates within a fixed identity, and the ego is precisely representative of sameness; within the self of phenomenology any impression of alterity or internal difference or negativity is an illusion (*ED*, 139). The experience of the Other is, for Levinas, primarily an experience of separation and distance, rather than of coincidence or community. Levinas takes pains to distinguish his position from the Heideggerian *Mitsein* (being-with), which, again like Sartre, he sees as a falsification of the true nature of human relations (*ED*, 134): we are not so much *with* others as separate from them for Levinas, and in conflict with them for Sartre. (According to Derrida, Levinas and Sartre are also both misrepresenting Heidegger, but this is not our concern at this juncture. See *ED*, 217, footnote.) So the face-to-face encounter is not a matter of mutual confirmation; on the contrary, it is the face that both initiates and stops violence: the otherness of the other as free transcendent subject both arouses my hostility and is also what causes it to cease, in so far as the face initiates an experience of transcendence and freedom which commands respect for the Other (*ED*, 154 and 218). And this respect is the primary ethical imperative: the 'incarnation' of non-violence (*ED*, 142). Derrida comments that the imperative is not a Kantian one: it is immediate, and does not pass through the universal or through respect (in the Kantian sense) for the Law.

All this is clearly a far cry not only from Kantian ethics but from most philosophical attempts at a formulation of ethical precepts. It might perhaps be seen as a return to first principles, in the sense of looking behind social, legal and religious systems in the search for what grounds them: ethics 'avant la lettre', to take up Derrida's phrase in connection with *archi-écriture*. Ethics for Levinas is without law or concept, it is not a Theory of Ethics, but rather an Ethics of Ethics, which may mean that it cannot give rise to any determinate ethics without being untrue to itself (*ED*, 164). And in a sense, this is exactly the problem Derrida himself appears to face: can deconstruction do any more than question ethical systems and beliefs? Can it ever pass beyond the negative phase – however ethically invigorating that negative phase may be – and make positive proposals, ethical or indeed political? If it can, it may be precisely in so far as it distinguishes itself from the unremitting negativity of Levinas's response to other attempts at ethical reflection. We have already seen Derrida defend Husserl's phenomenological *alter ego* against accusations of identity and reification. And he will go further and accuse Levinas in his turn of failing to take account of the necessary symmetry of human relations: if I experience the other as questioning my primacy as subject, for example, the other has the same experience of me (*ED*, 188); otherness has no meaning without a notion of the same. Levinas's rejection of phenomenology is itself necessarily phenomenological (*ED*, 195), he cannot escape entirely from the object of his critique if he is to speak at all: meaning depends on a transcendental ego (*ED*, 192–3). We have seen Derrida's awareness of this impossible dependence in the case of all the would-be original thinkers he explores, and have witnessed his attempts to grapple with it in his own philosophical discourse. Levinas's weakness, then, is certainly not his inability to escape the phenomenology which he criticizes and on which he depends; it is rather that he fails (or refuses) to recognize the fact of this dependence and all that it entails.

Similarly, Derrida considers Levinas's critique of Heideggerian ontology to be ill-grounded. The attempt 'to understand the Being of beings' is not the 'truism' that Levinas makes it out to be (*ED*, 198). It is an attempt to reach the simplicity of truth, but it is far from being a banal tautology. Nor are 'beings' subordinate to 'Being' for Heidegger, as Levinas claims: Being does not exist apart from beings, so it cannot have priority over them. And this is also, most importantly, why Derrida considers Levinas to be wrong in his belief that Heidegger subordinates ethics to ontology. Indeed, Heidegger's attempt to 'think the Being of beings' is not, properly speaking, an ontology at all, and certainly not a philosophy of first causes (*ED*, 201). It is other than ethics, but not a subordination of ethics; rather, Derrida argues, ethics would be impossible without it, for it conditions respect for the other as other. There is no sense in which Being could be said to 'dominate' beings; the very notion of ontic domination makes no sense in such a context, though of course it is impossible to avoid the use of ontic metaphors (*ED*, 203). For Levinas, violence is always perpetrated by the concept, and he interprets Heidegger's thought on Being as conceptual, despite Heidegger's insistence that it is necessarily pre-conceptual. In fact, Levinas's objection to the notion of ontico-ontological difference could be seen precisely as illustrating Heidegger's point about the forgetting of Being: ethics, as Levinas presents it, can give access to beings (in his own words, to man as substance or *en soi*, (*ED*, 210)), but not to Being. Derrida spends a good deal of time exploring the paradoxical affinities and oppositions between Levinas and Heidegger: they disagree on issues such as the relationship between language, violence and history, but they share the same eschatological aim of questioning and rethinking classical metaphysics and philosophy (*ED*, 210–24). In conclusion, Derrida poses the question of whether an experience of the other as Levinas envisages it is possible at all, or whether the concept of experience, in its very empiricism, is not necessarily (and paradoxically) dominated by a metaphysics of presence which leaves no room for alterity (*ED*, 225). If this fundamental question makes explicit the problematic or unthought-through elements of Levinas's ethics, Derrida's sympathy for him is none the less clearly apparent and itself requires explanation. It will be a long time before Derrida writes at such length again on ethical issues, and the 1964 essay remains a foundation. Indeed, the central question of the (im)possibility of ethics without a transcendental subject will be seen to underlie Derrida's thinking right up to his most recent political writings on issues such as responsibility and democracy.

Levinas's brief response to Derrida's critique in 'Violence et métaphysique' is to be found in 'Tout autrement', an essay published in a special issue of *L'Arc* (1973) devoted to Derrida. Derrida's second major discussion of Levinas is entitled 'En ce moment même dans cet ouvrage me voici', published in a collection of *Textes pour Emmanuel Levinas* (1980) and reprinted in *Psyché* (1987). To analyse this intermittent dialogue in any detail would take us too far from the central concern of this chapter. Very briefly, in 1973 Levinas attempts to turn the tables on Derrida, accusing him of falling into precisely the logocentric traps he uncovers in others, but then absolving him, at least in part, by the use of the distinction, developed in *Autrement qu'être*, between the *Dire* and the *Dit* (the saying and what is said). None the less, Levinas does seem to have taken on board some of Derrida's criticisms, in particular with respect to Heideggerian ontology, for he is at pains now to distinguish emphatically 'l'Être' from 'l'étant' ('Being' from 'beings') (*L'Arc*, p. 34). Derrida's 1980 essay is in the form of a bewilderingly disguised dialogue between a male and female speaker, and focuses, amongst other things, on questions of subjectivity, responsibility and sexual difference. In a collection of homage to Levinas, Derrida would perhaps not wish to be too overtly critical, but the essay appears to take issue with Levinas's masculinist discourse, though the piece is too fragmentary and playful for much to be deduced from it with any certainty. It is difficult to subscribe here to Critchley's belief in the importance of the 1980 text, and unfortunately his own account of the essay repeats rather than clarifies the obscurities surrounding it. But we will return to Levinas later in this chapter in considering the relationship between ethics and politics, when we examine Derrida's *Adieu: à Emmanuel Levinas* (1997), published shortly after Levinas's death.

Leaving the Derrida/Levinas exchanges for the moment, we will return now to Derrida's initial contention, outlined above, that the necessity and preservation of free questioning is what grounds ethics (*ED*, 119). This requires a brief examination of some of the texts published between 1964 and the 1980s – when the ethical question took centre-stage again in Derrida's writings – to see what they have to contribute to an understanding of the ethics of deconstruction. Broadly speaking, the texts of the 1960s and 1970s consider ethics only in so far as they attempt to show that deconstruction is itself ethical. They do not deal with ethical or political issues *per se*, but are rather concerned to defend deconstruction against accusations of indifference, neutrality or idealism, or a relativistic opposition to truth.

In *De la grammatologie* Derrida insists that he is not 'rejecting' logocentric notions of meaning and intelligibility, in the first place because nothing is thinkable without them, and secondly because they are necessary to 'shake up the heritage they are part of' (*Gram*, 25). Elsewhere he acknowledges that it is not, of course, possible to prove *philosophically* that such a 'shake-up' or 'transformation' is necessary (*Marges*, xviii). However, the 'prudent and meticulous discourse' of deconstruction will in time reveal the 'crack' ('faille') in the logocentric machine through which the as yet unnameable 'outre-clôture' ('beyond-closure') may be glimpsed (*Gram*, 25). 'The future', he writes in the *Exergue*, 'can only be anticipated in the form of absolute danger. It is what breaks absolutely with constituted normality and can only be proclaimed, *presented*, as a kind of monstrosity' (*Gram*, 14). Rigour gives way here to a brief apocalyptic vision in which deconstruction plays a leading role. Similarly, *différance* is referred to in terms of an aggressive strategy: it 'stirs up the subversion of any kingdom' (*Marges*, 22), threatening our desire for presence, and is defined as the 'destruction of the Hegelian *relève* [the dialectical overcoming of opposition] *everywhere* it operates' (*Pos*, 55). However, Derrida explains, *différance* cannot be infinitely extended, its effects decrease progressively in force; were infinite *différance* possible, it would make of life 'an impassive, intangible and eternal presence: infinite *différance*, God or death' (*Gram*, 191).

This stress on disruption and violence is ethical, not to say political – a response to the accusations of violence levelled against writing in logocentric discourse: the violence which writing supposedly does to the pure presence of speech, the violence Lévi-Strauss attributes to the arrival of writing amongst the Nambikwara, for example, or the catastrophe and perversion associated with the 'supplementarity' of writing for Rousseau (*Gram*, 195, 212). Not that Derrida denies the violence of writing, provided it is understood not in the narrow sense but rather in terms of his own broader notion of *archi-écriture*, that is the system of language itself, the iterability which both makes possible and yet 'erases' the subject: 'There is writing from the moment that the proper name is erased in a system; there is a "subject" as soon as this obliteration of the proper is produced, that is to say, from the first appearance of the proper and from the first dawn of language' (*Gram*, 159). Or, as he rephrases it a little later, 'access to writing is the constitution of a free subject in the violent movement of its own effacement and its own chain [*enchaînement*]' (p. 193), a movement which he considers literally unthinkable within the concepts of classical ethics, psychology and political philosophy. But the unthinkable is not contingently unthinkable; reason does not simply happen to be incapable of conceiving certain contradictions, it is in fact constituted by that very impotence. Reason is the principle of identity (p. 214).

Derrida does not pursue his allusion to the apparently paradoxical relationship between writing, violence and the constitution of a

free subject. But the question of the different historical and philosophical conceptions of the human subject is one which preoccupies
him from the outset and which will become increasingly
foregrounded in his work. Later in *De la grammatologie*, in his account of Rousseau's *Essai sur l'origine des langues*, the question returns in the guise of a consideration of what Rousseau calls 'le
propre de l'homme' (what is specifically human, the essence of
man) (*Gram*, 347). The logic of Rousseau's arguments on nature and
culture, and in particular the strange logic of supplementarity
which we have already discussed, lead to the conclusion that it is
the 'supplementary' that makes possible all that is prized as essentially human: speech, society, passion etc. But supplementarity is
not an attribute and cannot itself constitute the 'essence' of man.
The logic of supplementarity rather puts concepts such as 'essence'
into question; it is what prevents simple self-coincidence and
self-presence and thereby generates desire. Supplementarity disrupts the binary oppositions from which a simple conception of
the human might be generated: not only nature and culture but
also animal/human, child/adult, mad/sane, divine/human etc.
Supplementarity is simultaneously what permits and what prevents a definition of the human. This idea is further developed in
'La Mythologie blanche' of 1971 (collected in *Marges*), where
Derrida returns to the question of 'le propre de l'homme' in connection with the paradoxes inherent in the Aristotelian conception of
mimesis as constitutive of the human. These texts comprise the
'classical', paradoxical phase of deconstruction in which many of
Derrida's readers delight.[3]

The question of the human subject is clearly vital to any understanding of the ethics of deconstruction, and we must pursue it
further. In one sense, Derrida's early remarks on the subject are
arguably misleading. Like the structuralists before him, he tends to
set up the classical subject as an Aunt Sally waiting to be knocked
down. In his essay on 'Différance', for example, the subject is defined as 'self-identity or possibly consciousness of self-identity'
(*Marges*, 16), and Derrida asserts that 'just as the category of subject
has never been thought, and could never have been thought, without reference to presence as *hupokeimenon* or *ousia* etc., so the subject
as consciousness has never appeared other than as self-presence'
(*Marges*, 17). I have discussed this in some detail elsewhere[4] and will
not repeat my arguments here, except to reiterate briefly that the
notion of the subject as an autonomous, independent, spontaneous
foundation of knowledge, understanding, feeling and imagination

is easier to decry than to find in any of the supposed founders of the modern conception of the subject. Descartes does not ever use the term 'subject' in this sense, and what is more, depending on whether one focuses on the *Regulae* or the *Méditations*, he may be seen as founding opposing notions of the subject as on the one hand individualist and on the other transindividual or even impersonal. Furthermore, the Cartesian mind/body split which envisages the body as origin of the passions, emotions and sentiments, and the mind as origin of thought, can itself be interpreted as a form of split subject. In Kant the subject is explicitly rather than merely potentially divided: in his critique of rational psychology, Kant argues that we can know nothing whatsoever about the transcendental subject. Given the consequent impossibility of self-knowledge, we are left with a presumption of identity between the 'I that thinks' which is outside causation, and the subject of experience which is caught up in causality.[5] Husserl saw himself as correcting the errors of both Descartes and Kant with his conception of the transcendental ego which aims to avoid the subject–object cleavage and to close the gap between the abstract, rational, or noumenal subject and its concrete, empirical, phenomenal embodiment. We have already seen the problems created by Husserl's conception of a supposedly 'unproblematic' self-consciousness, problems highlighted by (amongst others) Derrida, Levinas and Sartre, but only to generate further dissension. Thus, in his essay on 'Les Fins de l'homme' of 1968 (collected in *Marges*), examined briefly in chapter 1, Derrida criticizes Sartre's humanizing readings of Hegel, Heidegger and Husserl, arguing that despite his intention of rethinking the question of 'man' by getting beyond the metaphysical heritage and substantialist tendencies clinging to the concept, Sartre never really questions its unity, and that consequently his phenomenological ontology remains a form of philosophical anthropology.[6] We saw that Derrida's representation of Sartre contrives to ignore the very close similarities between his own analyses of Husserl and Sartre's in *La Transcendance de l'ego* of 1936. Sartre is not the philosopher of self-presence and identity that Derrida would claim; on the contrary, the Sartrean subject is riven, fissured, constituted paradoxically by self-division and deferral, 'un perpétuel sursis' (*EN*, 713). Indeed, consciousness is defined by Sartre as 'a transcendental field without a subject' (*EN*, 291), for it is the reflexivity of consciousness that brings the subject into being. We will return to the Sartrean subject as a model Derrida was overhasty in rejecting, but we need first to disentangle the threads of Derrida's own thinking on the subject from the tissue of texts in which they are interwoven.

The essay on 'Les Fins de l'homme' follows the familiar deconstructive pattern: a presentation of authorial intention followed by a demonstration of internal textual self-contradiction. Derrida repeats for Hegel, Husserl and Heidegger the process he carried out for Sartre: despite their attempts to rethink the notion of man, all four fall back ultimately into humanist positions. Since Derrida is about to reveal the implicit humanism of Hegel, Husserl and Heidegger, it is important to him first of all to dissociate himself from the discredited 'anthropologizing' readings of them which prevailed in the 1940s and 1950s under the influence of Sartre. So he starts by acknowledging, albeit briefly, the claims of the three Hs to have rethought the notion of man. Hegel's *Phenomenology of Mind* is a science of the experience of consciousness, a science of the structures of the phenomenality of mind in relation to itself, and is rigorously distinct from anthropology. Husserl's transcendental phenomenology is an explicit critique of anthropologism, empirical or transcendental. Phenomenological reduction reveals transcendental structures which are never attributed to 'man', or the 'soul' or 'psyche' of man, and are not linked to society, culture or language. Indeed, as Derrida recognizes, Husserl is prepared to imagine not only a consciousness without a 'soul', but even a consciousness without man. And finally Heidegger, too, is acknowledged to have intended to direct his 'destruction' of metaphysics and classical ontology against humanism, though with only partial success.

Derrida's next move is to feign puzzlement as to why, given such strong evidence of their opposition to humanism, the three Hs were not reclaimed by structuralist thinkers from the anthropologizing emphasis given to them by Sartre; why their *anti*-humanist stance was not properly recognized. But this question is a rhetorical ploy, since Derrida's aim is, in fact, precisely to reveal the ways in which all three remain humanist, despite all their best intentions.

Hegel, in the first place, is caught up in the ambivalent dialectical process of *aufheben* (*la relève*) which goes beyond and transcends without destroying, which overcomes yet maintains, which overtakes and yet carries with it what went before. In short, although for Hegel consciousness takes over from the 'soul' or from 'man', and phenomenology takes over from anthropology, and is no longer a 'science of man', it is, by the implication of the dialectic, *still* a science of man. The teleology of Hegel's thought binds it to eschatological, theological and ontological assumptions. Hegel may be trying to think 'the end of man' but it is still *man* whose end preoccupies him. *La Voix et le phénomène* is devoted to Derrida's critique of Husserl, but the analysis in the 'Fins de l'homme' essay focuses in particular on Husserl's teleology of reason as it is at work in man, the rational animal, and argues that Husserl's critique of empirical anthropology is superficial and continues to promote a form of transcendental humanism. In the case of Heidegger, Derrida does not, of course, believe that *Dasein* can be simply identified with the 'man' of metaphysics, but Heidegger's humanism creeps back in through the notion of self-proximity. Man is the best example of Being because he *is* Being, both on a superficial, ontic level, but also, more seriously, at an ontological level; for when Heidegger says that *ontologically* man is distant from himself, divided from himself, this is not a distance that constitutes him (as it does for Sartre) but rather a fall from grace, a sign of inauthenticity. 'We see', says Derrida bluntly, 'that *Dasein*, if it is not man, is none the less nothing other than man' (*Marges*, 151). So in his meditation on Being, Heidegger is not moving away from a reflection on man; he is rather re-evaluating and therefore ultimately revaluing man's essence. Heidegger's opposition to humanism depends on his view that humanism has no real conception of the true dignity of man, and the aim of his opposition is a deeper recognition of man's humanity (*Marges*, 156).

In Derrida's view, then, none of the philosophers considered manage to sustain the rejection of humanism that they apparently propose: they are not able to sustain systematically either their anti-humanist discourse or the revised version which they would proffer in place of humanism. Derrida uses Husserl to show that presence cannot preserve itself against absence, division and difference. Difference and non-identity lie at the heart of even the most apparently unproblematic forms of presence. Difference, or *différance*, is precisely what prevents and replaces identity, and is, of course, one of the key terms in Derrida's deconstruction of the human subject. In all four senses Derrida ascribes to the term in his interview with Henri Ronse in 1967 (i.e. deferral and non-coincidence; differentiation; production of differences and ultimately of meaning; and the unfolding of, in particular, ontico-ontological difference, *Pos*, 17–19) *différance* appears as an impersonal agent, performing many of the functions previously attributed to the conscious subject. Derrida inverts the subjectivist position and describes subjectivity precisely as 'an effect of *différance'* (*Pos*, 40). In a later interview this 'effect' has a clearly positive dimension:

> The subject is not some meta-linguistic substance or entity, some pure cogito of self-presence; it is always inscribed in language and this very inscription constitutes a form of liberty . . . for it shows the subject that it is not tied to a single identity or essence, but lives in language, as *différance*, and is therefore perpetually haunted by the 'other'.[7]

Différance is based on what Derrida calls a 'paradoxical logic' which evades the law of the excluded middle, escapes the logic of identity, and attempts to deny what it posits, and posit what it denies. Derrida is employing in his use of *différance* a mode of transforma-tion closely akin to Hegelian dialectics, to Sartre's paradoxes about consciousness (consciousness is what it is not, and is not what it is), and to negative theology.[8] He is keenly aware of this kinship and even more keen to repudiate it. Indeed, as we have seen, *différance* is intended precisely as an attack on the recuperative dialectic: 'If there were a definition of *différance* it would be precisely the limiting, the interruption, the destruction of the Hegelian dialectic everywhere it operates' (*Pos*, 55). And whilst acknowledging all the apparent similarities between *différance* and negative theology, the connection, he maintains, is merely superficial: 'This definition of *différance* is not theological, not even of the most negative order of negative theology . . .' (*Marges*, 6).

What is clear from Derrida's tussle with Hegel and negative theology is that he is all too keenly aware of the precariousness of his own position. Just as Husserl found it impossible to preserve full self-presence, even in the intimacy of interior monologue, so, conversely, Derrida finds it hard to maintain the negativity and absence for which he is arguing, uncontaminated by presence, plenitude and identity. At one point he asks 'What would be the status of a negative which could not be transcended?' (*Marges*, 126). But *différance* is not so much the opposite of dialectical thought as the undermining of it. To oppose positivity and presence to a supposedly pure negativity and absence would be precisely to fall into the trap of transformative recuperation. Presence, identity, subject-hood are not denied in any simple sense. Derrida has only to introduce the worm of *différance*, of non-identity, non-self-presence, into the subject for it to be eaten away from the inside. The subject may not be an autonomous, original self-identical creator, on the theological model, but it does not need to disappear 'without trace'. Indeed, as we saw in chapter 4, when Derrida elaborates his notion of the 'trace' as undermining presence and therefore the subject which depends on presence, he makes explicit that it is only a certain 'classical' conception of the writing subject that he is refuting: 'The "subject" of writing does not exist if we understand by it some sovereign solitude of the writer. The subject of writing is a system of relationships between layers: the mystic writing pad, the psyche, society, the world. Within this scene, the "punctual" simplicity of the classical subject cannot be found' (*ED*, 335).

It is not easy to find in philosophy any real examples of this so-called 'classical' subject, self-identical and self-present, and Derrida's critique of the 'sovereign solitude of the writer' might best be viewed as a definition by opposition. When questioned about 'the subject of writing' by Guy Scarpetta, he insists that he never maintained that there was no subject, and no subject of writing. His intention is rather to invite a reconsideration of the whole question of subjectivity by envisaging it as an effect of *différance* (*Pos*, 40), an element in a relationship, rather than an originary source. When he refers to 'the effect of subjectivity as it is produced by the structure of the text' (*Pos*, 122), 'text' should be understood in the broad, deconstructive sense of 'general text'. Moreover, 'effect' is not to be understood in this context as the simple binary opposite of 'cause'. Derrida argues explicitly for a new concept of 'effect' which would borrow from the old opposition without being reducible to it (*Pos*, 90). In the second half of this final chapter on ethics and politics, I will argue that it is his understanding of the subject as effect which lies at the root of Derrida's aporetic conception of ethics. His conception of the subject seems uncannily stuck in what he himself might call the 'reversal phase'. It appears closer to the *non*-subject of structuralist discourse than to a radically deconstructed subject. Derrida's reluctance in the 1960s to acknowledge the full complexity of those conceptions of the subject he dismisses as 'classical' must surely have contributed to this apparent anomaly in his thinking. By 1980, however, he was himself disenchanted with the alacrity with which his critique of the classical subject had been adopted and simplified. The ten-day conference in Cerisy in that year devoted to Derrida's thinking took over the title of his 1968 paper, *Les Fins de l'homme*. It set out to ask not so much the old ontological question, 'What is man?', but rather the Heideggerian question, 'Who is man?', and aimed to reopen a question whose closure had tended to result merely in the reintroduction of a naive, reactive humanism:

> Between a 'disappearance of man', too well known today not to be badly
> known, a general critique of humanism too commonly accepted not to be,
> in its turn, worth questioning, and the shamefaced, naive or reactive
> humanism on which so many discourses fall back in the end . . . it may
> well be the case that the question of 'man' needs to be asked afresh today,
> in a philosophical as well as a literary, ethical or political sense – and that
> it needs to be asked as a question of *ends* (*Les Fins de l'homme*, p. 20).

Many of Derrida's essays, especially those concerning literary
writers, question implicitly and sometimes directly, the authority of
the subject. Derrida's considerations of *signature*, of intertextuality
and of the problems of authorial intention, which have already been
explored in earlier chapters, all form part of his deconstruction of
the subject. But it is not until *Psyché* and *De l'esprit* (both 1987) that
the question is again foregrounded at such length and with such
intensity. *Psyche* is the soul. It is also a kind of mirror which Derrida
claims to offer to the 'modern Narcissus'. A similar ambiguity in-
habits the subtitle of the collection, *Inventions of the Other*. Is the 'of'
a subjective or objective genitive? Is the other the inventor, the
absolute initiator, or does the phrase refer rather to my inventions
of the other, what I imagine him or her to be in my psyche, my soul,
or the mirror self? The title essay begins with a meditation on
reflexivity (p. 17), on self-reflection (p. 25), on mirror-images (p. 27),
and on the Psyche of fable. It continues with a discussion of the
notion of invention which, Derrida argues, has always been considered as the prerogative of the human: God creates, animals discover, only man as subject invents (p. 36). Derrida proposes to
deconstruct the notion of invention, firstly by deconstructing the
ambiguity of the genitive in the phrase 'inventions of the other'
(p. 53), and more generally by rethinking the whole question of
invention as a humanist supplement. In theological terms man is
seen as a supplement to God, as the *psyche* of God, his soul and his
mirror, his need and his desire (p. 58). So if invention always depends on a human subject, is Derrida seeking to reinvent invention
along with the subject? His answer is as teasing as his question: yes
and no, or rather, yes, but in no simple sense. For what, he asks, can
he – or we – be seeking, if it is the subject of seeking which is itself
being questioned?

> It is another 'we' who is given up to invention – not the 'we' who is
> identifiable with a community of human subjects . . . but a 'we' who is
> nowhere to be found and who doesn't invent itself: it can only be
> invented by the other. For the other is always another origin of the world,
> *we* are to be invented. And the being of *us*, and being itself. . . . For the

other can no longer be confused with the God or man of ontotheology nor with any of the figures of that configuration (the subject, consciousness, the unconscious, the self, man or woman etc.). (*Psyché*, 60)

The continuity between *Psyché* and Derrida's 1964 essay on Levinas will be apparent in the stress on the priority of the other over the self, but a change of emphasis is evident in the plural 'we'. The other is now charged not only with inventing *me* but rather *us*. Derrida's thinking is clearly still ethical, but it would seem to have lost its apparently paradoxical individualist emphasis.

Politics

The question of the relationship between ethics and politics as Derrida envisages it has been tackled by Richard Beardsworth in *Derrida and the Political* (1996), which gives an account of Derrida's relation to politics up to 1994, and also of the philosophical precursors and antagonists of Derrida's ethico-political enterprise, in particular Kant and Hegel. The book forms part of a series edited by Simon Critchley, and develops certain aspects of Critchley's account of the ethical implications of deconstruction. Just as Critchley argued that there could be no ethics of deconstruction, so Beardsworth argues that there can be no politics of deconstruction. But he rightly takes issue with the extent to which Critchley assimilates Derrida's ethics to those of Levinas, and argues that this assimilation leads ultimately to an underestimation of the political implications of deconstruction. What is more, Beardsworth sees Levinas's ethics as a singularly bad model for any attempt to move towards the political, arguing precisely that Levinas's overt refusal of politics itself becomes political, but in a narrow, even partisan sense. Levinas's opposition between Greek and Jewish thinking leads him, for example, to identify the 'authentically human' as the 'being Jewish in every man' (p. 124).[9] When we examine Derrida's latest account of Levinas in *Adieu* (1997) we will see that his response to this aspect of Levinas's work diverges significantly from Beardsworth's analysis of it.

In *De l'esprit* (1987) and 'Comme le bruit de la mer au fond d'un coquillage: la guerre de Paul de Man' (collected in *Mémoires: pour Paul de Man*, 1988), Derrida faces the task of responding to the violent political controversy surrounding one of the most influential precursors of deconstruction, Martin Heidegger, and one of its best-known exponents outside France, Paul de Man, who was a personal friend of Derrida's. Both Heidegger and Paul de Man were accused of fascist/Nazi sympathies, though their cases are rather different: Heidegger lived on after the accusations were first levelled at him, and neither denied his sympathies nor apologized for them; Paul de Man was dead when his early, arguably anti-Semitic newspaper writings were uncovered, and so was not able to respond, but he had made clear during his lifetime his intense hostility to, and rejection of, fascism and totalitarianism. Deconstruction was, in the popular press and imagination, gleefully tarred with the same brush of Nazi sympathy apparently uncovered in both its philosophical predecessor and its Belgian practitioner. Derrida's difficult task was to discuss the accusations and dissociate himself from the taint of fascist politics without betraying Heidegger or de Man by an overhasty or facile dismissal of them. In the case of Heidegger, which arose first, Derrida approaches the question through the notion of what Heidegger calls the *Geist*, or spirit, a term which was studiously and explicitly avoided in the early and late Heidegger, or at least treated with caution and put in 'scare-quotes', or inverted commas, the written equivalent of kid gloves. But at the time of the Rectorial Address and the *Introduction to Metaphysics* (i.e. 1933–5), the term *Geist* appears in Heidegger without any apparent distancing devices, and Derrida sets out to explore the implications of this rhetorical change.

In *Being and Time* (first published in 1927), Heidegger invites the reader to a great wariness with respect to the *Geist* or spirit. The term *Geist*, he warns, is part of a very misleading series, or semantic field. The series is that of spirit, soul, consciousness, person, all terms which appear to *oppose* the reification of the subject, but which, in Heidegger's view, fail to come seriously to terms with the real question of the being of *Dasein*. Descartes, he argues, was led astray by setting out from the idea of a self and a subject which were immediately given. The same strictures are also applied explicitly to Hegel's 'phenomenology of mind' and implicitly to Husserl's transcendental phenomenology. The subject is, as Heidegger presents it, bound to be hypostatized and misunderstood if its being, and the Being of beings, remains unquestioned. Derrida explains how it was, at the time of *Being and Time*, quite common to oppose substantialism and reification, but this opposition was, as Heidegger demonstrated, no more than an empty gesture if it left the nature of Being itself unquestioned (*De l'esprit*, 34). Contrary to appearances, the concepts of subject, soul, psyche, consciousness and spirit remain at best problematic, and at worst dogmatic. They belong precisely to the *subjective* series that Heidegger wants to question or avoid: they are linked ultimately to the Cartesian subject, even when they are most eloquent in their opposition to it (p. 38), and in their 'modern' rejection of all reification of the human: 'In that case', Derrida writes, 'it is futile to protest against the substantiality of the soul, the reification of consciousness, or the objectivity of the person, if one continues to give an ontological determination of the *who* as a subject subsisting in the form of presence (to hand)' (*De l'esprit*, 40). Derrida argues, as he did for Husserl, that it is a vulgar notion of time that makes of the 'who' a kind of enduring substance, but we will not look again now at his analysis of time.[10] Our aim here is rather to try to assess where Derrida himself stands in relation to the logic he is deconstructing. Having commented on Heidegger's conviction that even the most anti-substantialist views of man fail because they do not genuinely question the nature of Being, Derrida goes on to show Heidegger himself lapsing seriously in a more disturbing sense at the time of his Rectorial Address. In the address, the term *Geist* (and its adjectival derivative *geistig*) is used repeatedly, not in the sub-stantialist usage deconstructed in *Being and Time*, but in a way which comes frighteningly close to 'spiritualizing' Nazism in its praise of spiritual grandeur and will-power (pp. 60, 64). Derrida does not however permit himself the luxury of uninvolved critique, or sit back to show the trail of failures behind him, the trail of philosophers who have not managed to live up to the stringent demands of deconstruction. He does not conclude with a sad peda-gogue's 'could-do-better', or a virtuoso deconstructor's tour de force. On the contrary, he presents us with the more dismaying prospect of a humanist aporia or impasse. For it seems that the weapons to oppose racist, fascist or totalitarian conceptions of man are only to be found in those very areas deconstruction has been trying to leave behind. Politically at least, there seems no escape from humanist metaphysics, despite the demise of its philosophical credentials (pp. 65–6). And Derrida's exploration of the inevitable contamination undergone by all attempts to oppose noxious politi-cal regimes concludes with what seems like a pessimistic acceptance of the inevitability of humanism, and a call to vigilence, which is worth quoting at length:

> I do not intend to criticize this humanist teleology. It is certainly more urgent to remember that despite all our denials and avoidances of it, it

has remained up till now (that is, the time . . . of Heidegger, but things have not changed radically today), the price to pay for the ethical and political denunciation of biologism, racism and naturalism etc. If I am analysing this 'logic', the aporias and limits, the presuppositions and axiomatic decisions, the inversions and contaminations, especially, in which we see it trap itself, it is rather in order to reveal and formalize the terrifying mechanisms of this programme, all the double constraints which structure it. Is it a matter of fatality? Can we escape it? There's no sign of this either in 'Heideggerian' or 'anti-Heideggerian' discourse. Can we transform the programme? I don't know. In any case, we can't simply avoid it, and must recognize it in its most abstruse ruses and its most subtle mechanisms. (pp. 87–8)

De l'esprit is one of Derrida's most concerted attempts to engage with the question of the relationship between deconstruction on the one hand and ethics and politics on the other. In his essay on Paul de Man a year later, he goes back over a very similar terrain. The main argument of the essay concerns the ambiguity and complexity of de Man's political positions during the war, as evidenced in a selection of about twenty-five of his newspaper articles. Derrida seeks to understand how de Man could have entertained ideas which appear, fifty years later, so collusive with fascist ideology. He makes concessions to the fluidity and youthful *insouciance* of de Man's writings, but his conclusions are sombre in tone when he forcefully dissociates himself and deconstruction, as well as the de Man he knew so well, from the offensive anti-Semitism of the juvenilia in question. He is, however, at pains to stress his own refusal to condemn a man who is now dead, and whose mature life was politically irreproachable. Moralistic condemnation of someone who is no longer in a position to defend himself seems to Derrida to participate in the very logic it is condemning (*Mémoires*, 221), and the same criticism can be made of the confused attempts to tar deconstruction with the brush of fascism. One of the most interesting moments in the essay occurs in a lengthy footnote dealing with this apparently widespread determination to discredit deconstruction (pp. 220–8). Why, Derrida asks rhetorically, do we witness such hostility to a mode of analysis which attempts precisely to 'deconstruct the foundations of obscurantism, totalitarianism or Nazism, of racism and of authoritarian hierarchies in general?' (*Mémoires*, 224):

Why do people not understand that the exercise of responsibility (theoretical and ethico-political) demands that nothing should be excluded *a priori* from deconstructive questioning? For deconstruction is, in my view, the very implementation of that responsibility, especially when it analyses the traditional or dogmatic axioms of the concept of responsibility. Why do people feign not to see that deconstruction is anything but a nihilism or a scepticism, as is still frequently claimed despite so many texts which demonstrate the opposite *explicitly, thematically, and for more than twenty years*? Why the accusation of irrationalism as soon as someone asks a question concerning reason, its forms, its history, its mutations? Of anti-humanism as soon as a question is raised concerning the essence of man and the construction of the concept 'man'? I could multiply examples of this sort, be it a matter of language, of literature, of philosophy, of technique, of democracy, of all institutions in general etc. In short, what are they afraid of? Who are they trying to frighten? (*Mémoires*, 224)

Derrida points out a pattern which he mockingly describes as a 'law' according to which such criticisms are always (supposedly) carried out 'in the name of . . . a democratic ethics of discussion . . . and of transparent communication' (p. 225), precisely when the most elementary rules of discussion and argument are being flouted. The moralizing appeal to 'consensus' always produces a shameless transgression of the classical norms of reason and democracy. As he does in *Limited Inc.*, Derrida uses Habermas's ill-informed critique of him in *The Philosophical Discourse of Modernity* as one example of blatant misreading and misrepresentation. In chapter 3 I suggested that this phenomenon was not simply explicable in terms of the fear of deconstruction, as Derrida argues, but also in terms of the sheer difficulty of Derrida's own texts. There is more to be said about this difficulty and its relationship to fear. The fiercest critics of deconstruction are those whom Pascal would have referred to as the 'demi-habiles', those who have partially understood. The ignorant, Pascal argues, respect the law because they believe it embodies truth; the 'habiles' (those who understand) respect it as a necessary fiction, a man-made means of keeping order; the 'demi-habiles' recognize that it is man-made, and therefore are unable to respect it, but do not go beyond this position and grasp that the law corresponds not to 'reason' but to 'la raison des effets'. Derrida's own writings on the law discuss the wisdom of Pascal's views, but before we turn to them, let us briefly draw the moral of the story, as I understand it. Deconstruction does arouse intense fear and hostility amongst many liberal or conservative thinkers precisely because it pulls the carpet out from under their feet: it questions the comfortable assumptions of common sense, and replaces them with the questions themselves, rather than a new set of answers; it dismantles the liberal consensus, shows up its illogicalities and simplifications, but it puts no new ideology in its place; indeed, it argues that there is no firm ground or foundation to our most cherished preconceptions. Derrida, and perhaps you and I, may find this exciting and liberating, we may delight in the attempt to found an ethics and politics on the shifting sands of a subject which is an effect not a cause, but the accusations of nihilism, however misplaced, are hardly surprising. And indeed the move from the deconstruction of subjectivity to ethics, or from 'the ethical' to concrete political positions is as difficult to justify for Derrida as it was for Sartre, who was similarly accused of 'immoralism'.

In 1989 Derrida makes another attempt to explain his position on the question of the 'subject' in an interview, this time with a friend and colleague, Jean-Luc Nancy. His first move is to reproach Nancy for speaking of the 'liquidation' of the subject, insisting rather that it has been 'reinterpreted'. He reiterates his conception of the relationship between *différance* and subjectivity but more explicitly than in previous formulations:

> The relation to oneself can only be one of *différance*, that is to say of alterity or trace. Not only does this in no way attenuate obligation, but on the contrary it constitutes its only possibility, which is neither subjective nor human. Which does not mean that it is inhuman or subjectless, but that it is starting from this dislocated *affirmation*... that something like the subject, man, or whoever it may be, can be figured. ('"Il faut bien manger"', 95)

But for being more explicit, the explanation is no less problematic: we are presented with a conception of obligation which is neither subjective nor human, but from which the subject may be 'figured'. The subject is once again an effect of *différance*. Derrida now insists that it is naive to speak of 'the Subject' as if it were a mythical entity that has only recently been abandoned. The 'subjects' of Descartes, Kant, Hegel and Husserl are not themselves simple but involve paradoxes and aporias that deserve renewed consideration. Derrida would like to 'de-homogenize' the subject. Nobody, he maintains, ever seriously believed in the classical, humanist subject, autonomous self-sufficient, spontaneous. 'The subject never existed for anyone... the subject is a fable' (p. 97). Furthermore, current work on the subject may well form part of a deconstructive enterprise:

> We were speaking of dehiscence, of intrinsic dislocation, of *différance*... etc. Some might say: but precisely, what we mean by 'subject' is not absolute origin, pure will, self-identity or the self-presence of

consciousness, but rather this non-coincidence with self. Here is a response to which we should return. By what right may this be called a subject? Conversely, by what right may we forbid this to be called a 'subject'? I am thinking of those who want to reconstruct, today, a discourse on the subject that no longer has the form of self-mastery, of self-adequation, centre and origin of the world, etc., but which would rather define the subject as the finite experience of non-self-identity, of the underivable interpellation that comes from the other ... We will come back to this train of thought later. (p.98)

The problems Derrida is confronting come out quite clearly in this interview, and they are the problems I alluded to earlier in this chapter: he is torn between the recognition that no one ever really believed in the autonomous, classical subject, and the continuing desire to define his own views in opposition to it – 'a discourse that *no longer* has the form of self-mastery . . .' (my italics). There is much to say about the ambivalence of this 'no longer', an ambivalence which stops him recognizing his description of the subject 'today', as it is deconstructed, as extraordinarily close to the subject of *L'Être et le Néant* fifty years earlier. I am not sure whom Derrida is referring to (Jean-Luc Nancy himself, perhaps, or Levinas?),[11] but it is certainly not Sartre. We saw *La Voix et le phénomène* repeat in part, and probably unwittingly, Sartre's own deconstruction of the Husserlian subject. Twenty years on, Derrida seems just as reluctant to acknowledge Sartre as a forerunner of much of what deconstruction has to say about the subject. By 1996, however, there seems to be a partial change of heart. In the fiftieth anniversary issue of *Les Temps Modernes*, Derrida devotes the introductory essay to a reappraisal of Sartre, in which he expresses his delight in rediscovering, fifty years later, aspects of Sartre's writings which he remembers exciting him as a young teenager, but which he has entirely forgotten since. His revision concerns primarily *Situations II*, that is to say Sartre's arguments in the late 1940s for committed literature, and he finds there much that he can respond to, for example, the way Sartre is torn between the humanism expressed in 'Écrire pour son époque' and the anti-humanism ascribed to Roquentin in *La Nausée* of 1938. These texts were separated by nearly ten years, but even within the 'Présentation des Temps Modernes' itself, Derrida senses the same tension: on the one hand Sartre writes of literature as a means of human 'deliverance' or 'salvation'; on the other he denounces the discourse of fraternity as a 'myth' fostered by 'bourgeois charity' ('Il courait mort', *Les Temps Modernes*, 587 (1996), pp. 10–11). And Derrida comments on how, when he wrote

Politiques de l'amitié (1994), he had quite forgotten Sartre's own strictures on the rhetoric of fraternity. He goes on to generalize about this forgetting in a way that is of the greatest interest in the present context:

> As I multiplied recently, in *Politiques de l'amitié*, my questions concerning the authority of this fraternalist schema and all that it stands for in our culture, I had forgotten how, in an entirely different way, of course, Sartre had already challenged the rhetoric of fraternity. This forgetting, which must happen to me more often than I realize sometimes afterwards, is, at heart, the theme of this letter: a strange transaction between amnesia and remembering [*anamnèse*] in the heritage which makes us what we are, and which has already suggested [*donné à penser*] what we have not yet thought, as if our heritage was always a spectre yet to come, a spirit returning [*revenant*, literally 'ghost'], running ahead of us, and after which we run, breathlessly, running in our turn to our death, towards death and the loss of breath. ('Il courait mort', 11)

These delicately phrased comments on the recognition of the forgotten, which suggest that all is 'toujours déjà . . .' (always already . . .), are echoed a few pages later in Derrida's account of his rediscovery of *Qu'est-ce que la littérature?* (in *Situations II*), once so important to him, later discarded as insufficient and limited, only to be reread fifty years on as a text 'of an admirable and impressive lucidity, of an almost intact modernity (*actualité*), sometimes even ahead of us, exemplary' (p. 23). Derrida's reappraisal of Sartre is generous-spirited, dignified, and an appropriate tribute from one of the two most influential French philosophers of the twentieth century to the other.

Derrida's obituary essays on Levinas are equally generous; they also have the moving quality of a deep-felt sense of bereavement. *Adieu* (1997) addresses directly the subject of this chapter: the relationship between deconstruction, ethics and politics. It also refers to Derrida's 1980 essay, 'En ce moment même dans cet ouvrage me voici', in terms which appear to take a clear distance from some of his own earlier criticisms of Levinas. Derrida reassesses his interpretation of Levinas's linking of the feminine with the domestic and suggests that an alternative reading might not so much focus on the implicit 'androcentrism' of Levinas's account, but would rather point to Levinas's attempt to go beyond the gender-stereotypes of biological male and female towards a notion of feminine alterity that is not restricted to women (*Adieu*, 82–3).

The two essays of *Adieu*, the eponymous funeral oration of 27 December 1995, and the more substantial 'Le Mot d'accueil', given at the Sorbonne a year later as the opening address in a two-day *Hommage à Emmanuel Levinas*, are both concerned with more general questions of ethics and politics. 'Adieu' itself addresses Levinas's prioritizing of ethics over ontology and politics, and his persistent reflection on the destiny of Israel, but is primarily a brief meditation on death and on the multiple meanings of the term 'adieu'. 'Le Mot d'accueil' reflects on the Levinasian theme of hospitality and its relation to both ethics and politics. Ethics, Derrida suggests, *is* hospitality (etymologically) since in Greek *ethos* means the customs of a place, and he asks whether Levinasian ethics can found a politics or even a law of hospitality in the sense argued for by Kant in his essay on 'Perpetual Peace'[12] (*Adieu*, 43). If law and politics *cannot* be deduced from Levinas's ethics of hospitality, Derrida proposes to interpret this impossibility not as a failure but as indicative of the need to think differently about the relationship between ethics and politics, that is in terms of the very conditions of responsibility and decision-making. Derrida explores the relationship between the notions of *accueil* (welcome) and 'response' to the other in Levinas's texts, and is particularly interested in the notion of 'discours' as justice: 'Nous appelons justice cet abord de face, dans le discours' (*Adieu*, 60, citing *TI*, 43: 'We call justice this approach to the face in discourse'). By the time of *Autrement qu'être* (1974), justice has come to be associated by Levinas rather with 'le tiers', the third person, who interrupts the face-to-face encounter with the other. Unlike Sartre who also envisages 'le tiers' as disturbing the mutual recognition of a twosome, Levinas gives the interruption a positive sense, for it is 'le tiers', another other, who necessitates the move from primordial ethics to questions of justice or political and juridical responsibility (*Adieu*, 64–5).[13] Indeed, 'le tiers' holds the paradoxical position of preventing the potential violence of the face-to-face meeting of two subjects at the same time as he violates the purity of the unique ethical encounter (p. 66). This paradox may be seen as a double bind or an aporia; it is a scandal, Derrida maintains, in so far as it implies that ethics and justice[14] are inaugurated by an originary, quasi-transcendental interference with an implicit oath of allegiance, or what he calls a *parjure* ('perjury'). And it is precisely this 'parjure' or 'perversion' which is the paradoxical condition of Goodness, Justice, Love etc. (p. 69). It is ultimately impossible to separate justice from injustice, impossible to control or set precise boundaries or limits between them, and the very risk of perversion and treachery is what enables ethical enquiry. If there were a *rule* to follow, ethics and justice would be a matter of determinism and technique not responsibility and 'hospitality'.

Derrida is also intrigued by Levinas's identification of intentionality (in its phenomenological sense) and hospitality (pp. 87–8). He contrasts Kant's conception of universal hospitality as necessary for 'perpetual peace' in its interruption of warlike 'natural' instincts, with Levinas's conception of both hospitality and peace as ethical and originary. For Kant, peace is a political and juridical conception, whereas for Levinas it both precedes and goes beyond the political (p. 93). In Levinas's terms, intentionality is hospitality and hospitality is ethics; even hostility is a negative manifestation of hospitality.

Similar paradoxes attend the Levinasian conception of the subject: it is the subordination of the freedom of the subject, for example, which marks not only his or her 'subjection' but also the subject's freedom itself. The subject is both an *hôte* (host *and* guest) and an *otage* (hostage). Responsibility for the other is not a contingent and secondary condition for the subject, it precedes his essence and his freedom. The subject is responsible to and for the other, and vulnerable before him (p. 105). This is where the relationship between ethics and politics comes into play. Ethics is described by Levinas as *par-delà* (beyond) politics (p. 113): his reflections on Sinai, the Torah and the history of Israel are envisaged by him not as narrowly political, but rather as ethical meditations on the universal history of humanity (p. 118). This is the kind of position that leads Beardsworth, writing of course well before the publication of *Adieu*, to argue that Levinas's refusal of the priority of politics risks becoming inappropriately political, in so far as his meditations on Israel are bound to entail or encourage empirical political positions, despite Levinas's claims to the contrary. Levinas himself sees a universal message in the special calling of Israel, and attempts, through the triple concepts of fraternity, humanity and hospitality, to construct a kind of *a priori* messianism, which he envisages not so much as ahistorical as beyond the empiricity of history (pp. 120–1).

Levinas considers the current situation of world politics, with its ethnic wars, refugees and exiles, to transgress the duty of hospitality which constitutes the very basis of ethics. His writings, Derrida maintains, are deliberately contradictory, aporetic and dialectical: simultaneously for and against 'le principe étatique'

(p. 135); what he calls 'messianic politics' are somehow 'beyond politics', that is, politics in the traditional Western sense. Levinas considers Judaism's relation to politics to be very different from Christianity's, arguing that the latter is often a state religion whereas the former never is. Derrida is evidently unhappy with the dogmatic assurance of this argument, but he does not pursue the debate. Levinas's paradoxical phraseology is intended to subvert simple political interpretation, but it can also be seen as betraying a profound unease with his own position. 'Au-delà de l'État dans l'État', for example, which implies both transcendence (*au-delà*) and immanence (*dans*), may be viewed as an attempt to have a political cake as well as to eat it. The phrase is not easy to translate since besides its literal meaning, 'Beyond the state in the state', it has a second sense in so far as 'l'État dans l'État' is also an idiomatic expression meaning, in English, 'a law unto itself', and therefore, by implication, somehow beyond the law. The double 'beyond' which makes a good English version impossible also shows up the problematic nature of Levinas's thinking, and his strenuous will to maintain the (almost) unmaintainable. Levinas is also concerned to promote the 'democratic state' as the only state open to perfectibility, and the 'only exception to the tyrannical rule of political power' (p. 139). His feelings about the foundation of the state of Israel in 1948 are mixed: he neither approves nor disapproves of it, and he interprets it as an engagement and a beginning rather than as an end. 'Realist' Zionism he judges to be narrowly political and possibly inadequate to the 'prophetic ideal' it should be embodying (p. 143).

While distancing himself from some of the detail of Levinas's account of the situation of the state of Israel, Derrida interprets Levinas's determination to analyse Zionist commitment and aspiration, rather than its actuality, as evidence of the philosopher's desire to go beyond politics and to think a peace which would also be more than purely political. But Derrida questions the very conception of the 'purely political', a fiction which is part of Levinas's ongoing attempt to argue that Israel transcends politics in the name of 'political inventiveness', an inventiveness which Derrida admits he awaits with increasing scepticism in the light of the tragic fortunes of the ill-named 'peace process' (p. 148). Derrida returns to the contrast between Kant and Levinas over the question of peace, the former implying that even peace bears the traces of hostility, the latter that peace is primordial, and argues that their positions can be reversed in so far as the primordial ethical encounter with the face of the other is also what inaugurates violence. Levinas, Derrida believes, runs the risk that his texts could be used to argue that war ultimately witnesses to peace, just as forgetfulness of the transcendence of the other bears witness to that transcendence. The barrier between ethics and politics which was never impermeable, *pace* Levinas, has lost for ever its indivisible simplicity, as what transcends politics is reincorporated within it (peace, hospitality, paternity etc.). Eternal peace will be only a mask for violence if it comes at the price of life, as in Kant's ironic story of the inn sign, 'Zum Ewigen Frieden' (For Eternal Peace), bearing the picture not of a dove but of a cemetery (p. 175).

The question of the relationship between ethics and politics is repeatedly raised in *Adieu*, and its urgency is stressed, even if it cannot ultimately be resolved: 'The relation between ethics and politics, ethics and justice or law is necessary' (p. 198), Derrida insists. He speculates as to whether, perhaps, politics might best be considered as the accomplishment of an ethical possibility (p. 182), whilst acknowledging that he cannot speak for Levinas on this issue. It is true that Levinas concedes, with apparent reluctance, that 'political civilization is "better" than barbarism', but his scarequotes demonstrate unequivocally his belief that the 'better' is not equatable with the 'good', but rather with the 'less bad' (p. 194). Indeed, Levinas's writings cannot provide answers to these vital questions, for they remain resolutely silent over the 'rules' or 'schemas' which might mediate between ethics and politics. However, Derrida is determined not to leave the matter there: for him Levinas's texts are eloquent despite, or, more accurately, *because* of their silence. Ethics, he argues, entails politics and law, inevitably and unconditionally, but the political and juridical content is necessarily undetermined: it is beyond knowledge and concept, it is a singular matter of each person's responsibility, and it must always result from an analysis which is simultaneously urgent yet interminable, unique yet general. Levinas's silence on the relationship between ethics and politics is precisely a measure of that relationship: it implies a hiatus, not so much an absence of rules as a leap necessitated at the very moment of ethical, political or juridical decision. Without that discontinuity there would be the risk of a programme to follow, and any programme would necessarily be totalitarian and irresponsible in so far as it would replace responsibility for decisions with a predetermined rule (p. 201).

Derrida, then, has a very different view from Beardsworth about the implications of Levinas's silence; but clearly, like the undecidable nature of Levinas's androcentrism/feminism, Levinas's resolute refusal to draw a politics from ethics is open to radically opposed interpretations. Derrida's *Adieu* takes a rather Sartrean line on the paradoxical strength of weakness, the eloquence of silence, and the value of non-self-coincidence, non-self-identity and discontinuity. But we have already seen this development of the early implications of *différance* in Derrida's recent writings on the subject.

Finally we need to turn to some other of the specific ethical and political questions that Derrida has explored over the last ten years: friendship, democracy, Marxism, law and justice. But first a necessary caveat: since 1990 alone he has published over twenty books, not to mention numerous essays in various collections. Some of these are lengthy, major works, some are brief and will probably be collected together for republishing later, some are vast collections of interviews etc. It will not therefore be possible to do more than describe briefly a few of the subjects covered in the thousands of densely argued pages of Derrida's latest writings.

The pattern of argument in Derrida's most recent texts is recognizable from the early works, but the element of surprise and pleasure for the reader remains none the less. Anticipation of the reversals and complexities of the deconstructive approach does nothing to dull its edge. In *Politiques de l'amitié* (1994), for example, Derrida traces the theme of friendship from its Greek and Roman roots, through Montaigne's paradoxes ('O mes amis, il n'y a nul ami', 'O my friends, there is no friend'), to modern social theory; and reveals friendship to be 'phallogocentric' and 'homofraternal' (*Politiques*, 340), in the sense that its paradigm is always brotherly love, friendship between males. What is more, it is the model at the root of almost all definitions of democracy. The model is, in theory, inclusive: friendship and democracy are extended to all, but in fact its very 'extension' to women, cousins, etc. has the effect of neutralizing and, in that sense, marginalizing them (*Politiques*, 13). Derrida explores issues such as Aristotle's attempt to define friendship, the question of the best possible number of friends (not too many) (p. 37), the differences between love and friendship, between active and passive, and the consequences for a definition of friendship of taking the lover or the beloved as paradigmatic (pp. 25–6). It would seem that for Aristotle, individual singularity and particularity were paramount, but equally important were notions of community and of majority decisions taken by stable, identifiable subjects; so the ideal democracy was in fact irreconcilably torn between two tragically incompatible goods (p. 40). Similar contradictions are rife within friendship itself: 'better love than be loved' implies a dissymmetry that lies uneasily with the notion of the friend as another self. The continuity of preoccupations from Derrida's earlier work (particularly on Levinas) is clearly evident here.

Friendship and democracy are, Derrida argues, always practices of the 'Same': they protect themselves from the otherness of the other, deeming him enemy (or foe),[15] and potentially, at least, seeking his death. War, homicide, genocide, are all the reverse side of a politics of friendship. Who decides, Derrida asks, who is a friend? And this question is itself further complicated by the deconstruction of the subject which means not only that the 'who' is not simple, and that friendship itself must be thought without presence or proximity (p. 53), but that the nature of decision itself is put in question: no longer the active, free, conscious and voluntary act of a sovereign subject (p. 16). In fact, the subject as traditionally understood would be incapable of deciding: its self-identity and permanence would render illusory any apparent decision-making (pp. 87, 220–1). 'My'/'our' responsibility (for deciding) is not then annulled by the deconstruction of the subject – indeed it is made possible by it – but it is by the same token problematized (pp. 56–7, 256, 268).[16] Even the communality at the heart of community is put in question, as the internal contradictions of the notion come into focus: the rareness of the common, for example, as in Baudelaire, *l'homme des foules* ('man of the crowds'), and in Nietzsche (p. 64), which is one of the reasons behind Derrida's avowed unwillingness to speak in terms of 'community' (p. 338). Derrida is once again walking what appears to be an impossible tightrope: deconstructing the concepts of friendship and democracy in the name of an (impossible?) ideal, or, as he puts it, revealing the self-deconstructing force within the very theme of democracy (p. 129). In the end he feels obliged to spell out what he might have hoped was self-evident, were there not so much contentious and bitter evidence to the contrary in the continuing attacks on the alleged corruption of deconstruction: in deconstructing the concepts of friendship, fraternity, community and democracy, Derrida is not, he insists, *opposing* them; he believes in the merits of a democratic system. *L'Autre Cap* (1991) deals explicitly with this question in its relation to European politics. What deconstruction shows is that friendship is not simple or 'pure', and that democracy does not yet truly exist; nor can it, for it will always be a promise, an ideal that would no longer be an insult to the ideal of friendship on which it is based, a model to strive for but never, by definition, fully actualizable (*Politiques*, 338–40).

Derrida's approach to Marxism also differentiates between Marxism as it exists, or existed, and Marxism as it may be understood as a possible (or impossible) goal. *Spectres de Marx: l'état de la dette, le travail du deuil et la nouvelle Internationale* (1993) argues that there is more than one spirit of Marx, and attempts to move beyond the current disavowal of Marx to explore his alternative legacies, which it is still open to us to reaffirm. The title comes from the opening lines of the *Communist Manifesto:* 'A spectre haunts Europe – the spectre of Communism', which is then related to a wide and unexpected series of other spectres or ghosts, and especially the Ghost from *Hamlet*. Ghosts are, of course, particularly suited to deconstruction; after all, they do not exist, they are on the margins of being and non-being, they have 'no substance nor essence, nor existence, they are never present as such' (*Spectres*, 14). 'Spectrality is not nothing, it exceeds and thereby deconstructs all the ontological oppositions, being and nothingness, life and death' (*Adieu*, 193). Spectres put our ethics and politics to the test most acutely: to be *just* our principles must respect others who are no longer or not yet present. Our responsibility cannot disregard those who are absent, be it in time or space. *Spectres de Marx* criticizes what it calls the 'new dogmatism', that is the intolerant dismissal of Marxism in a frantic attempt to stabilize a fragile neo-liberal hegemony by dwelling on the demise of the political opposition. Derrida uses Freud's notion of the triumphalist phase of an incomplete act of mourning to explain the gleeful celebration of and obscene insistence on the end of an era in terms of *dénégation*, 'disavowal' (*Spectres*, 116, 118). This 'exorcism' attempts both to neutralize the spectral remains of Marxism and to deny its 'spirit' any future. Derrida's contention is that its future is our responsibility.

Derrida's text has, as always, a multiplicity of focuses, one of which is the question of ends, and of the end of history in particular: he compares the 1990s vogue (Fukuyama et al.)[17] for proclaiming the end of History, Man, Philosophy, Marxism etc. with that of the 1950s, arguing that these notions were popular and exciting to young intellectuals forty years ago, but necessarily seem less new to them today (*Spectres*, 37). Derrida takes Blanchot's novel, *Le Dernier Homme* (1957), and his article, 'La Fin de la philosophie' (1959), which deals with half a dozen books by French ex-communists or ex-Marxists in the 1950s, as witness to this situation of *déjà vu*, though he is not maintaining that the phenomena are identical. He is inviting us rather to contemplate the notion that 'the time is out of joint', a phrase from *Hamlet* which, rather like the phrase from Marx on spectres, is made to yield a vast panoply of different meanings. It is precisely the 'out of joint'-ness of time that permits the play in the mechanism on which deconstruction depends: a perfect fit would leave no room for manoeuvre[18] (*Spectres*, 65). It is the mismatch between law and justice, between justice as (in Levinas's terms) 'the relation with the Other' (*Spectres*, 48) and law as rules, norms and juridico-moral representations which is the very (paradoxical) condition of justice, and, as Derrida already hints, of deconstruction itself (p. 56). Being out of joint may entail the 'possibility of evil', but without that possibility all there would be is 'the necessity of the worst' (*la nécessité du pire*). The disjunction between law and justice is an evil that saves us from something worse: totalitarianism and immobile self-identity; and Derrida sees it as the unconditional ethical and political duty of deconstruction to dismantle totalizing philosophical responses which flee rather than seeking to open up a space for questioning (p. 59). As we saw in *Adieu*, these issues remain Derrida's major preoccupation in his latest work.

Marxism, Derrida argues, 'remains both indispensable and structurally insufficient' (p. 101). It is in this sense that he wishes to deconstruct the old messianism of Marxism while recognizing that aspects of it such as its emancipatory promise remain irreducible to deconstruction, and indeed akin to it in their structure, offering an unrealizable ideal of justice or democracy (p. 102). What is vital is to differentiate between the empirical and the ideal, unlike Fukuyama who confuses them, contriving to argue simultaneously that true democracy is a future ideal, *and* that it has been fully realized in the liberal democracies of Europe or the United States (pp. 107, 118). For Derrida, a 'true' democracy could never be empirically realized because it would involve the incompatible ideals of an infinite respect for the singularity and alterity of the other, as well as a quantifiable equality between anonymous singularities (p. 111). But a recognition of this very impossibility and incompatibility is essential to any striving for justice, just as undecidability is the paradoxical condition of responsibility and decision (p. 126). This is why Derrida claims that deconstruction has never been either Marxist or non-Marxist, but is rather faithful to 'a certain spirit of Marxism' (p. 127); though he recognizes that he will please no one by this position which will be criticized on the one hand as a belated rallying to the Marxist cause, and on the other as attempting to deconstruct what should be beyond deconstruction. None the less, he points out, Marxism itself has always claimed to be ready to undertake its own self-criticism, and indeed some Soviet philosophers have argued that they consider the best translation for *perestroika* to be precisely 'deconstruction' (p. 146). Whilst reaffirming that he 'is not a Marxist' (p. 143), Derrida still maintains that deconstruction would have been impossible without Marxism, and that it is a radicalization of Marxism (p. 151).

The first section of *Du droit à la philosophie* (1990), an essay of a hundred pages entitled 'Privilège. Titre justificatif et remarques introductives', deals with closely connected issues. The title of the book has a wide range of possible meanings, including both the relationship between law and philosophy, the question of who has a right to philosophy, and, once again, who decides? With these very questions both philosophy and democracy are initiated, and Derrida makes the connection with 'Violence et métaphysique' twenty years earlier (*Du droit à la philosophie*, 27; see *ED*, 118). He returns again to his preoccupation with the deconstruction of the 'subject', and describes it, as we already just seen him describe democracy, as having the structure of a 'promise': 'The self (*soi*), the *autos* of legitimating and legitimated auto-foundation *remains to come* [*reste à venir*], not as a *future* reality but as what will always keep the essential structure of a promise and can only come about as such, as *to come* ['à venir'; 'avenir' as one word is, of course, the future]' (*Droit*, 41. See also pp. 53, 70). The promise means, paradoxically, that what is 'to come' will never be present, even in the future. Its structure is precisely its futurity. We may feel as frustrated as Alice when she learnt the principle of 'jam tomorrow but never jam today', but we will also be as enlightened.

The law has been one of Derrida's recurrent concerns for at least the past fifteen years, from his contribution to the Cerisy Colloque devoted to Lyotard in 1982, 'Préjugés – devant la loi' (collected in *La Faculté de juger*, 1985) to two of his most recent works, *Du droit à la philosophie*, just referred to, and *Force de loi: le 'fondement mystique de l'autorité'* (1994). We might return briefly at this point to Pascal's remarks on the ungrounded status of the law:

> Justice, force. – It is just that what is just be followed, it is necessary that what is strongest be followed. Justice without force is impotent, force without justice is tyrannical. . . . So justice and force must be united; to ensure that what is just is strong, or that what is strong is just . . . one person says that the essence of justice is the authority of the legislator, another the convenience of the sovereign, another current custom; and

> this is the most certain: nothing, following reason alone, is just in itself; everything changes in time. Custom makes the whole of equity, for the simple reason that it is acknowledged; that is the *mystical foundation of its authority*. Whoever takes it back to first principles, destroys it. (*Force*, 27–9, citing Pascal, §298)

Pascal is quoting Montaigne's comments on the 'mystical foundation' of laws, obeyed not because they are just, but because they are law (*Force*, 29). Derrida is interested in these comments not so much for their apparent relativism, and certainly not in order to interpret them in terms of the cynicism of a La Fontaine ('La raison du plus fort est toujours la meilleure', 'The reason of the strongest is always best', p. 31), but rather in so far as they prefigure a modern critique of juridical ideology and can be interpreted as attempting a deconstruction of the very foundations of the law. The ungrounded, or self-grounding, nature of the law does not make it 'unjust' or 'illegal', but it certainly differentiates it from justice. Kant too assists in the deconstruction of the law when he shows that, unlike morality, it exerts an external constraint: it should be obeyed not because it embodies a categorical ethical imperative, but because it is the law (*Force*, 39; *Du droit à la philosophie*, 77–8). Unlike Deleuze,[19] Derrida does not use Kant's break with the Aristotelian conception of the law as a reflection of what is good, just and true to argue that the law is irrational and arbitrary. The lack of a transcendental foundation does not undermine it, except in the eyes of the *demi-habiles*.

Derrida is careful in these later works to spell out that deconstruction is not in any way a nihilistic undermining of truth, but rather an exploration of the prejudices and preconceptions that underlie much of what we generally accept without question. Deconstruction is therefore on the side of truth. Consequently, his recent writings contain fewer of the shocking 'quotable quotes' that earned deconstruction a bad name in the 1960s and 1970s. However, some can still be found, though they are far from having the playful (and youthful) tonality of the earlier essays.[20] In *Force de loi*, for example, we find the maxim with which I shall end my analysis: '*Deconstruction is justice*' (p. 35; Derrida's emphasis). What does this mean? Derrida is arguing that the fact that the law is open to deconstruction, whether because of its textual nature, which renders it always open to reinterpretation, or because of its lack of external grounding, is no bad thing. On the contrary, it may be seen as the one political hope of historical progress. But what is more, it is the deconstructibility of law, and of justice as embodied in the law, that makes deconstruction possible. This apparent circle needs thinking through. Justice itself, Derrida argues (adding the caveat 'if it exists') is not deconstructible, any more than is deconstruction ('if it exists') (p. 35). 'If it exists': the fact that the phrase is applied not only to justice but also to deconstruction should alert us to its rather special meaning; clearly both justice and deconstruction 'exist' in the usual, common-sense meaning of the term, but Derrida is asking rather if they can be said to exist in a pure form. It is as embodied in the law that justice can be deconstructed, precisely because it was 'constructed' in the first place. And this makes deconstruction possible in so far as deconstruction is always necessarily concerned with questions of law. Deconstruction takes place, Derrida maintains, in the space between the indeconstructibility of justice and the deconstructibility of the law. Like justice, deconstruction is impossible, or rather 'it is possible as an experience of the impossible' (*Force*, 35, 38). What makes deconstruction and justice possible is the aporetic nature of both (p. 38).

Far then from being a 'quasi-nihilistic abdication in the face of the ethico-politico-juridical question of justice and the opposition of justice and injustice' (p. 44), deconstruction implies a responsibility that is limitless in the face of the impossible infinity of its object. Furthermore, the responsibility of deconstruction necessarily includes the deconstruction of responsibility, along with the associated concepts of intentionality, will, freedom, conscience, subject, community, decision etc., in a way that might make it appear irresponsible precisely at the moment when it is most highly involved in the responsibility of its task (p. 45). This appearance of irresponsibility is not entirely unfounded; it corresponds to what Derrida calls the *epoche* – Husserl's term for the bracketing off of the empirical and contingent in the search for essences. And the essential moment of deconstructive *epoche*, a moment which is a structural rather than temporal necessity if it is to keep us from returning to our 'dogmatic slumber' (p. 46),[21] is a moment of suspense and anguish (*angoisse*). But who ever claimed justice could be achieved without any anguish, Derrida asks rhetorically, reminding the reader inevitably of the existential anguish in the face of the exhilarating recognition of the inescapability of freedom, and also, perhaps, of the alternative, *non*-Nietzschean response to the infinite potential for interpretation eschewed at the end of 'Structure, Sign and Play' (*ED*, 427). Is Derrida more sympathetic now, in his sixties, to the yearning for security that he tended to mock thirty years earlier? Or is he simply more of a consummate politician in the light of his repeated experience of the intense fear and hostility his writings have aroused? What is certain is that he considers the recognition of the distinction between law and justice as vital to any hope of political progress: it is *because* we recognize that laws do not ultimately embody justice in its pure state that we can continue with projects of emancipation. Like democracy, and like the subject, justice is always still to come (*à venir*, p. 60).

Derrida dissociates himself from the contemporary tendency to disqualify discourses of liberation and emancipation: these may need deconstructing in the light of the heterogeneity of law and justice which he has been exploring, but they will always be essential as new areas of excluded marginality become apparent.[22] The evident targets for deconstructive analysis are not simply the large-scale issues of international politics, such as the huge refugee problem, which he tackles in his recent essay, *Cosmopolites de tous les pays, encore un effort!* (1997), but also areas that are closer to home, such as current legislation on the military use of scientific research, abortion, euthanasia, organ transplants, bio-engineering, medical experimentation, the social stigma of Aids, the politics of drug trafficking, homelessness and the treatment of and status accorded to animals (*Force*, 62–3). *L'Animal autobiographique* (July 1997), the latest 'Colloque de Cerisy' to explore questions raised by Derrida's work, was devoted entirely to this latter issue. Derrida's own paper, 'L'Animal que donc je suis', lasted two intensive days, and examined the question of man's relation to animals, and in particular the systematic presumption of animal inferiority and denial of animal suffering in philosophical texts from Descartes through Kant and Heidegger to Levinas. The issue can be seen, in a sense, as the necessary culmination of Derrida's exposure of the repression and exploitation which we carry out 'unwittingly' against all we deem to be 'inferior'. This chapter started by asking whether deconstruction's relation to ethics could ever be anything more than an eschewing of the prescriptive and an undermining of ethical certainties. In the 1990s, at least, deconstruction appears to be pursuing a very different ethical and political agenda, and one which arguably supports Derrida's bold claim that deconstruction is justice.

Notes

Apologia

1 So we read in ch. 1 of *De la grammatologie* of modern linguistics 'working on the deconstruction of the constituted unity of the word "to be" [être]' (p. 35).
2 See, for example, John M. Ellis in *Against Deconstruction* (Princeton, Princeton University Press, 1989).

Chapter 1 Phenomenology

1 See Richard Kearney, *Modern Movements in European Philosophy* (Manchester, Manchester University Press, 1986), p. 114. Kearney is citing his own interview with Derrida.
2 Collected in *L'Écriture et la différence*, 1967.
3 *Gestalt* theory envisages perception as entailing 'configuration' or *Gestalt* (form or structure) rather than merely a sum of individual elements. Its main thesis is that the whole of any perceptual organization determines the appearance of its parts.
4 The theory of *Verstehen* rejects mechanistic models of psychological and historical analysis and seeks to understand social phenomena in terms of human intentions and meanings, grasped as synthetic wholes.
5 See also 'La Forme et le vouloir-dire' (*Marges*, 187): 'Phenomenology criticized metaphysics . . . only in order to restore it.'
6 See the end of the present chapter. The notion of questioning will be further considered in ch. 6.
7 Ideal objects – such as circles – exist as ideas rather than as empirical objects.
8 Translated into English as *The Crisis of the European Sciences and Transcendental Phenomenology* (Evanston, Northwestern University Press, 1970).
9 J. Derrida, 'The Time of a Thesis: Punctuations', in *Philosophy in France Today*, ed. Alan Montefiore (Cambridge, Cambridge University Press,

1983), p. 39. (The essay is the translation of Derrida's defence of his thesis in the Sorbonne on 2 June 1980.)

10 Derrida later used the word *différance* to convey the many-layered notion of differing, deferring and differentiation. See below, chs 3 and 6, for a more extensive account of *différance*.

11 See n. 10.

12 See n. 6.

13 See Colin Davis, *Levinas* (Cambridge, Polity Press, 1996), for an excellent account of the development of Levinas's thought.

14 See ch. 6.

15 Earlier in this chapter (p. 15), we saw the same phrase used by Hyppolite. The subject had clearly been put in question long before the assault on it by structuralism. See also n. 17.

16 For another, more technical, view of this question, which draws a somewhat different conclusion, in part by representing Sartre as a dialectician rather than a philosopher of paradox, see Daniel Giovannangeli, 'La Phénoménologie partagée: remarques sur Sartre et Derrida', *Les Études Philosophiques*, 2 (1992), pp. 246–56.

17 See in particular, 'Conclusion: Sartre and the Deconstruction of the Subject', in *The Cambridge Companion to Sartre*, ed. Christina Howells (Cambridge, Cambridge University Press, 1992), pp. 318–52.

18 See ch. 6.

Chapter 2 Structuralism

1 See also Paul de Man's *Blindness and Insight: Essays in the Rhetoric of Contemporary Criticism* (New York, Oxford University Press, 1971), for a brilliant discussion of related topics.

2 See Claude Lévi-Strauss, 'Structuralisme et critique littéraire' (1965), in *Anthropologie structurale II* (Paris, Plon, 1973).

3 See ch. 1, n. 10, and chs 3 and 6.

4 See ch. 6, p. 129.

5 See ch. 3, pp. 61–2.

Chapter 3 Language: Speech and Writing

1 Collected in E. Levinas, *En découvrant l'existence avec Husserl et Heidegger*, 3rd edn (Paris, Vrin, 1974; first edn, 1949; with additions, 1967).

2 I.e. a science of written characters.

3 See Rousseau's *Dialogues: Rousseau juge de Jean-Jacques* (London, Ed. Cazin, 1782).

4 See ch. 1, p. 24.

5 See ch. 2, p. 40.

6 See ch. 4, p. 78, and ch. 5, p. 97.

7 Christopher Norris's term in *Deconstruction: Theory and Practice* (London and New York, Methuen, 1982), p. 36.

8 John Ellis fails to understand this in his scathing if somewhat naive critique of the whole Derridean enterprise in *Against Deconstruction* (Princeton, Princeton University Press, 1989). See especially p. 25.

9 In ch. 1 we saw Husserl blaming the metaphorical aspect of language for apparent inconsistencies in his own theory of language.

10 See ch. 4.

11 See J. L. Austin, *How to Do Things with Words*, ed. J. O. Urmson (Oxford, Clarendon Press, 1962).

12 See ch. 2, p. 30.

13 *Glyph*, 1, Johns Hopkins Textual Studies (Baltimore and London, Johns Hopkins University Press, 1977).

14 I cannot agree here with Christopher Norris who believes that Derrida's playfulness means that he did not intend to meet Searle's 'arguments with reasoned opposition at any point'. See *Deconstruction: Theory and Practice*, New Accents (London and New York, 1982), p. 114. On the other hand, John Ellis's conviction that Derrida 'was smarting under what he had felt to be some damaging blows' seems equally implausible (see *Against Deconstruction*, p. 14, n. 10).

15 The misreadings are not, however, all on one side. Here, for example, Derrida seems to believe that Searle is attributing the permanence argument to him. Readers must make up their own minds by examining Searle's 'Reply' for themselves, but I am convinced that Derrida is wrong here. Searle's argument is simpler than Derrida can quite believe: he is just going back to the old conception of *scripta manent*. See *Glyph*, 1 (1977), p. 200.

16 *The Philosophical Discourse of Modernity: Twelve Lectures*, trans. Frederick Lawrence, (Cambridge, Mass., MIT Press, 1987; German original, 1985).

17 Presumably quoting Harold Bloom.

18 See ch. 6 for a further exploration of this question.

Chapter 4 Deconstructing the Text: Literature and Philosophy

1 See also *Diss*, 32 and *Pos*, 112.

2 See also 'Genèse et structure' (first published 1959) (*ED*, 242) for an earlier reference to Gödel and Husserl.

3 See ch. 3.

4 'La critique thématique' usually refers to a particular school of criticism, represented by Jean-Pierre Richard, but can also refer to thematic or 'content-based' criticism in general. See below.

5 See also *Diss*, 56.

6 See Harold Bloom, *The Anxiety of Influence* (London, Oxford and New York, Oxford University Press, 1973).

7 Derrida is referring to Sartre's *La Transcendance de l'ego*, first published 1936. In fact Sartre is arguing against Husserl that the ego is transcendent rather than transcendental, a point Derrida also seems to have overlooked here.

8 Charles Baudelaire, 'Le Spleen de Paris,' in *Oeuvres complètes* (Paris, Éditions de la Pléiade, 1961), p. 285.

9 G. W. F. Hegel, *Philosophy of Nature*, vol. 1, ed. and trans. M. J. Petry (London, Allen and Unwin, 1970), § 259, p. 235.

10 J.-P. Sartre, 'L'Universel singulier', in *Situations, IX* (Paris, Gallimard, 1972), p. 166. See also *Critique de la raison dialectique* (Paris, Gallimard, 1960), p. 103: 'The conflict between Hegel and Kierkegaard finds its resolution in the fact that man is neither signified nor signifier, but both signified-signifier and signifying-signified.'

11 See 'De l'économie restreinte à l'économie générale, *Un hégélianisme sans réserve*', in *L'Écriture et la différence*.

12 J.-P. Sartre, 'L'Engagement de Mallarmé', *Obliques*, 18–19 (1979), numéro spécial, *Sartre*, ed. M. Sicard, p. 94. See also *Glas*, p. 225: 'The critique (of a logic) which reproduces in itself (the logic of) what it criticizes will always be . . . an idealist gesture.'

13 Jean Genet, 'Ce qui est resté d'un Rembrandt', in *Oeuvres complètes*, vol. IV (Paris, Gallimard, 1968).

14 'Sa' is also the abbreviation for the *signifiant*, the signifier, and an ironically (in)appropriate way of expressing what would certainly fit the label of Transcendental Signified. 'Sa' may also be read 'ça' – it, the id – the very hint of which casts a shadow over *Savoir Absolu* as Thought thinking itself.

15 See also *Saint Genet* (Paris, Gallimard, 1951), pp. 209–10.

16 J. Genet, 'Ce qui est resté d'un Rembrandt', pp. 22, 25, 28.

17 J.-P. Sartre, *Les Mots* (Paris, Gallimard, 1964).

18 For an uneven but occasionally brilliant study of *Glas* which attempts to enter into its textual web rather than unravel it, see Geoffrey Hartman, *Saving the Text* (Baltimore, Johns Hopkins University Press, 1981).

Chapter 5 Deconstruction and Psychoanalysis

1 See below, in connection with 'Spéculer – sur "Freud"', Derrida's essay on Freud's *Beyond the Pleasure Principle*.

2 Sarah Kofman writes very clearly about the gap between Freud's intuitions and his concepts in *Lectures de Derrida* (Paris, Galilée, 1984). See especially the section 'Graphématique et psychanalyse' (pp. 51–114).

3 See *Pos*, 120 and *Diss*, 300, n. 56.

4 Kofman, *Lectures*, pp. 72ff.

5 See Kofman, pp. 76–90.

6 See ch. 4 on literature and philosophy, p. 79.

7 J. Lacan, 'Situation de la psychanalyse en 1956', in *Écrits* (Paris, Seuil, 1966).

8 Marie Bonaparte is named, the others are alluded to only implicitly.

9 Lacan takes over, without acknowledgement, Bonaparte's observation that Baudelaire's translation has misplaced the letter 'above' rather than 'beneath' the little brass knob in the middle of the mantelpiece (*CP*, 474).

10 Barbara Johnson, 'The Frame of Reference: Poe, Lacan, Derrida', in Geoffrey Hartman (ed.), *Psychoanalysis and the Question of the Text* (Baltimore, Johns Hopkins University Press, 1978). Originally in *Literature and Psychoanalysis*, a double issue of *Yale French Studies*, 55/6 (1977; repr. Baltimore, Johns Hopkins University Press, 1982, 1985).

11 See Marian Hobson, 'Deconstruction, Empiricism and the Postal Services', *French Studies*, 36 (July 1982).

12 Shoshana Felman, 'The Case of Poe: Applications/Implications of Psychoanalysis', in *Jacques Lacan and the Adventure of Insight* (Cambridge, Mass., and London, Harvard University Press, 1987).

13 Fredric Jameson, 'Imaginary and Symbolic in Lacan: Marxism, Psychoanalytic Criticism and the Problem of the Subject', in *Literature and Psychoanalysis* (see n. 10).

14 See below.

15 The German term *Todestrieb* (death drive) raises considerable problems of translation. Strachey uses 'instinct' in the English *Standard Edition*, but this conflates *Trieb* and *Instinkt*, which are distinct in German, the former belonging to the dynamics of the human mind, the latter to zoology. The French term *pulsions* was chosen, indeed specifically created, in the early years of the century, to translate *Triebe*, but risks confusion with other less fundamental impulses (such as Freud's *Partialtriebe*). Lacan suggests the paleonymic *dérive* (literally, 'drift'), punning on the French and English terms 'drive', *dérive* and 'derive'. I shall follow what seems to be the currently prevailing preference for the term 'death drive'.

  For further discussion of this question see Malcolm Bowie's *Lacan*, Fontana Modern Masters (London, Fontana, 1991), pp. 161–2, and J. Laplanche and J.-B. Pontalis, *Vocabulaire de la psychanalyse* (Paris, PUF, 1967). I am indebted to both these works for their clarification of this question.

16 'Remarks on Deconstruction and Pragmatism', in Chantal Mouffe (ed.), *deconstruction and pragmatism* (London and New York, Routledge, 1996), p. 79.

17 Malcolm Bowie's view of Freud's procedure is somewhat different from Derrida's: he sees Freud's paradoxes and aporias not as evidence of a refusal to accept the consequences of his speculation, but rather as part of an astounding exercise in attempting to think the unthinkable. We have not room here to do more than refer to this alternative and more generous interpretation of Freud's strategy.

18 Derrida is doubtless alluding here to M. Blanchot's *Le Pas au-delà* (Paris, Gallimard, 1973).

19 J.-F. Lyotard, *La Condition post-moderne* (Paris, Éditions de Minuit, 1979).

Chapter 6 The Ethics and Politics of Deconstruction and the Deconstruction of Ethics and Politics

1 See ch. 1, p. 25.

2 Derrida defines it as follows: 'Le visage est, en effet, l'unité inaugurante d'un regard nu et d'un droit à la parole' (*ED*, 211).

3 See chs 2 and 3.

4 See my 'Sartre and the Deconstruction of the Subject', in *The Cambridge Companion to Sartre*, ed. Christina Howells (Cambridge, Cambridge University Press, 1992), pp. 318–52.

5 See *Critique of Pure Reason*, pp. 361 (A,396), 334 (A, 350), 167 (B, 155). Also *Groundwork of the Metaphysics of Morals*, tr. H. J. Paton in *The Moral Law*, p. 123.

6 See ch. 1, pp. 27–8.

7 Richard Kearney, *Modern Movements in European Philosophy*, (Manchester Manchester University Press, 1986), pp. 125–6.

8 See my 'Sartre and Derrida: Qui perd gagne', *Journal of the British Society for Phenomenology*, 13, 1 (1982), reprinted in *Sartre: The Necessity of Freedom* (Cambridge, Cambridge University Press, 1988), and also 'Derrida and the Deconstruction of the Subject' (See n. 4).

9 E. Levinas, *A l'heure des nations* (Paris, Éditions de Minuit, 1988), p. 192.

10 See ch. 1.

11 Levinas's *Hors sujet* (Montpellier, Fata Morgana, 1987), for example, had appeared two years earlier.

12 I. Kant, 'Perpetual Peace: A Philosophical Sketch', in *Kant: Political Writings*, ed. Hans Reiss, trans. H. B. Nisbet (Cambridge and New York, Cambridge University Press, 1970).

13 See Levinas, 'Paix et proximité', in Jacques Rolland (ed.), *Emmanuel Levinas* (Lagrasse, Cahiers de la Nuit Surveillée, 1984), p. 345.

14 Derrida explains that he means justice as instantiated in law, as we shall see below, but this is his caveat, not Levinas's.

15 See Derrida's discussion of Carl Schmitt for the implications of this distinction, *Politiques*, 101–29, also p. 161 *passim* on Schmitt and Hegel on the enemy as absolute other.

16 See also *Force de loi*: 'a subject can never decide anything', (p. 53), and Derrida, 'Remarks on Deconstruction and Pragmatism', in C. Mouffe (ed.), *deconstruction and pragmatism* (London and New York Routledge, 1996):

> The question here is whether it is through the decision that one becomes a subject who decides something. . . . If one knows, and if it is a subject that knows who and what, then the decision is simply the application of a law. In other words, if there is a decision, it presupposes that the subject of the decision does not yet exist and neither does the object . . . the subject does not exist prior to the decision but when I decide I invent the subject. . . . That is why I would say that the transcendental subject is that which renders the decision impossible. (p. 84)

We will be reminded here of Sartre's discussion of the subject and of decision in *L'Être et le Néant*, and also perhaps of Kierkegaard's famous 'The moment of decision is madness', cited by Derrida first in 'Cogito et histoire de la folie' (*ED*, 51) and again in *Force de loi* (p. 58).

17 Francis Fukuyama, *The End of History and the Last Man* (New York, Free Press, 1992); translated into French by D. A. Canal (Paris, Flammarion, 1992).

18 See also Derrida's *Passions* (Paris, Galilée, 1993).

19 In G. Deleuze and F. Guattari, *Kafka: pour une littérature mineure* (Paris, Éditions de Minuit, 1975).

20 See, for example, the conclusion to 'Structure, Sign and Play', where Derrida writes of 'the affirmation of a world of signs without fault, without truth, without origin' (*ED*, 427).

21 Kant claimed that it was Hume who had awakened him from his 'dogmatic slumbers'.

22 See also Derrida, 'Remarks on Deconstruction and Pragmatism', pp. 76–88 (esp. p. 82), and his *Moscou aller–retour* (Paris, Éditions de l'Aube, 1995).

Bibliography

Works by Jacques Derrida, and English Translations

Adieu: à Emmanuel Levinas. Paris: Galilée, 1997.
L'Archéologie du frivole: lire Condillac. Paris: Galilée, 1973.
The Archeology of the Frivolous: Reading Condillac, trans. John P. Leavey, Jr. Lincoln and London: University of Nebraska Press (Bison Books), 1987.
L'Autre Cap; suivi de la démocratie ajournée. Paris: Éditions de Minuit, 1991.
La Carte postale: de Socrate à Freud et au-delà. Paris: Aubier-Flammarion, 1980.
The Post Card: From Socrates to Freud and Beyond, trans. Alan Bass. Chicago: University of Chicago Press, 1993.
Cosmopolites de tous les pays, encore un effort!. Paris: Galilée, 1997.
La Dissémination. Paris: Éditions du Seuil, 1972.
Dissemination, trans. Barbara Johnson. Chicago: University of Chicago Press, and London: Athlone Press, 1981.
'Donner la mort', in *L'Éthique du don. Jacques Derrida et la pensée du don*, Colloque de Royaumont, December 1990, ed. J.-M. Rabaté and M. Wetzel. Paris: Metailie-Transition, 1992, pp. 11–108.
Donner le temps 1: La fausse monnaie. Paris: Galilée, 1991.
Given Time 1: Counterfeit Money, trans. Peggy Kamuf. Chicago and London: University of Chicago Press, 1992.
Du droit à la philosophie. Paris: Galilée, 1990.
L'Écriture et la différence. Paris: Éditions du Seuil, 1967.
Writing and Difference, trans. Alan Bass. London and Henley: Routledge and Kegan Paul, 1978; repr. 1981.
'En ce moment même dans cet ouvrage me voici', in François Laruelle (ed.), *Textes pour Emmanuel Lévinas*. Paris: Éditions Jean-Michel Place, 1980; repr. in *Psyché: inventions de l'autre*. Paris: Galilée, 1987.
Éperons. Les styles de Nietzsche. Venice, Corbo e Fiori, 1976 (Quadrilingual edition). Paris, Flammarion, 1978.
Spurs: Nietzsche's Styles. Trans Barbara Harlow. Chicago, University of Chicago Press, 1979. Bilingual edition.

De l'esprit: Heidegger et la question. Paris: Galilée, 1987.
Of Spirit: Heidegger and the Question, trans. Geoffrey Bennington and Rachel Bowlby. Chicago: University of Chicago Press, 1989.
La Faculté de juger. Paris: Éditions de Minuit, 1985.
Force de loi: le 'fondement mystique de l'autorité'. Paris: Galilée, 1994.
'Force of Law: The "Mystical Foundation of Authority"', trans. Mary Quaintance, in Drucilla Cornell, Michel Rosenfeld and David Gray Carlson (eds), *Deconstruction and the Possibility of Justice.* New York and London: Routledge, 1992, pp. 3–67.
Glas. Paris: Galilée, 1974.
Glas, trans. John P. Leavey, Jr and Richard Rand. Lincoln: University of Nebraska Press, 1986.
De la grammatologie. Paris: Éditions de Minuit, 1967.
Of Grammatology, trans. Gayatri Chakravorty Spivak. Baltimore: Johns Hopkins University Press, 1976; 6th printing, 1984.
'"Il courait mort": salut, salut. Notes pour un courrier aux *Temps Modernes', Les Temps Modernes,* 587 (1996), pp. 7–54.
'"Il faut bien manger" ou le calcul du sujet', *Confrontations. Après le sujet QUI VIENT,* 20 (Winter 1989), pp. 91–114.
'Lettre à un ami japonais', in *Psyché: inventions de l'autre.* Paris: Galilée, 1987, pp. 387–93.
'Letter to a Japanese Friend', trans. David Wood and Andrew Benjamin, in Peggy Kamuf (ed.), *A Derrida Reader: Between the Blinds.* London and New York: Harvester, 1991, pp. 270–6.
Limited Inc., présentations et traductions par Elisabeth Weber. Paris: Galilée, 1990.
'Limited Inc. abc . . .', *Glyph,* 2 (1977). Baltimore and London: Johns Hopkins University Press, pp. 162–254. Reprinted in *Limited Inc.,* trans. Samuel Weber and Jeffrey Mehlman. Evanston: Northwestern University Press, 1988; repr. 1990.
Mal d'archive: une impression freudienne. Paris: Galilée, 1995.
Archive Fever: A Freudian Impression, trans. Eric Prenowitz. Chicago and London: University of Chicago Press, 1996.
Marges: de la philosophie. Paris: Éditions de Minuit, 1972.
Margins: Of Philosophy, trans. Alan Bass. Brighton: Harvester Press, 1982.
Mémoires d'aveugle: l'autoportrait et autres ruines. Paris: Louvre, Réunion des Musées Nationaux, 1990.
Memoirs of the Blind: The Self-Portrait and Other Ruins, trans. Pascale-Anne Brault and Michael Naas. Chicago and London: University of Chicago Press, 1993.
Mémoires: pour Paul de Man. Paris: Galilée, 1988.
Mémoires: for Paul de Man, rev. edn, trans. Cecile Linsay, Jonathan Culler, Eduardo Cadava and Peggy Kamuf. New York: Columbia University Press, 1989.
Moscou aller-retour, with Natalia Sergeevna Avtonomova, Valeri Aleksandrovich Podoroza and Michaïl Ryklin. Paris: Éditions de l'Aube, 1995.
L'Origine de la géometrie, de Husserl, Introduction et traduction. Paris: PUF, 1962.
Origin of Geometry (Husserl): Introduction, trans. John P. Leavey, Jr. Lincoln and London: University of Nebraska Press (Bison Book), 1989.

Passions. Paris: Galilée, 1993.

Points de suspension. Entretiens. Paris: Galilée, 1992.

Points . . .: Interviews 1974–1994, ed. Elisabeth Weber, trans. Peggy Kamuf. Stanford: Stanford University Press, 1995.

Politiques de l'amitié; suivi de l'oreille de Heidegger. Paris: Galilée, 1994.

Politics of Friendship, trans. George Collins. London: Verso, 1997.

Positions. Paris: Éditions de Minuit, 1972.

Positions, trans. Alan Bass. London: Athlone Press, 1987.

Le Problème de la genèse dans la philosophie de Husserl. Paris: PUF, 1990.

Psyché: inventions de l'autre. Paris: Galilée, 1987.

La Religion, Séminaire de Capri sous la direction de Jacques Derrida et Gianni Vattimo. Paris: Éditions du Seuil, 1996.

'Remarks on Deconstruction and Pragmatism', in Chantal Mouffe (ed.), *deconstruction and pragmatism*. London and New York: Routledge, 1996, pp. 77–88.

Résistances: de la psychanalyse. Paris: Galilée, 1996.

Spectres de Marx: l'état de la dette, le travail du deuil et la nouvelle Internationale. Paris: Galilée, 1993.

Specters of Marx: The State of the Debt, the Work of Mourning and the New International, trans. Peggy Kamuf, Introduction by Bernd Magnus and Stephen Cullenberg. London and New York: Routledge, 1994.

'The Time of a Thesis: Punctuations', trans. Kathleen McLaughlin, in Alan Montefiore (ed.), *Philosophy in France Today*. Cambridge: Cambridge University Press, 1983, pp. 34–50.

La Voix et le phénomène. Paris: PUF, 1967.

Speech and Phenomena, and Other Essays on Husserl's Theory of Signs, trans. David B. Allison. Evanston: Northwestern University Press, 1973.

Other Works

Baudelaire, Charles. *Oeuvres complètes*. Paris: Éditions de la Pléiade, 1961.

Beardsworth, Richard. *Derrida and the Political*. London: Routledge, 1996.

Blanchot, Maurice. *Le Dernier Homme*. Paris: Gallimard, 1957.

——'La Fin de la philosophie', *Nouvelle Revue Française*, 80 (August 1959), 286–98; reprinted as 'Lentes funérailles', in M. Blanchot, *L'Amitié*. Paris: Gallimard, 1971.

——*Le Pas au-delà*. Paris: Gallimard, 1973.

Bloom, Harold. *The Anxiety of Influence*. London, Oxford and New York: Oxford University Press, 1973.

Bowie, Malcolm. *Lacan* (Fontana Modern Masters). London: Fontana, 1991.

Condillac, Étienne Bonnot de. *Essai sur l'origine des connaissances humaines*, preceded by Jacques Derrida, *L'Archéologie du frivole: lire Condillac*. Paris: Galilée, 1973.

Corneille, Pierre. *Cinna* (Classiques du théâtre). Paris: Hachette, 1965.

——*Polyeucte, martyr*. Paris: Hachette, 1974.

——*Le Cid* (Classiques Hachette, 9). Paris: Hachette, 1991.

Cornell, Drucilla, Michel Rosenfeld and David Gray Carlson (eds). *Deconstruction and the Possibility of Justice*. New York and London: Routledge, 1992.

Critchley, Simon. *The Ethics of Deconstruction*. Oxford: Blackwell, 1992.

Culler, Jonathan. *On Deconstruction: Theory and Criticism after Structuralism*. London: Routledge and Kegan Paul, 1983.

Davis, Colin. *Levinas: An Introduction*. Cambridge: Polity Press, 1996.

Deleuze, Gilles and Guattari, Felix. *Kafka: pour une littérature mineure*. Paris: Éditions de Minuit, 1975.

de Man, Paul. *Blindness and Insight: Essays in the Rhetoric of Contemporary Criticism*. New York: Oxford University Press, 1971.

Descartes, René. *Méditations métaphysiques*, texte, traduction, objections et réponses par Florence Khodos, 3rd edn. Paris: PUF, 1963.

——*Regulae ad directionem ingenii: règles pour la direction de l'esprit*, revu et traduit par Georges Le Roy. Paris: Boivin et cie, 1933.

Ellis, John. M. *Against Deconstruction*. Princeton: Princeton University Press, 1989.

Felman, Shoshana. *Jacques Lacan and the Adventure of Insight: Psychoanalysis and Contemporary Culture*. Cambridge, Mass., and London: Harvard University Press, 1987.

Foucault, Michel. *Histoire de la folie à l'âge classique*. Paris: Gallimard, 1961.

——*Maladie mentale et psychologie*. Paris: Gallimard, 1962.

——*Les Mots et les choses*. Paris: Gallimard, 1966.

——*Histoire de la sexualité*, 3 vols. Paris: Gallimard, 1976–84.

Freud, Sigmund. *The Standard Edition of the Complete Psychological Works of Sigmund Freud*, 24 vols, trans. and ed. by J. Strachey. London: Hogarth Press, 1953–74.

Fukuyama, Francis. *The End of History and the Last Man*. New York: Free Press, 1992; French trans. by D. A. Canal. Paris: Flammarion, 1992.

Genet, Jean. *Oeuvres complètes*, vol. IV. Paris: Gallimard, 1968.

Genette, Gérard. 'Structuralisme et critique littéraire', in *Figures*. Paris: Éditions du Seuil, 1966.

Giovannangeli, Daniel. 'La Phénoménologie partagée: remarques sur Sartre et Derrida', *Les Études Philosophiques*, 2 (1992), 246–56.

Habermas, Jürgen. *The Philosophical Discourse of Modernity: Twelve Lectures*, trans. Frederick Lawrence. Cambridge, Mass.: MIT Press, 1987.

Hartman, Geoffrey (ed.). *Psychoanalysis and the Question of the Text*. Baltimore: Johns Hopkins University Press, 1982.

——*Saving the Text: Literature/Derrida/Philosophy*. Baltimore: Johns Hopkins University Press, 1981.

Hegel, G. W. F. *Phenomenology of Mind*, trans. J. B. Baillie, 2nd edn. London: Allen and Unwin, 1931.

——*Philosophy of Nature*, vol. 1, ed. and trans. M. J. Petry. London: Allen and Unwin, 1970.

——*Hegel's Logic*, trans. J. N. Findlay. Oxford: Clarendon Press, 1975.

Heidegger, Martin. *Introduction to Metaphysics*, trans. Ralph Manheim. New Haven and London: Yale University Press, 1959.

——*Being and Time*, trans. John Macquarrie and Edward Robinson. Oxford: Blackwell, 1967.

——'The Rectorial Address', in Gunther Neske and Emil Kettering (eds), *Martin Heidegger and National Socialism*. New York: Paragon House, 1990.

Hobson, Marian. 'Deconstruction, Empiricism and the Postal Services', *French Studies*, 36 (July 1982).

Howells, Christina. *Sartre: The Necessity of Freedom.* Cambridge: Cambridge University Press, 1988.

——(ed.) *The Cambridge Companion to Sartre.* Cambridge: Cambridge University Press, 1992.

Husserl, Edmund. *Philosophie der Arithmetik: mit ergänzenden Texten (1890–1901).* The Hague: Martinus Nijhoff, 1970. (First published 1891.)

——*Ideas: General Introduction to Pure Phenomenology,* trans. W.R. Boyce-Gibson. London and New York: Allen and Unwin, 1931; reprinted 1967.

——*Méditations cartésiennes,* trans. Emmanuel Levinas and Gabrielle Peiffer. Paris: Armand Colin, 1931.

——*Cartesian Meditations,* trans. Dorion Cairns. The Hague: Martinus Nijhoff, 1973.

——*Die Krisis der Europäischen Wissenschaften und die transzendentale Philosophie.* The Hague: Martinus Nijhoff, 1954.

——*The Crisis of the European Sciences and Transcendental Phenomenology: An Introduction to Phenomenological Philosophy,* trans. David Carr. Evanston: Northwestern University Press, 1970.

——*L'Origine de la géometrie,* présentation et traduction par Jacques Derrida. Paris: PUF, 1962.

——*Origin of Geometry,* Introduction by Jacques Derrida, trans. John P. Leavey, Jr. Lincoln and London: University of Nebraska Press (Bison Book), 1989.

——*Logical Investigations,* 2 vols, trans. J.N. Findlay. New York: Humanities Press, 1970.

Jameson, Frederic. 'Imaginary and Symbolic in Lacan: Marxism, Psychoanalytic Criticism and the Problem of the Subject', *Yale French Studies,* 55/6 (1977), double issue: *Literature and Psychoanalysis.*

Johnson, Barbara. 'The Frame of Reference: Poe, Lacan, Derrida', *Yale French Studies,* 55/6 (1977), double issue: *Literature and Psychoanalysis*; repr. in Geoffrey Hartman (ed.), *Psychoanalysis and the Question of the Text.* Baltimore: Johns Hopkins University Press, 1978.

Kamuf, Peggy (ed.). *A Derrida Reader: Between the Blinds.* London and New York: Harvester, 1991.

Kant, Immanuel, *Critique of Pure Reason,* trans. Norman Kemp Smith. London: Macmillan, 1929; reprinted 1980.

——'Perpetual Peace: A Philosophical Sketch', in Hans Reiss (ed.), *Kant: Political Writings,* trans. H.B. Nisbet. Cambridge and New York: Cambridge University Press, 1970.

——*Critique of Judgement,* trans. James Creed Meredith. Oxford: Clarendon Press, 1978.

——'Groundwork of the Metaphysics of Morals', trans. and ed. H.J. Paton, in *The Moral Law: Kant's Groundwork of the Metaphysics of Morals.* London: Routledge, 1991.

Kearney, Richard. *Modern Movements in European Philosophy.* Manchester: Manchester University Press, 1986.

Kofman, Sarah. *Lectures de Derrida.* Paris: Galilée, 1984.

Lacan, Jacques. *Écrits.* Paris: Éditions du Seuil, 1966.

Laplanche, J. and Pontalis, J.-B. *Vocabulaire de la psychanalyse.* Paris: PUF, 1967.

Laruelle, François (ed.). *Textes pour Emmanuel Levinas.* Paris: Éditions Jean-Michel Place, 1980.

Lautréamont, Comte de. *Oeuvres Complètes*. Paris: J. Corti, 1953.

Levinas, Emmanuel. *La Théorie de l'intuition dans la phénoménologie de Husserl*. Paris: Vrin, 1930; 1984.

—— *Totalité et infini: essai sur l'extériorité*. The Hague: Martinus Nijhoff, 1961; 1964.

—— *Autrement qu'être, ou au-delà de l'essence*. The Hague: Martinus Nijhoff, 1974.

—— *En découvrant l'existence avec Husserl et Heidegger*. 3rd edn. Paris: Vrin, 1974 (first edition, 1949; with additions, 1967).

—— 'Tout autrement', *L'Arc* (1973), special issue on Derrida; repr. in *Noms propres* (Livre de Poche). Montpellier: Fata Morgana, 1976.

—— 'Paix et proximité', in Jacques Rolland (ed.), *Emmanuel Levinas*. Lagrasse: Les Cahiers de la Nuit Surveillée, 1984.

—— *Hors sujet*. Montpellier: Fata Morgana, 1987.

—— *A l'heure des nations*. Paris: Éditions de Minuit, 1988.

Lévi-Strauss, Claude. *Race et histoire*. Paris: Denoi, 1952.

—— *Tristes tropiques*. Paris: Plon, 1955.

—— *La Pensée sauvage*. Paris: Plon, 1962.

—— *Le Cru et le cuit (Mythologiques*, vol. 1). Paris: Plon, 1964.

—— 'Structuralisme et critique littéraire', in *Anthropologie structurale II*. Paris: Plon, 1973.

Lyotard, Jean-François. *La condition post-moderne*. Paris: Éditions de Minuit, 1979.

Mallarmé, Stéphane. *Oeuvres complètes*, ed. Henri Mondor and G. Jean Aubry (Bibliothèque de la Pléiade). Paris: Gallimard, 1951.

Montefiore, Alan (ed.). *Philosophy in France Today*. Cambridge: Cambridge University Press, 1983.

Mouffe, Chantal (ed.). *deconstruction and pragmatism*. London and New York: Routledge, 1996.

Norris, Christopher. *Deconstruction: Theory and Practice* (New Accents). London and New York: Methuen, 1982.

Paton, H. J. (ed.). *The Moral Law: Kant's Groundwork of the Metaphysics of Morals*. London: Routledge, 1991.

Plato. *Phaedrus*, trans. R. Hackforth. Cambridge: Cambridge University Press, 1952.

Reiss, Hans (ed.). *Kant: Political Writings*, trans. H. B. Nisbet. Cambridge and New York: Cambridge University Press, 1970.

Ricoeur, Paul. *La Métaphore vive*. Paris: Éditions du Seuil, 1975.

Rolland, Jacques (ed.). *Emmanuel Levinas*. Lagrasse: Les Cahiers de la Nuit Surveillée, 1984.

Rousseau, Jean-Jacques. *Dialogues*. London: Ed. Cazin, 1782.

—— *Essai sur l'origine des langues*. Paris: Aubier Montaigne, 1974.

Rousset, Jean. *Forme et signification: essais sur les structures littéraires de Corneille à Claudel*. Paris: J. Conti, 1962.

Sartre, Jean-Paul. *La Transcendance de l'ego: esquisse d'une description phénoménologique*, first published in *Recherches philosophiques*, 1936; reprinted in edition by Sylvie le Bon. Paris: Vrin, 1965.

—— *La Nausée*. Paris: Gallimard, 1938.

—— *L'Être et le Néant: essai d'ontologie phénoménologique*. Paris: Gallimard, 1943.

—— *Situations II*. Paris: Gallimard, 1948.

—— *Saint Genet, comédien et martyr*. Paris: Gallimard, 1951.

—— *Critique de la raison dialectique, précédé de questions de méthode, I. Théorie des ensembles pratiques*. Paris: Gallimard, 1960.

—— *Les Mots*. Paris: Gallimard, 1964.

—— *L'Idiot de la famille: G. Flaubert de 1821 à 1857*. Paris: Gallimard, vols I and II, 1971; vol III, 1972; revised edn, 1988.

—— 'L'Universel singulier', in *Situations, IX*. Paris: Gallimard, 1972.

—— 'L'Engagement de Mallarmé', *Obliques*, 18–19 (1979), numéro spécial, *Sartre*, ed. M. Sicard, pp. 168–94.

Searle, John. 'Reiterating the Differences: A Reply to Derrida', *Glyph*, 1 (1977)

Yerushalmi, Yosef Hayim. *Freud's Moses: Judaism Terminable and Interminable*. New Haven and London: Yale University Press, 1991.

Index

Abel, Carl, 101
accidental, the, 16, 35, 40, 45, 46, 48, 53, 56, 58, 65, 84, 109, 110
affirmation, 41, 79, 90, 91, 93, 100, 142
alterity, 22–3, 26, 51–2, 65, 66, 87, 100, 124–8, 134, 136–7, 142, 143, 144–8, 152
  of animals, 156
  and the freedom of the subject, 124–5, 146–9, 150
anthropology, 26, 27, 34, 35–41, 42, 131, 132
archaeology, 48, 94, 120
archi-écriture, 49–51, 53, 73–4, 84, 120, 126, 129
archive, 99, 112–16, 120
  see also memory
Aristotle, 28, 45, 61, 63, 74–6, 79, 130, 149–50, 154
Arnold, Matthew, 24
Artaud, Antonin, 2, 73, 76–7
Aubenque, Pierre, 63
Austin, J.L., 64–9, 159 n. 11
auto-affection, 11, 23, 57, 59
autobiography, 3, 107–11, 156
  see also biography

Bachelard, Gaston, 61, 82, 104
Bataille, Georges, 2, 73, 91
Baudelaire, Charles, 3, 88, 89, 92, 103, 150
Beardsworth, Richard, 137, 146, 148
Benveniste, Emile, 63–4, 101–2
biography, 32, 107–11
  see also autobiography
biology, 34, 111, 112, 144
Blanchot, Maurice, 118, 151, 161 n. 18
Bloom, Harold, 159 n. 6, n. 17
Bonaparte, Marie, 104, 105
Bowie, Malcolm, 161 n. 15, n. 17
bricolage, 38–9, 42
Brunschvicg, Léon, 63

Cassirer, Ernst, 63
castration, 78, 100–1, 104, 105
Claudel, Paul, 34
Condillac, Étienne Bonnot de, 43–4, 61, 64–5
consciousness, *see* ego; humanism; phenomenology; psychoanalysis
Corneille, Pierre, 33
Crébillon, Claude-Prosper Jolyot de, 105